With compliments,

ANURAG HARSH

# THE PROFESSIONAL'S BIBLE

## NAVIGATING THE MODERN WORKPLACE

**Osborne Manhattan Publishing Group**
**300 Park Avenue**
**New York, NY 10022**



**The Professional's Bible/ Anurag Harsh**. -- 1st ed.
ISBN: 978-1-48359-803-1
eBook ISBN: 978-1-48359-804-8

*For Agustya & Vigyan*

*Today a reader, tomorrow a leader. Be a Fruit Loop in a world full of Cheerios*

*For Dad, late B.K Sinha*

*You inspire others to dream more, learn more, do more and become more*

# ACKNOWLEDGEMENTS

I have been influenced by a number of people in the making of this book. When I look back over the time spent writing this book, I realize the importance of my colleagues, professional network, and friends—without whom this book would simply not have been possible. I would like to extend my deepest gratitude to Ziff Davis CEO Vivek Shah, CXOTalk's Michael Krigsman, and one of the most insightful people I know in the business world Mr. Murli Buluswar.

And lastly, but most importantly, thanks to Andrew R. Calderon for his exacting and comprehensive editing. He pored over every line of this text, and it is all the better for it.

# INTRODUCTION

The modern workplace is recognizably different from the workplace of just 20 years ago. From the tools, the culture, and the demands to the career aspirations, leadership styles and employee expectations, the landscape is an Oz of surprises and transformation. For those born in the midst of digital transformation, the changes are part and parcel of learning how to succeed in today's market. For those taken by storm, the turning tide signals a commensurately radical shift in the way business has been done for, well, a very long time.

Some things haven't changed though. People are people. Today's workers are no different from the workers of a few decades ago in crucial senses. Workers today want to better themselves, make money, support their families and make time to enjoy them. They want healthy work relationships and once, in a while, their hard work lauded. In essence, at the personal level, the gap between then and now is not so vast. At the business level though, it's a whole new world.

A single company can have employees in different time zones, with expansive technological infrastructure supporting productivity and requiring new skills and expertise. That same company probably uses automation, AI, machine learning and robotics to offer new products, respond to market changes faster, and maintain highly coordinated supply chain segments operating in synchronicity. All the while, employees expect diversity, upward mobility, sustainable work relationships, job fulfillment, and furthering education. All of this in the context of a disruptive market terrain where competition is ruthless, and global.

For those legacy workers who came of age just 50 years ago, the modern workplace presents a tremendous challenge. They must constantly reevaluate their leadership style, develop genuine relationships with co-workers, be better salespeople, and learn how to market themselves, be innovative and entrepreneurial, achieve lofty project goals and maintain company priorities. They must learn new technology, new methods, and new business models, constantly reinventing themselves to remain relevant. Frankly, it's a lot.

*The Professional's Bible* is a simple guide to help people understand, navigate, and thrive in the modern workplace and answer the big question: What does it take to succeed in today's job market? At the heart of that question lies great uncertainty. This book is meant to quell that uncertainty.

The book takes the reader on a journey of short essays on Leadership, Self-Improvement, Career Development, Sales, Marketing, Innovation and Entrepreneurship. By the end, you should have the essential knowledge necessary to understand and master the modern workplace.

# CONTENTS

*Acknowledgements* .......... vii

*Introduction* .......... ix

**SECTION 1 -**
**LEADERSHIP** .......... XXI

**CHAPTER 1**
*Leading with Complete Optimism to Achieve Better Results* .......... 1

**CHAPTER 2**
*How to Revitalize Your Company and Give It the Boost It Deserves* .......... 6

**CHAPTER 3**
*The Power of Gratitude in Leadership* .......... 19

**CHAPTER 4**
*Understanding Power & Influence* .......... 24

**CHAPTER 5**
*Leading Up* .......... 30

**CHAPTER 6**
*Persuading People to See Your Way* .......... 36

**CHAPTER 7**
*Leaders Know Which Buttons to Press* .......... 50

**CHAPTER 8**
*Igniting Passion & Motivation in Employees* .......... 53

**CHAPTER 9**
*Bringing Disruptive but Lasting Change* .......... 65

**CHAPTER 10**
*Should Leaders Show Emotion?* .......... 73

**CHAPTER 11**
*The Illusion of Stability Blinds Leaders* .......... 75

**CHAPTER 12**
*The Role of Sleep in Leadership* .......... 78

**CHAPTER 13**
*Building and Leading Effective, High-performance Teams* ................83

**CHAPTER 14**
*The Best Leadership Literature. Ever.* ................90

**CHAPTER 15**
*Are You an "Antifragile" Leader?* ................94

**CHAPTER 16**
*How Leaders Use Comedy to Influence* ................96

**CHAPTER 17**
*Good Leadership Calls for Light and Shade* ................99

**CHAPTER 18**
*Why Creative Leaders Last Longer* ................101

**CHAPTER 19**
*Are You a Leader Who Pays Lip Service?* ................103

**CHAPTER 20**
*Leadership and Dealing with Workplace Adversity* ................105

**CHAPTER 21**
*Leadership Style That Fosters Creativity or Stifles Innovation* ................111

**CHAPTER 22**
*Leadership That Builds Synergy & Harmony in the Team* ................114

**CHAPTER 23**
*Pride, Leadership, and Business Relationships* ................124

**CHAPTER 24**
*Leaders Are Experts at Recycling* ................126

**CHAPTER 25**
*What Type of a Leader Will You Be?* ................128

**CHAPTER 26**
*How Do Leaders Manage the Room?* ................130

**CHAPTER 27**
*The Best Leaders Learn to Bite Their Tongues* ................133

**CHAPTER 28**
*Thoughts of a Scared Leader* ................135

**CHAPTER 29**
*Leaders Are Born in the Playground* ........ 138

**CHAPTER 30**
*IQ Is Worthless Without These Three Qualities* ........ 140

**CHAPTER 31**
*What Sort of Leader Are You?* ........ 142

**CHAPTER 32**
*The Triathlon of Leadership* ........ 145

**CHAPTER 33**
*Predict the Leadership Weather* ........ 147

**CHAPTER 34**
*Do You Know a Machiavellian Leader?* ........ 150

**CHAPTER 35**
*The One Word Leaders Never Use* ........ 153

**CHAPTER 36**
*"Soft Play" Is Not for Leaders* ........ 156

**CHAPTER 37**
*A Leader's A-Z of Body Language* ........ 158

**CHAPTER 38**
*Why Simple Ideas Are Often Best* ........ 162

**SECTION 2 – SELF-IMPROVEMENT** ........ 165

**CHAPTER 39**
*Self-Interest Is Tied to Shared Success* ........ 167

**CHAPTER 40**
*Life Lessons from the Rio Olympics 2016* ........ 175

**CHAPTER 41**
*Finding Your Inner Balance in Life* ........ 179

**CHAPTER 42**
*The ROI of Caring for Others* ........ 184

**CHAPTER 43**
*How to be Truly Innovative & Creative at Work and in Life* ........ 186

**CHAPTER 44**
*The Key to Great Business Relationships is to Understand a Person's Past* ..... 193

**CHAPTER 45**
*Does Authenticity on Social Media Matter?* ..... 195

**CHAPTER 46**
*Does Anger Have a Role in the Workplace?* ..... 197

**CHAPTER 47**
*How to Be More Productive Than Everyone Else* ..... 199

**CHAPTER 48**
*Six Simple Ways to Create Balance* ..... 203

**CHAPTER 49**
*The Art of Winning People with Words* ..... 207

**CHAPTER 50**
*Why Do We Work Best When We Have No Time?* ..... 213

**CHAPTER 51**
*How to Focus Under Pressure* ..... 216

**CHAPTER 52**
*Are Vacations an Opportunity for Business Development?* ..... 221

**CHAPTER 53**
*Will You Keep Coming Back?* ..... 223

**CHAPTER 54**
*Talking Your Way to Success* ..... 225

**CHAPTER 55**
*Developing the Mental Resolve for Success* ..... 236

**CHAPTER 56**
*Understanding Human Behavior for Success* ..... 245

**CHAPTER 57**
*The Social Media Marshmallow Test* ..... 254

**CHAPTER 58**
*You Buy from People You Like. Really?* ..... 256

**CHAPTER 59**
*You and Santa Need the Same Thing* ..... 258

**CHAPTER 60**
*Ten Phrases to Motivate Anyone* ....... 260

**CHAPTER 61**
*What to Do When Your Best Isn't Good Enough* ....... 263

**CHAPTER 62**
*Business Lessons from Black Friday* ....... 265

**CHAPTER 63**
*The Five-Step Mechanics of Creativity* ....... 267

**CHAPTER 64**
*Time for a Hackathon in Your Head* ....... 269

**CHAPTER 65**
*Don't Take Things So Personally* ....... 272

**CHAPTER 66**
*Look in a Mirror Before You Judge* ....... 274

**CHAPTER 67**
*The Ten Keys to Unlocking Inspiration* ....... 276

**CHAPTER 68**
*Productivity Hacks from Cheeseburgers* ....... 279

**CHAPTER 69**
*Your Imperfections Are Your Competitive Advantage* ....... 281

**CHAPTER 70**
*Personal Branding: The Power of You* ....... 284

**CHAPTER 71**
*Desperate Thirst for Exclusivity* ....... 287

**CHAPTER 72**
*Understanding the Dynamics of Groups at Work* ....... 290

**CHAPTER 73**
*Company Culture & the Public Image* ....... 296

**CHAPTER 74**
*How to Deal with Conflict at Work* ....... 302

**CHAPTER 75**
*Teamwork Lessons from Monkeys* ....... 312

**CHAPTER 76**
*Rise of the Collaborative and Shared Economy* ........ 315

**CHAPTER 77**
*Six Tricks for Amazing Presentations* ........ 318

**CHAPTER 78**
*Does Your "Tribe" Have a Shared Interest?* ........ 320

**CHAPTER 79**
*Seven Ways to Reduce Stress at Work* ........ 322

**CHAPTER 80**
*Work & Exercise* ........ 325

**SECTION 3 – CAREER DEVELOPMENT** ........ 329

**CHAPTER 81**
*Is Disruptive Learning Crucial to Transformational Career Progress?* ........ 331

**CHAPTER 82**
*Is Your Career Stuck in the Wrong Gear?* ........ 333

**CHAPTER 83**
*Does Doubt Help or Hinder Your Career?* ........ 336

**CHAPTER 84**
*Is Your Boss Taking You for Granted?* ........ 338

**CHAPTER 85**
*How Therapeutic Hobbies Can Power Your Career* ........ 341

**CHAPTER 86**
*Are You Likely to Lose Your Job?* ........ 343

**CHAPTER 87**
*Market Yourself: A Job Won't Find You Anymore* ........ 345

**CHAPTER 88**
*Are You Too Important to Be Ill?* ........ 347

**CHAPTER 89**
*Put Away the Recruitment Top Trumps* ........ 349

**CHAPTER 90**
*Meet Opportunities Before They Arrive* ........ 351

**CHAPTER 91**
*A Career Lesson from Bird Seed* ........ 354

**CHAPTER 92**
*Why Solopreneurs Will Rule the World* ........ 356

**CHAPTER 93**
*Is Grammar Important for Career Progress Anymore?* ........ 358

**CHAPTER 94**
*Seven Bad Habits That Get People Fired* ........ 363

**CHAPTER 95**
*Why Everything Is an Investment in Your Career* ........ 366

**CHAPTER 96**
*The Myth of Multitasking* ........ 368

**CHAPTER 97**
*Is "Likability" Truly Essential?* ........ 371

**CHAPTER 98**
*Surviving Office Politics* ........ 373

**CHAPTER 99**
*Why We Need Competition at Work* ........ 376

**CHAPTER 100**
*What Is Your Storytelling Quotient?* ........ 378

**CHAPTER 101**
*How to Cold Call a Hiring Manager* ........ 381

**CHAPTER 102**
*Ten Signs That You Should Leave Your Job* ........ 384

**CHAPTER 103**
*Managing Change in Your Career* ........ 387

**CHAPTER 104**
*Why Do Your New Recruits Keep Leaving?* ........ 390

**SECTION 4 – SALES** ........ 393

**CHAPTER 105**
*The Art of Closing: Top Sales Negotiation Strategies* ........ 395

**CHAPTER 106**
*Discover Your Inner Salesman* ........ 405

**CHAPTER 107**
*Redesigning the Broken Sales Function in America* ........ 408

**CHAPTER 108**
*Is It Time We Retired Sales Commissions?* ........ 421

**CHAPTER 109**
*Good Sales People Are Not Pond Scum* ........ 426

**SECTION 5 – MARKETING** ........ 429

**CHAPTER 110**
*How to Disrupt a Market* ........ 431

**CHAPTER 111**
*Why Do Consumers Purchase?*
*Understanding the Customer's Mindset* ........ 439

**CHAPTER 112**
*How to Keep Your Customers Loyal to You* ........ 446

**CHAPTER 113**
*Five Steps to Change the Perception of Your Brand* ........ 450

**CHAPTER 114**
*Money Can't Buy Love, or Even a Like* ........ 454

**CHAPTER 115**
*How to Really Influence Customers* ........ 469

**CHAPTER 116**
*Extracting Maximum Value When an Ad Goes Viral* ........ 478

**SECTION 6 – INNOVATION** 481

**CHAPTER 117**
*Innovating in the Internet Age* 483

**CHAPTER 118**
*Never Let Innovation Become Normal* 490

**CHAPTER 119**
*The Nine Ingredients of Innovation* 492

**CHAPTER 120**
*How Can Companies Innovate in the Digital Era?* 495

**SECTION 7 - ENTREPRENEURSHIP** 499

**CHAPTER 121**
*Start-Ups Need Momentum More Than Money* 500

**CHAPTER 122**
*Lost Your Entrepreneurial Mojo?* 502

**CHAPTER 123**
*Entrepreneurial Lessons from Black Swan Events* 505

**CHAPTER 124**
*How Will Entrepreneurs Solve Their Problems?* 507

**CHAPTER 125**
*Your Product Is Destined to Fail* 509

**CHAPTER 126**
*The Five Golden Rules for Freelancers* 511

**CHAPTER 127**
*The Entrepreneur's Epitaph* 514

**CHAPTER 128**
*The Top Ten Hires for Any Start-Up or New Project* 516

**CHAPTER 129**
*Where Do Entrepreneurs Get Their Energy?* 519

**CHAPTER 130**
*Entrepreneurs Have to Learn to Kill* .......... 522

**CHAPTER 131**
*Seven Reasons Why Investors Won't Back Entrepreneurs* .......... 524

**CHAPTER 132**
*Routine Is the Enemy of Entrepreneurs* .......... 526

**CHAPTER 133**
*Entrepreneurs Eat Failure for Breakfast* .......... 529

**CHAPTER 134**
*Why Every Start-Up Needs a Spring Clean* .......... 531

**CHAPTER 135**
*Seven Battlefield Tactics of Successful Entrepreneurs* .......... 534

# SECTION 1 - LEADERSHIP

# CHAPTER 1

## *Leading with Complete Optimism to Achieve Better Results*

Optimism is an underrated outlook on life that can often come across as fanciful or unrealistic. Those who describe themselves as optimists usually have a skeptical glance shot their way. In a sense, we expect cynicism, verging on pessimism by default. We suspect that anyone who believes in good outcomes, positive outlooks, and rosy dispositions most of the time must not be connected to reality.

Those who leer doubtingly are more likely to receive praise for their perspicacity and wisdom. It's a predicament in that we preclude optimism as a viable mentality, leaving it little room to flourish where it otherwise might have.

Fortunately, those who strive for optimism possess a resilience that cannot be undone by mere skepticism or cynicism. It's unsurprising then that optimistic people are far more likely to succeed than their dubious counterparts. Optimists are predisposed to look forward to new days, new opportunities, favorable prospects, and happiness. The optimist's mentality grants them the fortitude to cope with life's hardships and adversity without losing ground.

I strive to maintain an actively optimistic demeanor and mentality in all situations. I don't think that distances me from reality. It creates a new reality around me that invigorates my family, friends, and coworkers with positive energy. I am an antidote to their negativity, and in that way, together we create a medicine cabinet of optimism that allows us to counteract unproductive negativity. Both the negative and the positive mindset are self-fulfilling prophecies, and I'd much rather work toward the latter.

## Active Optimism Is a Practice

It isn't easy to be optimistic: particularly when those around you are the opposite. It can feel like the world is conspiring to bring you down. It isn't. That's just pessimistic rhetoric parasitical to your self-narrative. With a few guideposts to follow we can steer clear of the pitfalls of pessimism.

1. Remember that your optimism increases the likelihood of good outcomes. It isn't just because you see things positively, but because you seek out opportunities positively.

2. Break down larger tasks into smaller ones. We can feel overwhelmed by all we have to do because we don't have a clear sense of what we have to do.

3. Ask for assistance whenever a task is unmanageable for you.

4. Encourage the people around you with solution-oriented positivity. It isn't enough to say positive things. You must follow through with positive actions and provide positive solutions to real problems.

5. Exercise self-control and be mindful of your habits. We spend years developing habits unwittingly. They can sometimes be the reason for our failure. Be aware of them.

6. Optimism starts with the individual but can only thrive in a community of optimism. It isn't to say that such a community would have no place for negativity or pessimism. It would; but not as the baseline.

The list above is meant to cover individual and community aspects of optimism, in addition to common pitfalls. The best way to avoid the pitfalls and ensure the success optimism in your life and the lives of the people around you is to spread it around.

## Inspire Optimism in Others

First, start with the assumption that the best possible realities are attainable. Temper that with the belief that they are only accessible to groups and not individuals. The reason being that we are entrenched in social environments, which means that we affect and are affected by those around us. If you want to live the life of a positive hermit, so be it. If not, to live an optimistic life is inevitably a social activity.

The three key ingredients to form an optimistic community are purpose, meaningful work, and extraordinary people. The purpose informs our efforts while concurrently community building. When there is purpose, there is meaning. When those are present, specific and perceptible reasons for doing what one does are readily identifiable. When that happens, we unlock what's extraordinary in others and ourselves.

However, optimism is a potent force that can sometimes bowl us over without notice. Be wary of the signs and outcomes of excessive optimism:

1. When only good news is acknowledged and any bad news is swiped away to avoid conflict or dispirited faces, confusion can ensue. Tackle difficult conversations head on.

2. The country club effect is when a team grows isolated from the realities of business enough that the detachment generates losses, conflicts, and unfeasible plans. This can happen with any mindset.

3. Over-reliance on advocates who speak on your behalf. Don't give your voice in a group to someone else, no matter how much you agree

with what they say. Your words will differ and shine light on darkened corners.

4. Inflexible methods that emerge from complacency and comfort. Stirring things up when necessary isn't a bad thing. Just make sure you have a purpose—hopefully a noble one.

## Learners Are the Best Optimists

Leaders should be learners, not stewards of established beliefs, norms, and practices. The attitude of a learner is fertile ground for constructive optimism, optimism that won't fall prey to the four excesses I listed above. A learner recognizes that their current knowledge is not the end-all-be-all. They recognize the importance of listening to others, of coalescing different modes of thinking, and of the inherent value in all ideas. Value, therefore, becomes a function of perspective rather than power, authority, or verbosity.

We should all endeavor to be learners at all times. There is a certain amount of selflessness that is needed to be a successful learner. You must identify when to put aside your knowledge and experience to just absorb new perspectives and information, as opposed to seeing how to fit the new information into your existing framework—or how to refute the new information. This takes optimism, fearlessness, a desire to change for the better. And none of that is simple, nor is it easy off the bat. With practice, though, it gets much easier.

Too many people lack this learner's disposition, and when the leadership lacks it, then organizations suffer because they stagnate and corrode from the inside out. Inflexibility is a manifestation of negativity. We hold on to what we know for fear of change. But we only fear the change because we don't know if bad outcomes will accompany it. With an optimistic outlook, we can change with the forethought that even if bad outcomes arise, so too will good outcomes. We change in search of the good, not the bad. Don't let the fear of bad outcomes force you to sacrifice all the good that exists.

## Believe in Self-Improvement

Be self-confident and positive in all that you see and do. Before you can set an example for others to follow, you must be solid in your beliefs, even if they change over time. The one belief that should persist no matter what ideological shifts you experience is this: I can be better, and together, we can be the best.

The emotional energy that that belief exudes will infuse the space and people around you, inspiring them to better themselves. They will choose positive thinking in the same way you chose positive thinking. When we do so, we motivate the people around us through rewards, purpose, and meaning, and not through fear, rules, and incentives. People will incentivize themselves so long as they have a good reason.

What better reason to wake up every day, go to work, and give all of yourself if not to secure a better you and the best us for the future.

# CHAPTER 2

## *How to Revitalize Your Company and Give It the Boost It Deserves*

Those of us who preach to others about corporate culture, disruption, and the digital age throw around the word "pivot." It's a term that recently slipped into political discourse, and long ago left the corporate world bitter and disillusioned. Without going into detail, a pivot is a change in direction, presumably to rectify or avoid a structural or operational error.

Pivoting is not a simple act, nor is it all that clear, yet we tote it like a saving grace. What's worse, despite a plethora of articles that attempt to breakdown the concept in practicable terms, I, for one, can't make heads or tails of it. So, I decided to put together an article that holistically covers all the basics of pivoting, but with different packaging.

From here on out, *forget* pivot and *think* revitalize.

Why swap out one term for the other? The pivot is all about making bottom-up and top-down changes because of an underlying assumption a company is floundering, pale, and sickly. If that's the case, then what good will it do you to pivot if you are falling apart inside? When we rely on metaphor, we might as well do it properly. Your business doesn't need to shift direction; it needs to be revitalized. You need to breathe life into it.

The purpose of this article is to help you devise a revitalization plan that explores and takes advantage of your passion, vision, creativity, story, and core competencies.

When you arrive at content you are familiar with, feel free to skip it. Make this article your own. After all, customization is the spirit of the digital age.

## Draw Up Your Personal Revitalization Plan

We all know what it feels like to hit proverbial rock bottom. In the lurch, it can seem that no amount of effort can save us. Escaping the rut can often mean overcoming yourself. We all engage in some degree of self-sabotage. Unaware, we blame the system, our team, or life. An effective revitalization must start, first and foremost, with yourself.

1. *Set a clear vision.* Map out your goal in the utmost detail. Ask yourself: How will that end-state feel? What will it look like to others? How will your surroundings look? How will it affect those around you? The true power of imagination relies on a cognitive flaw. The brain is inadequate at distinguishing real and fictive musing, so use that to spur yourself into action.

2. *Do a gap assessment.* As you daydream about the desired end-state, identify improvements, changes, or supplements necessary to achieve your goal. Make a list. Moreover, take stock of costs and sacrifices. It's critically important to be honest. All things worth doing require sacrifice and exact a cost. Be fully cognizant of those from the start.

3. *Find mentors.* Knowing what you lack is part and parcel of knowing what others have that you want. I don't mean envy; I mean admiration. Find people who can teach you and empower you with knowledge and sound advice.

4. *Conduct a premortem.* From the onset conceive of all the ways you could fail or falter. Don't forget to include your own personal and historic stumbling blocks.

5. *Build accountability markers.* Establish a reliable system of rewards and punishments. It might sound archaic. It isn't. For optimal results get someone else to hold you accountable. (That's when things get really interesting!)

6. *Track, measure, refine.* Track your weekly performance and goal attainment. A diligent record allows you to make informed adjustments.

## Eight Principles of the Revitalization Spirit

A plan devised and implemented without guiding principles is doomed to fail. When you study successful organizations and individuals, you'll begin to see emergent themes. You'll see great courage, a contrarian mindset, an openness to risk-taking, and an attitude that feeds on limits rather than shies away from them.

After much analysis and research, I've distilled eight principles that typify the revitalization spirit:

1. *Let go of the past.* The past teaches us about the present in preparation for the future. It can also hinder us. Constant fear of past failure is a deterrent and a hindrance. To let go, you must trust in the lessons the past has taught you.

2. *Promote courage.* Celebrate new ideas and encourage people to uninhibitedly express them. Create a brave space where people can take chances without fear of backlash.

3. *Embrace failure.* We are surprisingly unforgiving for such flawed creatures. Failure is instrumental to discovery and learning. Recast missteps and mistakes as natural parts of the learning process, not as punishable offenses.

4. *Do the opposite.* A contrarian attitude, in modulated doses, can yield extraordinary results. When a person upends expectations, takes the

counterintuitive approach, or confronts what they most fear, conviction takes the wheel.

5. *Imagine the possibilities.* I said this above, but it bears repeating. Imagination is a creative gift that the practical among us has condemned as infantile. What an error of maturity.

6. *Put yourself out of business.* Successful companies improve design to put their own products out of business. You aren't just competing with the market; you are competing with yourself.

*Reject limits.* Limits serve their purpose. That does not mean they are inviolable. The path toward revitalization often breaches the boundaries of limitation. Aim beyond. Whether you are launching a product, opening a fashion boutique, seeking a job, or rebuilding a broken community, your focal point must be the sky.

With a plan and a spirit, we can step into the brambles. Into the technicalities, logistics, and details of business ownership. They are equal parts nuance, equal parts agonizing. Defeat comes one way or another. In those moments, we might wonder why not settle for traditional employment instead? Then again not. The very conviction to triumph is a fire unperturbed by passing rain clouds. It is an indescribable spirit. A revolution.

Now that we've covered the individual, I'll move on to the business.

In the remainder of the article I will explore multiple business strategies proven in business culture today.

## Cannibalize Your Own Product

Success can intoxicate even the most disciplined leaders and disorient them into thinking their advantage is unending. Instill in your company that successes should be celebrated while acknowledging their impermanence.

When you are thinking about revitalizing a product or service, look deep into the heart of it. Unleash your imagination and pull from as many sources of inspiration as you can. If that results in cannibalizing your own product or service, so be it.

As you probe and prod your offerings, bear in mind the following advice:

1. *High Value.* Any revitalization should increase value. If it doesn't solve a real problem, then forget about it.
2. *Original.* If it's already on the market, don't settle for marginal improvements.
3. *Significant.* People don't forget offerings that change the way they see or interact with the world.
4. *Emotionally Charged.* Connect with customers on an emotional level.

## Shake Up Your Operations

How did Toyota surpass GM to become the world's largest car company? How did Dell beat IBM in the computer industry? It wasn't product innovation, slick advertising or rock-star executives. It was a commitment to operational innovation. Operational innovation, coined by management consultant Michael Hammer, is the concept of completely overhauling the way a company does business in an effort to create a significant competitive advantage.

In a word, rebuilding.

Here is a quick and practical five-step process to kick off your operational revitalization efforts:

1. *Make the case for change.* Detail both the opportunity and upside that can be seized through a successful change, and articulate the true cost of stagnating.

2. *Set an audacious goal.* Challenge yourself and your team to solve bigger problems, and you will uncover bigger innovations.

3. *Do a friction audit.* Carefully examine each step of your processes and the way you do business. Where are the bottlenecks? What steps could be shortened?

4. *Bypass Who for What.* As old ideas are discarded, egos get bruised. Set the tone from the start that the mission is all about the What, about finding a better solution and driving the business forward.

5. *Borrow ideas from other industries.* Look for creative approaches to similar problems in other industries.

6. *Create vivid experiences.* The experience you create for customers is an area prime for revitalization. If your product or service is revitalized, and you've already optimized the way you do business, the *customer experience* is then another powerful playground for creativity and revitalization.

## The Five Senses Test

Companies are, by their nature, abstract entities, amorphous and difficult to imagine. And people are notoriously bad at empathizing with or envisioning large masses of just about anything. Companies that sideline customer experience remain abstract and analytic. Unengaged with the real world in a tangible way, these companies prevent their customers from building emotional bridges.

A sound starting point is to put yourself in the customers' shoes. Bear in mind the knowledge gaps. Customers don't know the board, the managers, or the strategy. Ostensibly, customers are outsiders. In lacking that insider knowledge, they also lack intimacy and experience the company detachedly. With a quick role reversal, you can attune yourself to the customer experience to see which touchpoints need revitalization.

Think of the touchpoints as sense experiences. When a customer enters a brick-and-mortar location, what do they see? What do they smell? What is the air quality? These are the latent attributes of a company that impress themselves on memory, becoming inseparably associated to the feelings evoked.

If you haven't done this already, chances are that you are missing out on huge opportunities to engage your customers.

Note that this approach isn't about volume or intensity. The senses are apertures, easily flooded and more easily overwhelmed. Customers, unlike companies, are people, not abstract entities. Use your common experience as humans with senses as a guide.

## Avoid the Curse of Inconsistency

As you start to plan the areas where revitalization is necessary, remember that less is more. You don't want to saturate your brand to the point of gimmickry. You especially want to avoid brand inconsistency. Brands like Starbucks predicate their success on brand consistency. Imagine a Starbucks. Now imagine another. And another. No matter what location you picture, the colors, aromas, amenities, offerings, and, if they are lucky, service will be the same.

And if you think that doesn't make a difference, think again.

The W Hotel has crafted a hotel experience that is calculated at every step. Enter one of its more than 50 hotels in 24 countries, and you'll immediately sense a special experience: ultrachic, elegant, minimalistic. From the funky bathrooms and techno music in the elevators, to the staff dressed in all black, customers never confuse a W hotel with a Marriott.

Now imagine that you checked into a W Hotel, strolled past the swanky entry, and arrived at your room, only to find a floral quilt and heavy, plaid curtains. What a buzzkill. While this will never happen at a W hotel, mismatches like this one occur throughout the business world with stunning regularity: a high-end apparel shop that uses cheap hangers, an American bistro that tries to peddle sushi. Even if you do 99% of things perfectly, it's the 1% mismatch that people will most remember.

To avoid this blunder, think of your brand as the full 100%, not just 99%. This crucial 1% differentiation, achieved by creating a consistent, positive experience at every customer touchpoint, plays a big role in your ability to grow and meet emerging competitive threats.

Now think about your own organization. Contemplate every experiential element that isn't making your customers say, "Wow!"

Is it the outdated paperwork you require customers to complete? The dimly lit parking lot?

Unleash your creativity by levying a significant overhaul on at least one area of customer engagement. The results will speak for themselves.

## Tell a Memorable Story

The sense engagement, the consistent branding, the overarching mission, and the emotion and motivation behind your brand are critical elements, necessary to draw in customers and create lasting memories. But all those elements lack potency without a story to carry them.

Think of story as a narrative. Story is a fundamental part of human life, and to some extent, we are all capable of discerning a "good story" from a "not-so-good story." Hone that intuition to tailor a narrative about your brand that resonates with customers. Yes, ads tell stories. Ads tend to tell stories in a vacuum, though. The brand story expresses why the company exists, what its origins and values are, and it reveals the minds and hearts of its creators and supporters. It is transparent and relatable.

Nick Morgan is a master storyteller who has written memorable and inspiring speeches for elected officials, business executives, and dignitaries. He categorizes stories into five types:

1. *Quests.* These begin with ordinary people in an ordinary situation. Then a problem arises or an event occurs that forces the hero to leave home or depart from the status quo in search of a goal—usually in the service of a larger moral purpose. It's trite, yet we are captivated.

2. *A Strange Land.* The protagonists (that's us) find themselves in a foreign land. Call it Pivotland. Regular people meandering an enigmatic terrain where the language and rules are disorienting. Along comes a leader (that's you) to proffer guidance, a new vision, a new set of rules, or a new way of coping. Hope is restored and a bold new horizon opens before us in this strange land. We applaud those who overcome insurmountable odds with deft mastery.

3. *Love Stories.* Two people meet, fall in love, fall out of love, learn a little more about each other, decide to stick together, and live happily ever after. The journey is about the lessons learned and the character development. If you're a leader with an idea about how people can better cohabitate, love stories are for you.

4. *Rags-to-Riches Stories.* These stories are more about ambition and perseverance than they are about wealth acquisition. They're about average people who, with a little luck and hard work, manage to succeed.

5. *Revenge Stories.* Many believe there is true evil in this world and that it takes goodly people to thwart its insidious advance on our otherwise pristine way of life. Revenge for injustice wrought is an all-consuming motivator. A good villain and justice served are enthralling ways for

leaders to persuade their followers that they have the right idea about life.

By writing your narrative with one of these five classic structures in mind, you can use storytelling to capture hearts and inspire action. This applies to both internal and external communications, marketing, and brand messaging. Great storytelling is the difference between the anecdotal and the legendary.

## Revitalize Your Communication

In a reductive sense, everything we have discussed thus far boils down to communication. Sure, we communicate using words. We also communicate with images, gestures, colors, sounds, symbols, and a range of other mediums—some more direct than others.

When it comes to written communication, there are six principals to keep in mind:

1. *Keep it simple.* Make your communications simple and compact. Jettison the jargon.
2. *Make it clear.* Uproot imprecision and plant the green seeds of concrete word choice. Palpable language is better.
3. *Speak to your audience, Not Yourself.* Speak in a language that your audience understands, and realize that they don't have the same knowledge and points of reference you do.
4. *Keep it brief.* Word count.
5. *Make it memorable.* People will remember stories and feelings far more than details and figures.
6. *Activate with action.* Start with the end-goal in mind, and make sure your communications all lead to the desired outcome.

The words you say speak to your mindset—or not. Companies and brands must be particularly careful when it comes to diction. Words have lives of their own, each one packaged in a context and containing a context of its own, rife in cultural connotations, lived experiences, and possible misperceptions.

## There Is No One-Size-Fits-All

The key to marketing today is customization on a massive scale. By creating customer personas and insightfully gaining intimate knowledge about your average customers' habits, preferences, and hesitancies, you can create marketing material that appeals directly to your customer base. There is no one-size-fits-all ad or buzzword. Your content must be highly targeted, highly specific, and largely evocative.

Beware! Don't get locked into specificity. Overly focusing on your core competencies can blind you to new business opportunities. Bella Donna is a case in point.

Bella Donna is Europe's first hotel floor designed by and dedicated exclusively to women. Every hospitality assumption was challenged when management designed a new style of bathroom. The bathrooms are stocked with exclusive products. High-powered hairdryers, full-length mirrors and healthy room service options are customized for their intended guests. Women traveling for business to Copenhagen have kept Bella Donna constantly booked to capacity and have given a big boost in exposure to the entire hotel property.

If you feel stuck, it's time to discover new customers and explore fresh ways to sell to them. Resort to your imagination.

Imagine that your customer base completely dried up, and your distribution practices became illegal. What new customers would you serve? Where would you find them? How could you sell and deliver in a new way?

This exercise is exactly what your competitors are doing right now, so it's your job to beat them to the punch.

## Learn the Six Rules of Creative Cultures

Revitalizing any part of your company, let alone all of it, takes creativity. It takes understanding creative processes and a willingness to try new methods that might seem primitive or impractical. When you tackle this challenge with others, it can ignite a culture of creativity where risk-taking and impracticality are linchpins of the creative process. The solutions needn't be impractical, but the road to them needn't be orthodox. Inspiration can be found in the most unlikely places.

There are six commonalities in companies where creativity is extolled as a virtue:

1. *Fuel passion.* Many great human achievements and advances happened by accident. Many more happened through passion and willpower. Passion, a devotion to a cause or outcome beyond reason, is an unstoppable force.

2. *Hunt and kill assumptions.* As organizations and industries progress, assumptions become unwritten rules. Over time these unwritten rules become norms and habits that constrain our creativity. Ferret them out and question them.

3. *Never stand still.* A hindrance to creativity is the assumption that it's inborn or requires no hard work. Creativity is a gradual process.

4. *Embrace oddball ideas.* Instead of shunning wacky ideas, explore them and encourage people to nurture them. You never know what might happen.

5. *Stick it to the man.* A healthy dose of skepticism is fertile ground for big dreams. Promote a modicum of irreverence in your team.

6. *Fight to win.* We will face obstacles, both internal and external. Stare them down until they shrink before you. When you decide on a course, stay the course.

## In Sum

Revitalization is about the human condition. It's about what we bring to the table from the get-go. Inside of us there are resources at our disposal that can breathe new life into a company if we are unafraid to test the waters.

Take some time out of your busy schedule to sketch out your operational structure, your customer journey, your story, your core competencies, your products, all the things that make your company what it is. Once you do that, pluck the dead leaves and revitalize.

# CHAPTER 3

## *The Power of Gratitude in Leadership*

The promise of lifetime employment no longer motivates people as it once did. In fact, it does the complete opposite. People seek opportunities to migrate, garnering more experience and knowledge to make themselves indispensable to their employer—only to leave again. Those who stay usually cite corporate culture, fair compensation, solidarity, and constructive challenge as their main motivators.

This reveals an emergent employer-employee relationship based less in monetary incentives and security, and more so in value and values. This is the Millennial Effect on the job market. True, this new generation of workers still wants money and benefits, but some are willing to stay at a company that offers less if it gives them a greater sense of meaning. At the beginning and end of the day, they can justify leasing their life to the company.

As leaders, if we tap into those emotions in earnest, we can affirm the vision of value, create unquantifiable potential profit, and muster a loyal and fulfilled workforce that can unlock innovation through passion rather than incentivization.

## A Culture of Values

Culture is a boon and a curse. In some cases, it can hinder progress, keep people in the dark ages, clinging to tradition and eventually causing their demise. Companies are keen on this now more than ever.

One of the salient questions at the conferences I've spoken at is, "How do I get the shareholders (in their 70s) to jump on digital transformation?" C-suite executives who want to upgrade their supply chains are stalemated by reticent and risk-averse boards who don't fully grasp the necessity of digital transformation.

But my point isn't about digital transformation as such. It's about reluctance to change.

In order to cook up a culture of values, two ingredients are essential.

1. The first is acceptance that change is an imperative.
2. The second is recognition.

I think this goes without explanation. The second requires some expansion.

Recognition is largely about gratitude. When we recognize, celebrate, appreciate, promote, and build-up the people in our community, we promote desired cultural values that grow over time. When employees and employers feel confident enough to recognize each other and express gratitude, it squelches the vices of competitiveness. Everyone is given permission to be themselves and be honest.

In turn, a culture of recognition engages, energizes, and empowers employees. And today it can mean the difference between failure and success.

## The Backbone of Gratitude

George Anders, a contributing editor at *Forbes*, notes that many of the fastest-growing jobs in the modern economy require a powerful sense of empathy. Empathy is the ability to put oneself in another's situation. Truly powerful empathy is the ability to understand and anticipate at a deep emotional level someone else's thoughts, feelings, perceptions, pleasures, and displeasures.

Silent empathy won't move a workforce. It must be expressed. The best way to express this is appreciation. At the most basic human level, recognizing effort and saying "thank you" has astonishing power to motivate others.

Payroll processing company ADP asked employees and HR directors in Great Britain, "Aside from pay, what motivates and engages you at work?" Fifty-nine percent replied, "Praise and recognition." That was by far the most important motivation after pay— more than employee benefits, clear paths for advancement, or even the flexibility to work where and when the employee wanted.

## How to Cook Up a Culture of Gratitude

There are five proven ways to generate a culture of gratitude:

1. Identify the right or desirable behaviors.
2. Give constructive feedback whenever someone is on the right track or accomplished a personal goal.
3. Praise people for breaking through social or emotional barriers.
4. Recognize trust and bond building. Reify your social bonds.
5. Inform people when what they have done makes you feel good.

*And of course, vice versa for all the above. Express gratitude whenever you see someone do these things for you.*

When gratitude permeates the workforce, all sort of change occurs. For one, wins are not centered on the individual, they become group wins. "We did this," rather than, "I did this." Losses, too, are displaced across the team and taken as opportunities for growth, because culpability loses its allure.

This list is intended as a starting point. Surely getting a culture off the ground takes much more work, especially in an organization. However, in pointing out tangible behaviors and practices, we establish a solid launching pad. When you then implement them throughout the company strategically at every level, you get social cohesion. And that's fertile soil for enduring culture.

## A Culture of Gratitude Makes People Happy

Happiness makes people work smarter, more engaged, and more productive. It can also give people a sense of meaning. For example, if part of your corporate goals includes creating a culture of gratitude to raise motivations and thereby profits, people will see their actions in a broader context, as part of a broader mission. If they stand behind that mission, then they will feel great about their time/energy investment. Everyone will feel that they belong to something bigger. That's a huge factor in employee retention.

Recognition as I described above has the power to make work a place of greater meaning and deeper happiness if gratitude is treated as a linchpin of the workplace.

## Potential Profits from Gratitude

What is the financial benefit of being a great place to work?

- The Great Place to Work Institute offers some statistics contrasting the performance of the 100 Best Companies against the U.S. average.

- The rate of attrition among the 100 best companies ranges from 50-65% ***lower*** than the U.S. median.

- The employee growth of Best Companies is ***five times*** the rate of the U.S. average (15.4% versus 3.2%).

- And lastly, there is a noticeable boost in ***recruiting reputation*** among these companies, which assures them less employee fugue, and ***more engagement*** from their present and prospective employees.

- The Hay Group, a global management consulting firm, shows that companies with top engagement scores have ***five times the revenue growth*** of companies with low scores.

In sum, gratitude and recognition will help guarantee the success and satisfaction of not only your company, but also your employees, by imbuing work with greater meaning and the gratification that only social appreciation can offer. We are, after all, inexorably human.

# CHAPTER 4

## *Understanding Power & Influence*

Recently, conversations about leadership, corporate culture, and management have revolved around the upheaval of command-and-control structures and approaches. It can be easy to forget that this upheaval comes with implicit assumptions that often condemn people's intentions.

For example, someone who is doing a job to wield influence may be seen as opportunistic, although they aren't necessarily a bad manager or leader. The ends do not justify the means, we have often heard; they also don't determine them.

In other words, there are many ways to accomplish a goal.

### Some Research on Influence

Research reveals that there are three predominant reasons why people go into management or accept administrative roles. The first is social affiliation, or the need to identify with and/or be liked by a group; the second is the need for achievement; and the third is the desire for influence, as in, power in a group.

## Being Political and Moral

There is a misconception that thinking about influence or acting politically is innately deceitful or fraught with disingenuousness. Certainly there are people who act in this way and do reprehensible things, but that isn't a function of acting politically, it's a function of sidestepping or stepping on people around you. It's a function of prioritizing ulterior motives over group priorities.

All that being said, if you want to compete in an environment infested with people like that, you need to know how to play the game, no matter the sector. That's why I have put together these tips. It's my attempt to arm you with the tools to compete and succeed in organizational environments.

## The Nine-step Plan

1. *Let people know about you.* The people in managerial and administrative positions in your workplace are probably so preoccupied with *their* own work that they don't have time to notice the finer points of *your* work. Don't assume that your boss is aware of your progress. Sure, they will notice big achievements or when you complete an assigned task well, but much is lost in the day-to-day.

   As such, the first order of business is to make sure that your boss notices your accomplishments and your effort. The easiest way to do this is to tell them. It's a simple matter of mere exposure.

   Social psychologist Robert Zajonc studied the mere exposure effect at length and described it as the phenomenon that people prefer, thereby choosing what is familiar to them.

   People like what they remember, and that includes you.

2. *Cultivate and hold onto influence.* People change over their lives. As you can change, you can develop qualities that help you cultivate influence

and eventually, hold onto it. The first step to any self-improvement is the belief that you can indeed change. You must believe that you can better yourself in deliberate and predetermined ways.

After that, you must assess your strengths and weaknesses dispassionately. Don't zero-in on negative traits more than positive ones; consider them on par and decide how to treat each one.

And, lastly, you must identify what traits are most important in your environment and work on harnessing those. Each space and culture will vary slightly so it's up to you to make those evaluations.

3. *Where you start affects where you will go.* Not all starting points are created equal, and not all career paths are the same.

   Some people have more advantages than others; some people create advantages for themselves; some people enjoy tremendous amounts of luck. The first and the last of these are largely out of your control, so there is little to no risk involved. The second is riddled with missed opportunities, risk, disappointments, and, alternatively, the satisfaction of a mission accomplished.

   When looking to place yourself in a position to succeed, you don't want to throw yourself into the shark tank immediately. You want to locate the places from where the shark tank draws its power and go there, or, identify niches where potential for growth exists that few people have stepped into.

4. *Staying silent is worse than being rejected.* You may not have heard of Reginald Lewis, but he taught me a valuable lesson. He was a successful African American corporate lawyer and founder of a buyout firm, TLC Group. Although his story isn't consigned to the history books, it is legendary.

   He was the first black man to own a company with revenues over $1 billion back in the 1980s. He grew up in a downtrodden part of

Baltimore, aspiring to study law at Harvard Law School. After he graduated from Virginia State University, he was accepted into a Rockefeller Foundation-funded program, where he discovered that those accepted were ineligible for admission to Harvard Law School. He defiantly approached the dean of admission, argued that his presence at the school would be mutually beneficial, and became the first person to gain admission to Harvard Law School before even applying.

Lewis understood that the worst that could happen from asking for something would be getting turned down. And if he were turned down, so what? People who ask and do not receive are no worse off than those who don't ask in the first place.

5. *Networking is about relationships.* Ever since I read this definition of networking from Hans-Georg Wolff and Klaus Moser, I never forgot it. Networking: "Behaviors that are aimed at building, maintaining, and using informal relationships that possess the (potential) benefit of facilitating work-related activities of individuals by voluntarily gaining access to resources and maximizing advantages."

   This covers a broad array of behaviors. What I like is that it emphasizes intention, and the key verbs of "building, maintaining, and using" informal relationships.

   The focus should always be on cultivating relationships with others, not exploiting them. There must be some reciprocity there for it to work.

6. *Safeguard your reputation.* Your reputation is the highest capital you have, so you should be deliberate about how others perceive you. Don't leave this to chance. Granted, you cannot wield full control over the perception that others hold, but there is a large degree of influence you possess here. Let your actions, words, and outputs always align with a predetermined moral compass, wherever it may point.

One way to safeguard your reputation is to not avoid conflict. Surely you don't want to create it, but when it arises, be prepared to confront it with temperance.

A few things to remember is that a little tenderness can go a long way, and so too can leaving people a graceful out. Do not let your emotions get the best of you. It's fine to feel them. It's not fine to let them steer. Also, don't take things personally.

7. *Don't get overconfident.* Studies have shown that those who believe they wield influence tend to get overconfident, which results in greater risk-taking, less social regard, stereotyping, and tendency to see others as means. I advise that any intimation of these feelings and beliefs be dispelled immediately. They only cause you—and others—harm.

8. *Politics aren't inescapably nefarious.* Many people have an aversion to politics. They like to think that there is some way of opting out of "office politics." As almost any Ancient Greek philosopher would tell you, we are political animals. Everything we do is part of the body politic, whether we want it to be or not. There is nothing inherently undesirable about that.

   Politics can take many forms. It's up to you to decide what kind of political animal you want to be. Some politics can support general wellbeing, job satisfaction, and career development, while others that prioritize power over people can engender cut-throat workplaces where dissatisfaction is high.

9. *Find the right place for you.* And last but not least, find the right place for you. To do this you must be brutally honest about your strengths, weaknesses, and preferences. Your motive should be self-enhancement and you cannot do that if you aren't happy at your workplace. Part of the reason some people express unhappiness about their job is because they feel confined. Don't let others trap you or coerce you into behaviors you don't condone. And always objectively analyze the workplace.

What opportunities are there? What room for growth is there? Who will you work with? How can they further your career? These are objective questions that help guide your decision-making and put you in a position to succeed.

# CHAPTER 5

## *Leading Up*

Recently, much talk about leadership has centered on the unhorsing of the boss figure by the leader figure. In simple terms, the sharp distinction between the two roles is that the former relies on a power structure, whereas the latter relies on a collaborative structure.

Much of the advice and conversation has emphasized the new role of the leader: what it should look like; how it should make team-members feel; what individual differences should be addressed first and foremost, and how. Most of these considerations are one-way, and teamwork is a two-way street. So, it begs the question: what about the path from team-members to leaders?

These new leaders are working to change their ways in order to increase efficiency, job satisfaction, and productivity.

How then do team-members fit into and amplify that resolve?

### Be Your Own Manager

The approach comes from John C. Maxwell's *The 360 Degree Leader*. He explains that each team-member's underlying strategy should be to support the leader. The best way to do that is to be attuned to oneself, and to manage oneself. That way, the leader can focus on overarching goals, tasks, and structures, while each team-member heads up their specific tasks that shore up larger efforts. In this way, team-members relieve the leader of administrative tasks, allowing them to focus more on supporting the team's efforts.

What's more, doing this consistently will increase group harmony and nurture trust. When your team leader and team-members know that you can manage yourself, and that you have a track record of tangible success, they will grow to trust you. This is a conduit to greater responsibility and autonomy within the group. It's a process—a transformational process—but everyone learns along the way.

## What Does Manage Yourself Mean?

It means moderating and tending to your emotions, time, priorities, energy, thinking, words, and personal life. One or any combination of these factors when unmanaged can encumber upon the group dynamic. When you successfully manage them with temperance and conviction, you sustain the right environment for collective triumph.

Here are some more concrete suggestions on how to manage yourself:

1. *First, do your own job well.* When you identify a problem, try to fix it. If you can't fix it or aren't allowed to, then bring it up to the person who can with solutions at hand. Sometimes that will mean railing against the status quo. So be it as long as your intention is the betterment of the team as a whole.

2. *Successful people do things that unsuccessful people are unwilling to do.* This is best typified as the "whatever-it-takes" attitude. It means not taking the easy way out, it means giving your all, it means saying the things that others don't want to hear, it means helping your team and its leaders acquire a new perspective so long as it comes from a place

of enrichment. It means acting because it matters, not because it looks good or will get you a promotion.

When, how, and to what extent you pursue each of these imperatives depends on the collective heartbeat. You can tell. You can take the pulse of the group. Once you learn what makes the group tick, what its weaknesses and strengths are, what its priorities are, who its constituents are, that is when you can learn how to align yourself in a profitable and productive way.

## Old Habits Die Hard and How to Survive Them

True, many bosses are changing their approach to leadership and management, but equally true is that others are not. Some bosses are unwilling or constitutionally unable to change their ways. That puts you in a polarizing position to either adjust or escape.

For scenarios like this one, I like the lion tamer analogy developed by Steven L. Katz in *Lion Taming*. Some bosses are lions. They roar, bite, and attack unpredictably. You should be a lion tamer. It's one of the best skills to develop when you are in a lion's den.

The lion tamer is constantly looking for optimal ways to work with the lions. Lion tamers want to have proactive and productive relationships without compromising their own wellbeing. The lion tamer recognizes that the lions think differently than everyone else and gets into their heads. They understand what shapes the lion's perception of the world: in most cases, lions see you as either prey, an enemy, or ignorable. Prey, they eat; the enemy, they kill; and everyone else, they disregard. What is left? Being on par with the lions without being a lion.

In essence, being a lion tamer means:

- Strengthening your self-perception and self-image.
- Playing a proactive, observant, and strategic role instead of having to feel that you are in a subordinate or weaker position.
- Recognizing who the lions are and what they want to be the lions of.
- Trusting your own intuition and instincts while verifying what others see and experience in similar situations.
- Observing more and reacting less.
- Establishing your own presence, reputation, and authenticity.
- Deciding with or for whom you want to work and why.

Many of these kernels of advice flow from the belief that you cannot be a lion tamer, you cannot be a vital team member, you cannot support your leader and your team if you do not recognize your own self-worth. When you do so, you remove psychological obstacles from your path and grant yourself permission to be, unapologetically.

## Embrace Your Value and Harness It

You aren't a cog. You weren't born a cog. You can feel like a cog, and others can make you feel like a cog, but that doesn't mean you are one. You have skills, experiences, and knowledge that can make you indispensable to a group. Part of that has to do with the group dynamic, and part of that has to do with embracing your own value.

I don't mean for this to come off fanciful. What I am communicating is that each person, within reason, should recognize what they contribute to the team and see their value in that context. Otherwise, they risk being short-changed, exploited, or undervalued.

All things being equal, this self-evaluation should center on material outputs. No, I don't mean how much money you make (although that can factor in). I mean what you *do*. What you do may not generate the greatest amount of relative revenue, but that doesn't mean that it isn't an essential element in the functioning of the team.

Remember the point about context? Context influences how action is perceived, and it influences how you perceive yourself. A work environment where unquestioning rule following is the norm will penalize autonomy; whereas an environment where independence and innovation is the norm will denigrate a "follow the leader" attitude.

This is a dramatic shift from just a few years ago, and it bears greatly on self-perception. At one point in time the American Dream included a directive to keep your head down, follow instructions, show up on time, work hard, suck it up, and wait to be rewarded.

The new American Dream looks a little like this. Be remarkable. Be generous. Create art. Make judgment calls. Connect people and ideas. And leaders will have no choice but to reward you.

You can't do any of those things though, if you don't reward and value yourself first.

## Tune in to Your Presence

Your presence is the combination of all these features. It's the confluence of your actions and contributions to the team, of your ability to grapple with lions, tigers, and bears, and your self-perception. When you have a positive outlook on these three features, backed by lived experience, you will have a powerful presence.

Granted, your presence is also the sum of countless features that inherently provide little value but superficially evoke respect, authority, or expertise; things like where you went to school, how you look, how articulate you are, and what you claim to know. In today's conversation on leadership we are undercutting the primacy of those once-pivotal attributes, but that doesn't mean they don't hold sway. We all fall prey to the smoke and mirrors, and that's all right. The problem is when smoke and mirrors is all you have.

The oldest Dale Carnegie technique in the popularity manual applies here: show interest, ask questions, listen, engage, add value, be empathetic, and, by all means, be yourself—your amplified self.

Like it or not, people will judge you, so if you can influence their judgment to a large extent without driving yourself mad, do so. But let it be a result of your hard work, your social adeptness, and your self-confidence.

# CHAPTER 6

## *Persuading People to See Your Way*

As an executive I am constantly in front of clients, customers, partners and investors. Every step of the way, I have learned to translate my vision so that others can see its merit and thereby be better aligned in thought. With time, study, experience, and practice, I have gathered a few tips on the art and science of persuasion that I'd like to share.

Persuasion is a grimy word to some. It connotes coercion, manipulation, and nefarious quick wit. If we take a moment to piece apart the definition of "persuade" offered by Merriam Webster, we'll see that persuasion isn't quite as seedy as some people may assume.

To "persuade" is to cause (someone) to do something through reasoning or argument. This suggests that there are different ways of persuading someone since reasoning and argument can take many forms. Some arguments appeal directly to the mind while others appeal to the heart, and yet others appeal to both. Surely there are unethical ways to influence mind and heart, but that is up to the persuader. In either case, persuasion is aimed at one thing: to change someone's perception or course of action toward something.

In that end-oriented sense, persuasion seeks to accomplish one of two things with respect to action. A persuader either wants to get someone to do or not to do. In some contexts, an intuitive and sophisticated understanding of persuasion is essential. It can mean eat or be eaten. In the contemporary work environment with so much competition, this skill-set is integral.

Moreover, persuasion is vital because of its deep tie to a basic social impulse. That is, the impulse to have things happens how we want them to. I'm sure that you've experienced this impulse in your professional life, in your family life, and in your friendships. You decide that a course of action is correct, so you set out to convince others, and when they do not agree, you become indignant and aggravated.

Given that persuasion is an inherent part of our relationships, we might as well glean how, precisely, to do it best.

## How to Identify a Persuasion Priority

The object of your persuasion is a "persuasion priority." The launching pad should always be, "Who is the person you want to hear yes from, and for what?" Whoever the person is, your persuasion priority must be evaluated against four criteria.

1. What would the impact of attaining that goal be to you or your organization?
2. Is it large enough to make a perceptible difference to your life or the lives of others?
3. Is it so large a request that it is unattainable?
4. How likely is it that more people other than me will benefit from the outcome?

In a professional environment, you may encounter people who exude confidence and charisma. In my experience, the most persuasive people tend to possess certain attributes, such as assertiveness, empathy, communicativeness, tenacity, and resilience. These people already know about priority points, although they may not consciously recognize them. The criteria above span the gamut of impacts, affective drives, social values, and perception. These are chief features to developing a persuasive line of reasoning and argumentation.

## Persuasion is Social at Heart

At heart, persuasion is a social act. The very act of trying to convince someone must finely balance psychological and sociological norms, assumptions, and expectations, in addition to compelling reasoning. There are two linchpins of persuasion that easily subsume the individual and group aspects of persuasion: reciprocity and congruency.

Reciprocity is about benefit, balance, and survival. When it comes to persuasion that pays deference to reciprocity, we must adopt a give-and-take mindset. This consists of your willingness to proactively pursue the self-interest of another person and your willingness to accept help from others. Not only must you give in equal measure, you must also take in equal measure.

Congruency is about unity. To effectively persuade someone, your actions must reflect your thoughts. You must believe in whatever you are advancing; otherwise, your words and your actions will fall flat. You must convince yourself before you can convince others.

A few brilliant people have spent a lot of time thinking about the features of persuasion: reciprocity, congruency, impact, significance, and practicality. Several theories of persuasion have sprung from their considerations, but there is one in particular that has stood out to me.

## Unified Field Theory of Persuasion, or Something Like It

Robert Cialdini is a professor emeritus of Arizona State University, and he created something quite like the seminal Unified Field Theory of Persuasion, but with a few twists.

He was inspired by Herbet A. Simon's approach to decision-making that emphasizes the influence of heuristics and biases. Biases, much like optical illusions, can sometimes confound us. Life with its unpredictability can also confound us. That is why we have evolved heuristics, which are mental shortcuts that allow us to make quick decisions accurately.

Armed with these concepts, Cialdini parsed out persuasion into six distinct categories: reciprocity, scarcity, consistency, liking, authority, and social proof. Think of them as "persuasion by way of…"

1. Reciprocity involves give and take. It involves mutual or collective interest.
2. Scarcity involves finitude. It entails leveraging the reality of limited resources, including time.
3. Consistency involves trust. People prefer predictability and people who do what they say they will.
4. Authority involves power. When you have expertise or insider knowledge, you are in a power position.
5. Social proof involves anecdotal information. Social proof comes in various forms. Whatever form it comes in, the core will be testimonial.
6. Liking involves likability. Simply put, when someone likes another person, they are far easier to persuade. Reflective glory, influencer marketing, and endorsement all thrive on this concept.

Positives as well as negatives can aid your persuasiveness. We must recognize the laudable features of decision-making, and so too must we recognize the failings. In this case, biases.

***Availability Bias.*** We tend to place greater confidence on the information that we recall more easily. When you keep key information fresh in someone's mind, they are more likely to trust it.

***Halo Effect.*** When we identify someone as having one positive attribute, we tend to apply that positivity unilaterally to other aspects of their lives.

***Confirmation Bias.*** When we hold a belief or conclusion to be true, we tend to seek out confirmation, despite evidence to the contrary.

## How Individual Factors Come into Play

Although the strategies, approaches, and categorizations above apply broadly to most human interactions, there are a number of individual factors that we must keep in mind also. This advice is akin to the adage "Know your audience."

The same kind of information or presentation will not have equal affective and persuasive force on every person. In the book *Personal Styles and Effective Performance,* David Merrill and Roger Reid identified four personalities based on the axes of assertiveness and responsiveness.

1. *Driving.* This personality type is characterized by power and autonomy seeking through facts and concrete information.

2. *Expressive.* This personality type is characterized as communicative and competitive.

3. *Amiable.* This personality type is characterized as relationship-oriented and cooperative.

4. *Analytical.* This personality type is technical and logistical. They want to know how, why, and who. They are risk-averse.

The advantage of identifying these personality types is that they can help us learn how to treat people the way they want to be treated.

For example, a Driver does not enjoy small talk. They prefer facts not feelings, and they appreciate concision. An Expressive enjoys high energy and fun. They allow for digression and story sharing. An Amiable prefers to get personal, and form a bond as quickly as they can. An Analytical leaves no question unanswered and makes sure to cite sources.

## Are You of the Digital Persuasion?

Technology plays a crucial role in just about every layer of human activity nowadays. Persuasion is not exempt. Take as an example Computer-Mediated Communication (CMC).

We use text messaging, emails, video conferencing, and phone calls to communicate on a near daily basis. Don't let these interfaces undercut your persuasive ability. Learn to adapt to the mode of communication by wielding emoticons, being concise, funny, and grabbing hold of your reader's attention.

## Persuasion as a Lost Art

Persuasion is also known as rhetoric. For some, rhetoric is an even dirtier word than persuasion. In truth, that depends on the perspective of the persuader. Persuasion isn't necessarily unethical, nor must it be. If your end is ethical and your means are ethical, then you should be in the clear. However, if your end is ethical but your means are reprehensible, then you are making a mistake. There is a rule of thumb (a heuristic) that

Daniel Pink offers for operating ethically. "Treat everyone as you would your grandmother." It's fine advice.

With that clearly established, we can move on to a more formulaic conversation on persuasion without running the risk of sounding hawkish.

## The Persuasion Equation

If you were to ask people what they think the secret to persuasion is, you'd have many different yet overlapping responses. What most people do not have is an equation. Your persuasion equation can be a guiding star.

This is a time-tested and evidence-based persuasion equation: A Great Business Case + Your Outstanding Credibility + Compelling Language. Let's break it down a bit.

## The Persuasion Equation: A Great Business Case

A *Great Business Case* refers to logic and emotion. If you want to appeal to logic, do so in quantitative terms. If you want to appeal to emotion, then do so in qualitative terms.

The former is much more difficult than the later. When you feel overwhelmed by numbers, figures, and stats, remember that you'll never attain your maximum persuasiveness being afraid of your calculator.

The latter is predominantly emotional. Qualitative reasoning can be used to accomplish at least six emotion-driven objectives.

1. *Provoke.* To cause a reaction, particularly anger.
2. *Invoke.* To give people positive expectation and a fulfilling reason for agreement.

3. *Awaken.* To cause someone to experience a novel emotion or realization.

4. *Arouse.* To get someone motivated about new ideas and possibilities.

5. *Touch.* To evoke sympathy or empathy.

6. *Ignite.* To spur people into action with a sense of achievement.

The goal is to incorporate at least one of these emotional strategies into your business case. This will help you connect with your audience on a deeper, more intuitive level.

A business case bolstered by an emotional strategy can amount to nothing, however, if the speaker does not win the trust of his audience.

## The Persuasion Equation: Your Credibility

Credibility and trust building are elemental to effective persuasion. If you do not possess expertise, a solid track record, or the respect of your audience, your attempts to convince someone to do things your way won't accomplish the intended effect. The good thing is that gaining credibility is much simpler than you might assume.

Social proof, as I mentioned above, is a potent conduit to credibility. When others believe in you, it is far more likely that strangers will too. Think about the success of reviews on platforms such as Yelp. Some businesses have staked their claim to fame on those reviews. Individual people are no different.

Another way to establish your credibility is by publicizing your success. This doesn't mean you should go on an ego trip, but be proud of your successes. Recounting your progress with humility can help increase credibility and self-satisfaction.

Accountability. I cannot overstate the importance of accountability. People must believe that you are genuinely devoted to your causes. It is easy enough to take credit when things go well. We should be equally as eager to accept responsibility when things do not. This is a power mechanism for credibility, trust, and reliability.

## The Persuasion Equation: Language and Body

In a rudimentary sense, persuasion is about language. Learning to determine what words to use and when is a skill. It takes time to develop. Without it, however, your persuasive ability may suffer tremendously.

One directive to bear in mind is that people are more inclined to believe what they can picture. Using adjectives and descriptive language can often help you bridge the gap between possibility and plausibility. Be careful not to wax rhapsodic, or you'll sound like you're full of fluff.

Another directive is to connect your language to your audience. If you have an opportunity to ask questions, discern what your words mean to your listener. Often we assume persuasion is mostly about quick wit and fast-talking. The dialectical approach to persuasion relies on question and answer. It shows you are open and listening. That can help establish credibility too.

The final directive is that language is communication, and communication is myriad. Sometimes a gesture, a look, or no body movement at all can communicate volumes. The power of nonverbal communication is astounding.

When it comes to persuasion, writers on the subject talk about bodily communication as poker players would. They talk about tells. Here are a few commons tells and recommended responses.

***Steady Eye Contact.*** The person is attending to your words. Don't miss the opportunity to engage by speaking directly and holding eye contact.

***Wandering Eyes.*** The person is distracted or shy. Don't make any sudden movements; don't speak loudly. Cordiality and a swift smile will do just fine. Make the process painless.

***Attentive Smile.*** When someone smiles at you, you smile back. Don't spend too much time looking at the person. Try to make the encounter amiable and casual. A smile usually means good will.

***Disbelieving Squint.*** Your target is on the move. They are skeptical, uncertain, or unconvinced. You'll want to deploy some emotional strategies and engage the heart.

***Standoffish.*** When someone keeps their distance from you, it means they are not receptive. Don't take it personally. That will shut you down. Take the signal to mean, "Get in and get out quickly." Say your piece and move on. The heart is blocked.

That's the Persuasion Equation in a nutshell. It has worked wonders for me. Granted, it is not easy to keep in mind all at once, but with practice and mindfulness you can plan each facet efficiently.

## Some Polish on the Equation

The Persuasion Equation is formulaic, which can be off-putting to some. Persuasion is not mathematical; it is human interaction, social. If it is easier for you to think about persuasion in less formulaic terms, then this next advice might make more sense to you.

## Engage. Explore. Reframe. Finalize.

It's a simple and clear-cut way to approach connecting with your audience and getting them to see through your eyes.

***Engage.*** Timing is everything. Find a time to discuss the topic at hand when your interlocutor is most approachable and receptive. In addition to when is how.

How you approach your interlocutor is very important. A face-to-face encounter is always preferable. Although it's a necessary evil, discard email, phone, and text conversations whenever possible.

***Explore.*** Once you've engaged, explore the topic at hand. You may not know your interlocutor well or at all. If you jump into the water too soon, you may find yourself in a turbulent tide with no escape route. This is how you take the temperature. You can gauge emotional response, degree of knowledge, level of significance and relevance, and, if applicable, financial situation.

This phase creates a solid rapport based on balance. Remember to ask, speak, ask. Don't underestimate the power of good questions.

***Reframe.*** This part of the process speaks to propositions. When you are presenting a proposal or some other proposition, make sure to give at least three options. Discuss the benefits and dis-benefits objectively. Furthermore, since you've gone through the exploration phase, you may already have a sense of your interlocutor's priorities. Be sure to address those too.

***Finalize.*** Do not fear objection or rejection. Objection especially is a sign of interest. The deadliest response is apathy. That means you didn't succeed at engaging your interlocutor either at the beginning or all the way through to the very end. If that happens, do not fret. Ask your interlocutor's opinion. Give them an opportunity to voice their concerns and the reasons for their dissent or disinterest. Then, take it from there.

## United We Stand, Divided We Decide

Seldom do groups decide together. They may discuss, debate, and argue together, but generally, the best way to ensure group satisfaction when it comes to decision-making is to have each person deliberate and decide independently. Often in groups, some people will feel drowned out or influenced by others, which can breed resentment after the fact.

The best advice I can offer when it comes to group persuasion is that what you need is a consensus, not unanimity. To do this you need to balance pragmatism, charisma, leadership, and credibility. These are the things that groups tend to demand from their speakers.

As for the specific strategy, the Persuasion Equation still applies.

## The Dos and Don'ts of Persuasion Success

We have spent all this time exploring how to persuade, what persuasion is, and what it is not. There is one more topic of importance that I like to refer to as the post-mortem.

Imagine that you've put together a tight pitch, crunched all your numbers, spoken measuredly and evocatively, and calculated all of your nonverbal communication. And then, your interlocutors agree. They are buying what you're selling. At this point, you can't afford to screw things up by making an amateur mistake.

There are five don'ts that I recommend.

1. Don't reply with incredulity.

2. Don't keep selling your case.

3. Don't review concerns.

4. Don't be unprepared.

5. Don't bask in the limelight.

And, naturally, there are the four dos of success.

1. Offer encouragement and satisfaction.
2. Provide next steps.
3. Get your client to follow through with an action.
4. Publicity means accountability.

## Persuasion Starts with You

The final part of this article is where you should start the entire process: you.

If you step into a situation or preempt it with negative self-talk, you are undermining yourself from the gate. Remember, you must believe in yourself and believe in what you are pitching. That candor and excitement will spill onto your audience.

Sometimes our internal dialogue is injuriously negative. Be cognizant of your internal dialogue and reframe negative thoughts.

Don't reprimand yourself, though. Keep an optimistic outlook and be pragmatic. This involves an honest self-review. Listing your strengths and weaknesses and adding experiential evidence to each assessment can help keep you realistic and grounded.

Grounding yourself is easier when you have a clear sense of what success means to you. Make sure to set-up small goals that aggregate to big wins. That covers much of the cognitive side of success.

Additionally, we shouldn't neglect our bodies. Proper rest, high dopamine levels from reduced stress, good food, and physical activity all enhance our persuasive abilities by maintaining a healthy brain and heart.

## Parting Words

Persuasion is social, but it starts with you. You must convince yourself of your value and of your ability. The first person who you need to sell on your pitch is you.

# CHAPTER 7

## *Leaders Know Which Buttons to Press*

Those of you who have kids or are kids at heart may have seen the film *Inside Out*. It is an animation about the adventures of five "emotions," five characters that live within a little girl's head and dictate her reactions to the events around her. The characters are Joy, Sadness, Fear, Disgust, and Anger.

It is a simplistic version of what really goes on in our heads, but there is much truth to the basic premise. The characters' work is based around a control panel, and they can press various buttons and pull certain levers to produce a suitable reaction in the girl. They don't always get it right, and this is what gives the film its charming and true-to-life quality.

The film also briefly lets us into the heads of the mother and father of the girl, and there we see slightly different versions of these five emotions. You are left with the impression that they are unique to each of us in our idiosyncrasies.

It made me think about some of the best leaders in business and how they seem to have a direct shortcut to the control panels of their teams. They understand how to influence each person on an individual level, and the key to this is that pressing a certain button for one person will not have the same effect as pressing it for another person.

One manager may be motivated by the fear of failure, and although this should not be abused, every now and again, a gentle hint as to the ramifications might do the trick. On the other hand, hinting at potential failure to someone else might cause them to freeze and back away; they might need more of an encouraging and coaxing hand.

Leaders learn about how their people react in certain situations by observing them and listening to them. They build up an "instruction manual" in their heads, and with every new experience, they are that little bit better informed as to which buttons to press in the future. Of course, it is impossible to get into someone's head entirely (unless you are a hypnotist), but the key is to understand someone's preferred behavior patterns. When the time comes, there is less doubt about which buttons to press.

I suppose that this could be seen as the key to influencing. Doing something or saying something, "pressing the button," elicits the desired reaction from someone. To influence, you have to be able to touch people right in their core, reaching the essence of who they are and appealing to their, "Oh yeah, I thought that" mentality. Once you have done that successfully a few times, they will let you in a lot more readily in the future, and it becomes ever easier to bring them on board—even when they may not have chosen to do it themselves.

In the film *Inside Out*, the two key emotions are Joy and Sadness, and the message of the film is that sometimes emotions have to work in tandem for a contented life. Sadness is natural when you have suffered a loss (in life or in business), so forcing a smile and acting as if nothing has happened won't help you get over it anytime soon. Sometimes you need to be "down" to be able to feel "up" again. Some may call this authenticity—being true to your emotions.

The best leaders are authentic and genuine with their people. They are upset when something has gone wrong, and they show empathy for their people when they are upset. There is nothing worse than the hyper-cheerful leader who doesn't let anything phase them. Life is hard sometimes; if you show your team that you feel it, they will appreciate your sympathy even more when they are having a hard time.

Getting into people's heads is easier when they can relate to you. If they feel that you are on their side, they will let you press their buttons.

# CHAPTER 8

## *Igniting Passion & Motivation in Employees*

I have been both an employee and an employer.

As an employee, I have seen myself at low points because of work-related stress and pressures. It took a fair share of introspection and reflection to regain my passion for a company or job that might have lost its luster over the course of time. It happens to the best of us.

As an employer, I have relentlessly tried to create an environment that allows my employees and colleagues to sustain their groove, kindle their passions, and learn more about themselves. This, without a doubt, is one of the biggest challenges that today's companies face. The bright side is that when it is done right, the rewards are endless.

In order to address these crucial issues of life and career, I set about trying to discover what great companies do with their employees that allow them to stay motivated and passionate. I spoke with many of my clients and customers, read books on the topic*, and evaluated my own experiences.

This article, I will warn, is not a short one like some of my other chapters, as this I felt this topic was just too important to gloss over.

## Work Culture Is Always in Flux

"You are the company you keep." Personal success and business success are functions of the company you keep. This ancient wisdom packs so much practical information and insight into the nature of human relationships that it is astounding how quickly we can forget it. The motivations and abilities of the people that you surround yourself with can push you far beyond your potential. In a company, this can mean greater success not only for you but also for everyone in the company. Over time, the habits and values of mutually shared success can mature into a full-fledged culture—a culture that places emphasis on sharing visions and goals, on communication and transparency, and on growth and innovation. A culture like that is much better equipped to thrive in today's economy and workforce. The reason is that in this environment certain values lose their appeal while others come to the fore.

## Old School

In the old-school model of corporate success, time and effort are construed as functions of money. Employer and employee are bound by a system of financial rewards devoid of fundamental satisfaction. Aside from the socio-emotional aspects, the model is simply unsustainable. The efficacy of this model is inextricably tied to the market. When there is job scarcity or the proffered wage is above market rates, for example, workers will acquiesce despite reservations. Conversely, when there is a market upturn, then employers find themselves in direct competition for workers. Whatever the economic reality, however, the common denominator is that workers are usually unhappy with their work when their sole reason for being these is money. I do not believe this is because people reflexively dislike work. I believe people can derive profound fulfillment from work, just not when it is solely about money.

## New School

Employers should endeavor to stoke the passions of their employees with other means than monetary incentives. There are many ways to do this that trigger higher levels of gratification, satisfaction, and loyalty. When that happens, engagement is born, and that is a force to reckon with. When employees are engaged, their passion ignites, ideas flourish, and the people around them are sparked into action. Their energy increases too. That yields great productivity, creativity, and performance. As you, the employer, see this all manifest, you'll be prompted to reward the person, promote them, and invest in their developments. This wonderful dynamic is the passion and motivation cycle, also known as positive reinforcement.

## Engagement and Passion Starts with You

The triumph of a passionate and motivational employer-employee relationship lies in commitment, focus, and effort. This triad of feel-good experiences stems from you, the employer. Why? "You are the company you keep."

Until you decide what kind of employer you want to be, what culture you want to create, and what steps will lead you to succeed, you won't choose the right people to surround yourself with. This isn't to say that everything is about you, but it surely starts with you.

Employees also have needs and desires. Those should be acknowledged. They should be respected. They should be adsorbed into your relationship. On the main, there are seven prevalent employee expectations that, when nurtured, can engender passion, motivation, and commitment:

1. Compensation

2. Alignment

3. Atmosphere
4. Growth
5. Acknowledgement
6. Autonomy
7. Communication

Consider these expectations the pillars of a transparent and human-oriented work culture. They are the cradles for success in today's economy. Google is an excellent example. So is Apple. They have cultures so successful that other companies strive to emulate them.

## Quid Pro Quo

The right compensation structure can yield tremendous gains in your company. As I mentioned above, that alone won't guarantee motivation. But, the wrong compensation structure will invariably yield unhappiness. It's an easy wager, really.

However, the goal shouldn't be to provide only monetary incentives. Those are easy to disregard and easy to compete with. If the only advantage you have over your competitors is pay, there are many ways a competitor can outdo you.

Compensation isn't limited to money. Compensation also means promotions, benefits, awards, and bonuses. There are three vital facets of a satisfactory compensation model.

1. *Transparency.* Some organizations—and people—are quite mysterious about their finances. This opacity undercuts transparency. When resources and praise are being distributed equally, don't hide it! Let everyone know what wages are like, what it takes to ascend within the

company, and specifically, what someone could do to reach their next benchmark.

2. *Overpay.* There are some companies that pride themselves on paying the highest wages in their respective industries. Research from Towers Watson shows that employees who believe they are paid fairly are 4.5 times as likely to be highly engaged when compared with their disappointed counterparts. Money isn't everything, but it is important.

3. *Achievement.* Share success throughout the company in a genuine and palpable way. Employees who feel their efforts are tied to the company's success tend to engage more in the company as a whole. An outcome-based approach focused an employee's self-improvement and development can lead to relationship building and heightened levels of motivation.

## I Walk the Line

Values are worthless when they aren't followed by action. Companies today are expected to uphold certain social values beyond consumer satisfaction. They are expected to be environmentally responsible and social conscientious. The acid test of whether companies are enacting their proclaimed values is their employee engagement. When companies enact the values that they preach, their employees tend promote the company. They advocate for it in public, which takes numerous forms nowadays.

This is the byproduct of employer-employee alignment. It's the byproduct of putting your money where your mouth is. No longer will consumers and employees accept empty rhetoric. You must show your true colors and let them fly. This starts with creating, revising, and reviewing your company's basic core values, and then asking yourself, "Are we promoting these values?" When you start this process, be sure to include your employees and to call upon your customers. You won't understand the distance between your self-perception and public opinion until you ask other people.

Once you have assessed and diagnosed your state, begin deploying strategies to sustain and enforce your values. Here are a few strategies of my own making:

***Interview.*** Interview based on your values. You should prime and filter people from the get-go.

***Train.*** Train in accordance with your values. Make sure they permeate every job function.

***Reprimand.*** Delineate clear consequences for violations of core values. You mean business.

***Evaluate.*** Provide employee evaluations that reference your core values.

***Demonstrate.*** Lead by example. Hypocrisy is intolerable from authority figures. You should embody your company's core values.

Morality alone won't keep employees motivated, but it's an important ingredient. Once you have a proper compensation system guided by core values, your employees will feel secure and at ease. They will also begin to feel more engaged.

## A Breath of Fresh Air

Atmosphere is an elusive concept. It's the result of myriad factors, including personal ones that you can't control as an employer. Relativity notwithstanding, it's an important component of motivation and passion, and one that shouldn't be left to happenstance. Atmosphere is a deliberate choice, and even if it isn't playing out as planned, the intention to create a particular environment can suffice to motivate and impassion employees.

A good starting point in this case is not you but rather your employees. There are six questions that employees often ask themselves about their employer:

1. *Is my employer doing everything possible to advance my safety?*
2. *Do I have what I need to excel at this job?*
3. *Do I like, respect, and trust my employer?*
4. *How do I feel about my co-workers on a day-to-day basis?*
5. *Do I feel energized in this environment, or do I just want to escape it?*
6. *Am I enjoying myself?*

I am not suggesting people ask themselves these questions precisely. I imagine they ask themselves some iteration of these. They all point at satisfaction, fulfillment, the quality of interpersonal relationships, and independence. I think every human shares a positive desire for these things.

## Growth Isn't Just for Plants

Growth is about development. It is less so about the ends than it is about the means. Employees want a chance to demonstrate their worth, their talents, and their stuff. At the same time, they want to feel challenged and spurred into action so that they can develop and grow.

Growth is even better when it is a shared experience. If the employer is not growing with the employee, then the relationship shifts from fellow learners to teacher-student, and that's a power dynamic that many employees do not enjoy. As is the norm, I have a five-step growth formula. These are some of the tricks I've picked up over the years.

1. *Growth Agenda.* Initially an employer and an employee will probably want the same things. Over time, their priorities and needs will

change. Setting a growth agenda with periodic reviews can ensure you stay on the same page in a mutually beneficial way.

2. *Timetable.* Just as a consensus of growth goals is important, so too is a consensus on a timeline. Without a timeline, there can be no accountability.

3. *Individualization.* Every growth agenda and timetable must cater to the individual who it's supposed to benefit. Every person also has different approaches, learning styles, and milestones that work for them. This must also be individualized.

4. *Celebrate.* Share in success together and celebrate each other's successful attainment of predetermined growth goals. This kind of shared experience can validate efforts and help maintain a healthy employer-employee relationship.

5. *Again.* Once a growth agenda is completed, start again!

## I See You and You See Me

Defying expectations can teach us lifelong lessons. Wegman's is a supermarket that defies all expectations yet teaches us a lesson in employer-employee relationships that we should carry with us. The employees who enter this chain supermarket store often enter with a "just another job" mentality. It is there that Wegman's has staked its claim to fame since 1998. Wegman's has ventured to create a culture that encourages loyalty through acknowledgement and pride.

Fortune's *100 Best Places to Work for* has listed Wegman's Food Markets since the list's inception in 1998. In 2012 and 2014, it was named best supermarket chain in the United States. The culture of acknowledgement and pride is ingrained into everything they do.

Acknowledgement is an important word to apprehend. Acknowledgement has a unique psychological texture; It is active, congratulatory, and exalting. When you acknowledge someone for something, you communicate its extraordinariness and its worth.

Furthermore, acknowledgement goes beyond accomplishments and gets at a person's admirable attributes. It indicates their character.

There are four touchstones of acknowledgement.

1. *Personal.* Any acknowledgement must be evaluated against the backdrop of that individual person's capabilities. Not everyone should be weighed on the same scale.
2. *Proportional and Pertinent.* An acknowledgement must be proportional to the thing acknowledged. The same goes for rewards. It must also be related.
3. *Prompt.* Don't wait too long. It'll seem disingenuous.
4. *Public.* Tell the world.

Wegman's couples this acknowledgement model with a customer-first model. This is a killer combo. When you have a happy employee who puts your customers first, then you have happy customers.

## I Am My Own Person

Independence is a correlate of freedom, and most people crave it from the moment they begin to walk. There are numerous societal guide posts that ever-increase the range of our freedom. As we get older, that freedom decreases. For some people, entering the workforce marks a significant reduction in their independence, and consequently, in their freedom.

Employers are sometimes nervous to confer increased independence in the workplace because of the potential risks. The notion that oversight is necessary to assure that employees will do their jobs properly and efficiently is endemic to most industries. The downside is that employers who operate under this assumption tamper with trust building. Employees will not feel autonomous, they will not feel trusted, and they will not feel connected to the company or their employers. All this will undermine motivation and passion.

To undo this vicious cycle, employers should strive to cultivate a more entrepreneurial environment in their workplace, where employers provide conditions to empower their employees. The conditions should be conduits for self-direction and expertise-building that channel them toward mutual success.

The basic tenets of company entrepreneurship are independence, creativity, passion, and a desire to succeed. When you find ambitious employees, they will tell you where they want to go. What you need to do is figure out how to help them get there, and, concomitantly, how they can help you along the way. It's autonomy with a mutually assured benefit.

Companies that promote autonomy need to set concrete goals and parameters. Jointly established rules, expectations, and areas for growth are requisites. There are nine ways to nurture a culture of autonomy in the workplace:

1. *Our Vision.* Employers and employees must have overlapping visions.
2. *Goal Setting.* Delimiting concrete and realistic goals, meeting them, and celebrating them is key.
3. *Tell Me Why.* Don't just bark directives. Explain your reasoning. You'd be surprised what explaining your madness can accomplish.
4. *You Decide How.* Let your employee decide how they accomplish something. They know themselves better than you know them. You should provide guidance whenever necessary.

5. *Delegate.* Many hands make for light work. Learn to leverage your resources. Let your employees identify where they could use assistance and help them delegate accordingly.

6. *Trust First.* Be upfront about giving your employees trust before they have earned it. It places the burden of reciprocity on them.

7. *Problem-Solving.* Encourage employees to find solutions to their problems first. Self-sufficiency is key.

8. *Accountability.* When you set goals with another person and hold each other responsible, accountability is generated. That is a good way to stay on track.

9. *Acknowledgement.* I said a lot about it above. Tell people when they have done something well.

## Talk to Me

I've written on the importance of communication at the personal and organizational levels. We all know—or so I would like to think—that this is old hat by now. The problem with conventional wisdom is that we usually recognize its significance without actually dissecting it into implementable terms.

To make a long story short, here are a few basic points about communication that I think stimulate healthy employer-employee relationships and instill motivation and passion in employees.

***Need to Know.*** There are certain things that employees need to know, like safety protocols, legal procedures, and contract terms (mostly legal and liability information).

***Want to Know.*** Employees do not like being in the dark. In fact, most people dislike being in the dark—fear of the unknown and such. Employees want to know what their work amounts to. They want to know what your plans for the future are and how they might fit into them. Employees want to know how they can improve. Employees want to know things that you might not be able to foresee, so you should ask. Ask them what they want to know. It's communicative and transparent.

***Should Know.*** Employees should know that you are invested in their success and that you are always willing to listen or make time. Employees should know that your relationship is professional, but it doesn't just stop at work outputs and paychecks. The most successful companies rely on strong interpersonal connections and sharing information to cultivate trust, open communication, and long-lasting bonds. Those are the ties that resist change.

## You Are the Company You Keep

I said it above, and I have now said it below. As an employer, you are in control of the people who surround you. You can decide the kind of team you want to build. That team can grow its own unique culture that meets the needs, desires, and aspirations of its constituents. It can also take you on a journey toward success and fulfillment. When you find a group of people who also want to take that journey with a clear set of values aimed at growth, open communication, fair compensation, and collective spirit, innovation can happen.

# CHAPTER 9

## *Bringing Disruptive but Lasting Change*

When you want to change your circumstances, you have to commit fully. Action cannot wait. Taking the time to consider the pros and cons, cook up a strategy, and weigh out the evidence is not a precursor to change, but rather, a concerted effort to bring to life a vision that only exists in your mind.

From the onset, change-seekers must be courageous. There will be setbacks; there will be customs to confront; there will be resistance; there will be lessons to learn about communication, sensitivity, reciprocity, and solidarity; and there will also be discomfort. There is much at stake, which is why change shouldn't be an *ad hoc* process. In a journey into uncharted territory, it's best to be prepared.

So, the rub is that if you want to change your life or your company, you need courage and a strategy.

### How to Smooth the Way for Change That Defies Convention

There will always be reasons that assail you from every direction to stop pursuing the change you seek. Your inner voice and even the people around you will try to dissuade you.

Society is full of prohibitions and rules. That's an inexorable part of social environments that can sometimes hinder individual progress. If what you're proposing is a bold move that defies accepted norms, overcoming resistance from wherever it arrives will require constant effort.

When you are face-to face-with detraction, remember a few things.

***Repetition.*** A simple, concise, and repeatable summary that captures the end-goal of the change you seek has numerous benefits. A summary can ease communication, make the change feel more real, and increase persuasive power, while also serving as a guidepost and a motivational wellspring. The summary should communicate the inspiration behind the change too. Be it your employees, your friends, or your significant other, the listener should readily grasp why this vision of the future is most desirable.

***Communicate the Change.*** Whatever the change is, you are its mouthpiece and therefore, the best person to communicate the steps necessary for acceptance. According to Kevin Eiken Berry and Guy Harris in *From Bud to Boss*, the fulcrum point of great change from a leadership perspective is often how well you communicate the change to those you want to convince. Their ten-point strategy is an excellent litmus test to apply before presenting your idea:

1. *Draw in imagination.* Drawing people in requires one-on-one, personal conversations. Remember, people choose to change based on their beliefs. Helping them to see the dissatisfaction you see, believe in the vision, understand the steps, and reduce apparent risk is likely more about conversation and less about the beauty of your PowerPoint.

2. *Inspire ownership.* You must help people identify their place in your vision. A self-serving future lacks mass appeal. A collective vision with clear benefits for all possesses solidarity.

3. *Show process.* One of the biggest mistakes that leaders make in communicating change is falling prey to the Curse of Knowledge. As originator, you are intuitively familiar with the process that brought you to

conclude change is necessary. Others must be shown that process in a broken-down and relatable way.

4. *Call it a journey.* Especially if the change is large and complex, you must mollify intimidation by emphasizing that change is a journey, slow-going and gainly. Assure that the change will take time, and supporters will have time to learn and adjust incrementally.

5. *Ask questions.* Use questions to open lines of communication. Questions get people talking. Ask questions to understand their feelings about the change.

6. *Small bites.* Build a new status quo gradually. By advancing on the change a little bit at a time, you allow people to adapt to novelty.

7. *Ask questions.* Why is this here again? It's here again because it's that important for effective communication.

8. *Give it words.* Naming a thing grants power and confidence: you help people grasp the concept and make it easier for everyone—you included—to talk about it.

9. *Celebrate progress.* Celebrate any and all gains. Completion, effort, and personal challenges are all candidates for celebration. If you want to maintain and build momentum, as well as keep people on track, you must celebrate progress.

10. *Take responsibility.* As a leader, own success and failure. Don't displace blame, but rather, use shortcomings as opportunities for growth and proportionately revel in triumph.

Just as crucial as *what* you say and *why* you say it is *how* you say what you say. Some general tips on communication that I've picked up from others and my own experience are speak with—not at—people ; ask open-ended questions, not accusatory ones; demonstrate respect by default; speak about what you want rather than what you don't want; use "and" more than "but" (the former amplifies while the latter disqualifies); keep the listener's self-interests in mind; and listen deeply, not just actively (conversation is not two simultaneous monologues).

## Deviation from the Norm Can Be Uncomfortable

The nature of the change you seek can be a great source of discomfort. Discomfort can hamper dialogue and undo attempts at honest and transparent communication. We are prone to avoid discomfort. It's in our nature because we don't like to feel exposed or vulnerable. This can present a stumbling block to change, causing dissent, disgruntlement, or fraction.

Talk-friendly is an approach to tame the elephant in the room. It underscores the importance of acknowledging feelings of discomfort and both the implicit and explicit assumptions and beliefs at play in any given conversation. This may sound aggressive, and it will probably be perceived as aggressive, which is why the general rules I listed above are vital.

The Talk-friendly approach is a three-part process:

1. Identify the source of doubt or discomfort.
2. Uncover underlying assumptions in an open and curious manner.
3. Make it safe for the person to share perspectives without fear of backlash.

Keep at the forefront of your mind that true, enduring change is never insular. It may start with the individual but invariably includes other people. It's social. It occurs among real people with issues that have consequences. The greater your sensitivity to context, the greater your chances of success.

Sensitivity to context is both intuitive learned. I believe that there are common and predictable underlying sources of tension that can eek out of us when we are uncomfortable or in disagreement. In *Leadership and the Art of Struggle*, Steven Snyder points out some of these common sources of tension.

He explains that tension spawns from a number of sources, some tensions being so deeply ingrained that even the feeler fails to recognize their source. Tension can arise from individual or institutional traditions (past), from aspirations (future), as well as from outward (relationships) and inward (core identity) traits.

Tensions of tradition arise when one confronts established customs, practices, norms, and habits. Tensions of aspiration arise when one confronts visions of the future that clash with our own. Tensions of relationships arise when one confronts power dynamics, personal scripts, and identity politics. Tensions of identity arise when one confronts values, beliefs, history, allegiances, emotions, and spirituality.

The two straightforward, yet complex, antidotes to tension that Steven Snyder proposes are to (1) reimagine the conflict and (2) focus on how you are contributing to the tension such that you might change.

I'll say a little on those strategies momentarily. I want to get a word in about frame of reference. We often get caught up in the moment when tensions arise. Conflict has the power to absorb us and to distort our perceptions. Remember that tensions are fears and that getting through those tensions can lead to a better future, inclusive solutions, and the change you wish to see in the world.

As for the strategies, the goal is to self-reflexively look at tensions as disconnects that are bridgeable through creativity and receptivity. Sometimes the solution is to recast the tension in new terms, with a metaphor, or to get a second opinion. Tensions are not problems, although they are problematic. They are foibles that make us human. And when they are released, so too is great motivation and energy.

## Setbacks Are Everyone's Problem

There are noticeable early warning signs that your proposed changes are going to encounter resistance. Broadly stated, resistance is anything that impedes forward progress. That said, resistance isn't always intentional, but it is a setback.

As the change-seeker, you must equip yourself with patience, temperance, communicativeness, and a vision to handle and surmount resistance. If you are especially adept, resistance can be transformed into fuel that drives your change.

*Confusion* is a conspicuous setback. No matter how clearly you express the journey and vision, some people might not grasp any of it. Combat confusion by asking questions.

Another culprit is *silence*. That's a tough one to handle. Don't assume that silence means acceptance. It can be a loud form of dissent. Again, ask questions. Prod your audience.

*Diversion* is another culprit of resistance. You'll frequently encounter members of the "yeah, but…" tribe. As is the case with resistance, some diversions are deliberate while others are unconscious. Acknowledge diversion openly to turn it around. Don't shy away from dissent; embrace it to disarm it.

It isn't easy to confront resistance. When we are opposed, criticized, rebuked, or misunderstood, it elicits a spate of emotions: anger, vengeance, frustration, shame, or disillusion. Remember that no matter how good your plan is you will always face resistance of some kind. Don't take detraction personally.

In *Choosing Change*, Walter McFarland and Susan Goldsworthy caution that change-seekers should expect setbacks and commit to pushing through them. Beyond that they should find ways of exploiting setbacks.

Some typical setbacks are

1. *Reduced priority of the change effort over time.* The realities of business stealthily supersede and distract from the change effort. When the primacy of a revolutionary change effort begins to flounder, the effort is jeopardized.

2. *Loss of vision.* The main motivator of a change can be obscured for a number of reasons. Often the effort required to effectuate change can discourage people from continuing, as they prefer the known inconformity. Keep everyone looking forward to avoid myopia.

3. *Senior leadership opposition.* Senior leadership consensus is critical to wide-scale change in an organization. Although grassroots movements can help set the stage, eventually senior-level support will be requisite. The senior leadership must be on board.

4. *Ineffective change leadership.* It's important to recognize whether you are the best person to spearhead the change. You don't have to take the sidelines, but realistically, not every person is adept at moving masses. After some self-analysis, if you realize that's the case for you, align with someone who can be the *ying* to your *yang*.

5. *Derailers.* Also known as unexpected occurrences that threaten the success of change efforts. Derailers arise from the growing complexity of the competitive environment: increasing globalization, unprecedented competition, more or different stakeholders, economic uncertainty, energy constraints, resource scarcity and political instability.

## How to Bring About Lasting Change in the Workplace

Change is a journey to learning, whether the end is success or failure. There are enduring lessons to be gleaned from simply embarking on an unlikely course in the earnest pursuit of collective, positive change. As I said, all change is invariably social: the more people are on-board, so too the more conduits there should be for information exchange and reflection.

1. *Encourage learning.* Act as an intermediary who provides context and perspective. You are not a micro-manager. Let people find their own path so long as their vision is clear.

2. *Encourage team-building.* Act as weaver who takes the attributes and skills of others and combines them in new, holistic, and vision-driven ways.

3. *Encourage intra-organizational sharing*: Act as architect who builds the structures and processes needed to share and mobilize learning across the organization. Without shared learning, there is no sustainable change.

## In Sum

Bringing about change, above all else, is a personal challenge that makes demands on your mind, body, and spirit. It takes great courage and empathy. It summons your biases and forces you to confront the vices and virtues of others. It creates gaping divisions and lasting bonds. But when it's successful, the journey to change can remake lives and reveal previously unseen potentials.

# CHAPTER 10

## *Should Leaders Show Emotion?*

There is a difference between showing emotion and using emotion.

While it might not be the best idea for a leader to show their raw emotions without restriction, selectively revealing their genuine emotions to invoke an emotional response in others is the hallmark of the very best leaders.

Unfortunately, we live in a world of sugar coating and polishing. Messages are carefully constructed to achieve the desired effect, and true feelings are hidden deep down, lest they hinder the corporate cause. Many believe that they have to toe the "political" line to progress in their careers, and we betray our true feelings so often that it almost becomes our second nature. Expressing our genuine emotions and feelings becomes rare in the modern office.

That is what makes them so powerful. Emotions are critical to everything a leader must do: focus their team, change strategies, solidify relationships, foster trust, communicate a vision, make compromises, and learn from failure. Without the power from genuine emotions, there are so many initiatives that would simply fall flat. Sometimes it can seem a little clumsy and uncomfortable when a leader "opens up" to their team, but that can make it all the more effective. When leaders show their "human" side, people will join their cause.

The first step, however, is to be more aware of our emotions ourselves. In a business world where logic has dominated, we have suppressed our emotions to such an extent that sometimes we don't even understand what we are truly feeling. When we are angry, we bury it deep down. When we are upset, we try not to show it. When we are excited, we temper it. When we are inspired, we dumb it down. How many times have you done this? How many times has the external reaction not been reflective of the internal urge?

Emotions are not only as important as logic—without them, no logical endeavor would ever come to pass. To make something happen, someone has to "feel" that it is meaningful. When leaders let their emotions out, they let other people get in. This takes a certain amount of bravery, but the "control" of a true leader is about inspiring their people and then backing off for them to do their own thing.

There is the famous proverb in the ancient Chinese collection of philosophical writings titled *Xunzi* from Xun Kuang, the third century B.C. Chinese philosopher known as "Master Xun" ("Xunzi") which is generally true to life: 不闻不若闻之，闻之不若见之，见之不若知之，知之不若行之。Translated, it means,

*Tell me, and I'll forget. Show me, and I may remember. Involve me, and I'll understand.*

Maybe we could add another line (suggested respectfully),

*Make me feel, and I'll follow you.*

# CHAPTER 11

## *The Illusion of Stability Blinds Leaders*

When you work 10 or 20 years to earn a leadership position at a successful company, you probably are not eager to acknowledge that everything about your position is temporary… but it is.

Let me illustrate what I mean with a picture that changes endlessly. I generated the image you see above—and all those below—with a program on OpenProcessing.org. The program reacts to the movement of your cursor over the image. These movements reveal the countless data points (seen as white dots) that underlie all these images.

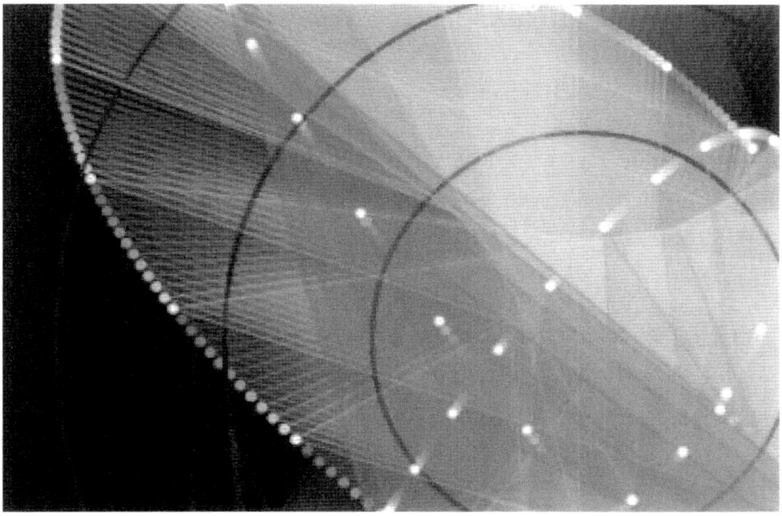

Your company is also comprised of an enormous number of data points. They represent the movements of raw materials, assets, employees, customers, and vendors. These movements are governed by a wide range of processes and rules, as well as by events in the world at large.

When you look at your own company, it's easy to see a stable image, like the one below. But if you look at it carefully, it is different from the one above.

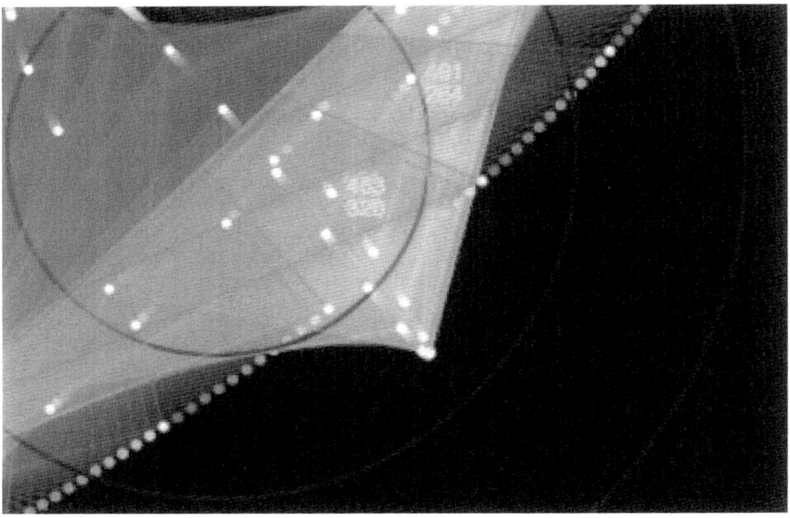

In fact, you work hard at creating a stable image, through the use of a logo, branding, and active marketing programs. But such an image masks a tremendous number of unending movements.

The greater your ability to recognize that everything is temporary, the more adept you will become at managing change. In other words, the better you will be at managing.

For example, you will realize

- Your most talented employees increasingly see themselves as free agents, who no longer trust that loyalty to the company means they will experience loyalty in return. The best workers are willing to leave and test their value in the marketplace, while the worst are most content to stay.

- Product designs and processes decline in value as time passes. To maintain your company, these assets need to constantly be reinvented and replaced.
- Investors may have a fleeting interest in your company; their time horizons and interests may be very different from other stakeholders.
- Your most valuable customers are most likely to be approached by your competitors.
- Your own tenure as a leader is finite in nature, and you should treasure every opportunity to make an impact.

When I first stumbled upon this program, it seemed like a fun but somewhat mindless diversion. But when you interact with the program, you get a vivid reminder that all complex systems are constantly in flux.

Stability is an illusion. You have a nice office, healthy compensation, and a full calendar. It's easy to get comfortable, relax, and congratulate yourself.

By all means, be proud of your success, but do not become complacent. Your success is not permanent, and neither is your company.

To lead, you must be highly cognizant of the temporary nature of all that you oversee.

Treasure all that revolves around or close to you. Be grateful for the contribution of every person, and consider yourself to be on an incessant quest for talent.

# CHAPTER 12

## *The Role of Sleep in Leadership*

Sleep. There are people who relish it so much that they consciously and skillfully manage their sleep every night. They recreate the perfect conditions ritualistically: the right lighting, the right aromas, the right sheets, the shower, the meal, tea – all of it carefully thought out and planned. They seldom awake drowsy, dissatisfied, or late for work.

Then there are their careworn and caffeinated counterparts who treat sleep carelessly. To these zombie people, sleep is an encumbrance on productivity. It isn't a priority. They loathe sleep. These people race through their day assuming their irritability, lack of patience, and disengagement is the result of anything but an erratic and unhealthful sleep-wake cycle.

Sleep (mis)management is increasingly detrimental and worrisome. We live in a hyper-connected world that makes excruciating demands on our attention and our brains. At a basic level, there is only so much energy and carrying capacity that we can devote to the mass of information that flies at us daily. It takes a toll on our brain circuitry and systems. Add to that a lack of sufficient nutrition and rest, and you've entered an unsustainable situation. The least we can do for our overloaded brains is give them adequate and profound sleep.

I recently came across a fascinating TED talk titled "How to Succeed: Get More Sleep" by Arianna Huffington that you should check out on

YouTube. In fact, she's got a great new book *The Sleep Revolution* on the subject that I would also recommend reading. In it she says, and I quote,

*There is now a kind of sleep deprivation one-upmanship.... if you try to make a breakfast date, and you say, "How about eight o'clock?" they're likely to tell you, "Eight o'clock is too late for me, but that's okay. I can get a game of tennis in and do a few conference calls and meet you at eight." And they think that means that they are so incredibly busy and productive, but the truth is they're not, because we, at the moment, have had brilliant leaders in business, in finance, in politics, making terrible decisions. So, a high I.Q. does not mean that you're a good leader, because the essence of leadership is being able to see the iceberg before it hits the Titanic. And we've had far too many icebergs hitting our Titanics.*

## We Lose More Than Sleep

Research has unequivocally shown that sleep-deprivation causes a reduction in brain processing, gives rise to several serious health issues, and leads to emotional instability, among other impairments.

The most recent part of our brains to evolve was the neo cortex. It's responsible for higher-level executive function, such as problem solving, reasoning, organizing, inhibition, planning, and executing plans. This brain region is particularly susceptible to the ill effects of sleep deprivation. Basic visual and motor skills also deteriorate from sleep deprivation, but not nearly as much as higher-level executive functions.

Research shows that after roughly 17 to 19 hours of wakefulness (let's say at 11 p.m. or 1 a.m. for someone who got up at 6 a.m.), individual performance on a range of tasks is equivalent to that of a person with a blood-alcohol level of 0.05 percent. That's the legal drinking limit in many countries. After roughly 20 hours of wakefulness (2 a.m.), this same person's performance equals that of someone with a blood-alcohol level of 0.1 percent, which meets the legal definition of drunkenness in the United States.

The tragic paradox of lack of sleep is that our impaired judgment allows us to rationalize it. "I do not need sleep," or "I'm doing fine with a couple hours of sleep," become reprisals against an instinct and basic need. Business leaders who have identified this trend and sought to remedy it are doing so from within their institutions. Some companies integrated naps, in-house restoration areas, and sleep therapists on-site. The economic motivation behind this integration is the belief that happy, healthy, and well-rested employees work better and with brighter dispositions; in addition, they generate creative outputs and increase potential for innovation. There is substantial research to back up this belief.

## Sleep Makes You More You

One study has shown that a good night's sleep leads to new insights: participants who enjoyed one were twice as likely as those who didn't to discover a hidden shortcut in a task. Likewise, an afternoon nap has been found to aid creative problem solving; subjects who took a nap after struggling on a video-game problem were almost twice as likely to solve it as subjects who stayed awake.

Other research has discovered that creative thinking is especially likely to take place during dream sleep, enhancing the integration of unassociated information and promoting creative solutions. A wealth of scientific studies has also highlighted the impact of sleep on all three stages of the learning process: before learning, to encode new information; after learning, in the consolidation stage, when the brain forms new connections; and before remembering, to retrieve information from memory.

Sleep positively contributes to many wonderful brain processes. It increases our empathy and our ability to recognize emotional, facial, and bodily cues. It increases our patience and tolerance for new ideas and challenges. It allows us to consider more possibilities at one time by sharpening our short-term memory.

Much of it happens while we sleep. Many studies have shown that the brain consolidates new information during particular and identifiable stages in the sleep cycle. It's fascinating. It all underscores the import of a good night's rest, that thing we often shirk or bemoan.

## A Rest-first Mentality

If businesses, governments, and schools truly respected and understood the importance of sleep, they would make aggressive changes to their schedules and protocols now.

Companies and governments are especially vulnerable to the pitfalls of sleep deprivation. To counteract 24/7 work cultures, companies have structured workflows that use global networks to enable healthy sleep schedules among their employees. For example, IT help desks shift locations every eight hours. Other companies alleviate work pressure by creating "tag teams" of employees who seamlessly hand over the reins to teams in different time zones at the end of their shifts. Simply knowing an employee's preferences toward sleep can help reinforce a sleep-friendly culture.

Several companies have imposed blackout times on work emails. A large European car business, for example, programs the smartphones of its non-management employees to switch off work emails automatically between 6 p.m. and 7 a.m. In many companies, particularly knowledge-based ones, this would be disruptive and counterproductive, but provided there are overhauls, such a policy can send a clear signal of management's intent.

The common thread in all those approaches is that good sleep must be planned if not forced -- a planned night off without emails, work, or smartphones.

## A Word from Bill

Former US president Bill Clinton once admitted, "Every important mistake I've made in my life I made when I was tired." Business people have often lagged behind others in both their willingness to acknowledge the issue and their readiness to act on it. But history is riddled with the incidence of tired-related folly.

It's time for organizations to find ways of countering the employee churn, lost productivity, and increased healthcare costs resulting from insufficient sleep.

If it is true that some millennials care less about high salaries and more about work–life integration, then the next generation of employees will demand solutions even more strongly.

# CHAPTER 13

## *Building and Leading Effective, High-performance Teams*

"Team" is a word that gets thrown around frivolously. People often think that a group of people working toward a common cause is a team, much like a group of people with a commonality is a community. This is fallacious and misleading. It leads people to assume that all you need for teamwork is an end and determined roles. Anyone familiar with teamwork knows that's just untrue and inaccurate.

It's time to consider teams systematically and scientifically. If we better understand what a team is, why some teams are more successful than others, and how we can form successful teams, companies, causes, and progress alike, we will be triumphant and grow more of the time.

### Teams and Technology

For all the talk about technology and our fast-paced society, we understand it very little. The effects of this new and historic milieu are still insensible to us: they elude our senses and our apprehension.

Here's a fastball.

Our technology and the rate of invention outpace our biological capabilities. To borrow from engineering, we're a gating factor, as in a roadblock, to faster progress. So, when we talk about pumping technology into an organization or a country, what good is it if the people can't keep up or exploit it? I've argued elsewhere that the United States in particular needs to devote more resources to technological education in its population, or risk falling further behind the curve.

That aside, my point is that we are biologically handicapped in our ability to cope with fast-paced change, let alone change at a technological pace. So, when a wide-scale change is demanded, we often freeze or trap ourselves in irrational decision-making. In the attempt to adapt, we sacrifice internal cohesion, system efficiency, and sometimes fall apart. All institutions and organizations face this problem.

On the flip side, we have copious technological resources that facilitate communication and collaboration. We also have computer programs designed to help us calculate a number of factors, data, and possibilities simultaneously so as to yield the "best" decision. We are using technology to guard against our shortcomings.

Nevertheless, it is important to understand our flaws so that we can guard against them and not become entirely reliant on computers and algorithms to save us from ourselves.

The first step is to understand the nature of leadership and teamwork—our most primitive super powers.

## The Nature of Leadership

I'm a proponent of knowing where you stand before taking a step. If we want to address the nature-given inefficiencies mentioned above, first we should endeavor to understand them completely.

Leadership researchers found that effective leadership isn't solely contingent upon charisma and socio-emotional intelligence. To an extent, it is a numbers game. They found that even the best leaders have a limit to their successful span of control, usually around six to ten people. Beyond that it is difficult for even the most adept leader to sustain the bandwidth required to nurture each person in the group. Therefore, smart leaders place other leaders at different levels to direct critical areas on their behalf.

Another fact of leadership is structure.

In a molecule, you have at least two atoms. Not all molecules are equally stable, however. Their stability is a function of the atomic bonds of the constituent atoms and the structure of the molecule. Although all atoms in a molecule are vying for stability, the overall structure may not be stable, try as they might. Teams of people exhibit similar combinatorial attributes.

Some teams are considerably stable. Pairs, of course, are the stablest of all, not just because of their simplicity, but also because they mirror those most basic of all human relations: friendship and marriage.

But add a third team member and things become much more complicated--sometimes even explosive. Trios work, of course, but often it seems they do so only by serial pairing. After all, history doesn't show many triumvirates and troikas, especially among rulers, that have survived for long.

Beyond three, there is no consensus, except on what the upper bound is. Some say that groups of five to seven people are optimal; others say four to nine; others still say 12, at most. The upper bound, now known as the Dunbar Number, is 150. Of course, 150 is no longer a team, but rather a tribe or clan.

The estimate arises from a concept known as clusters of intimacy. The concept is premised on the idea that optimality comes from connection and intimacy. If you are not connected to the people around you, then you won't feel intimacy, and therefore, no compulsion toward cohesion or self-identification with the group.

All this has a biological, evolutionary, and neurological basis. The short of it is that we are prone to social cohesion and self-organization by design. But we have a threshold.

That being the case, how do we create teams that are optimally composed and structured?

## Optimal Team Structure and Composition

Teams these days are not just being studied statistically or as part of isolated experiments, but in real life and while they are in operation.

The director of MIT's Human Dynamics Laboratory Alex Pentland and his team have used "sociometers" to measure data on communication patterns and productivity of teams in real organizations.

According to Pentland, great teams do the following:

- Team members communicate frequently.
- They talk and listen in equal measure.
- They communicate informally.
- They look for ideas and information outside the group.
- They adjust their patterns of communication.

More conclusions drawn from their research are that teams need both independent and socially attuned thinkers. Leaders also need to know the distributions of the different types of thinkers on the team and manage accordingly. Studies have found that the optimal balance of people on radical-innovation teams requires that 50% of the members have the following distribution of personality types:

- *Creative.* 20-30%. Teams with too many creative types struggle with implementation. That's because (surprise!) creatives are not always practical, unconcerned with rules, and may initiate conflict.
- *Conformist.* 10-20%. Conformists are the backbone of a team. They are there to support and identify issues of implementation. They make teams predictable in a good way.
- *Detail-oriented.* 10% at most. Detail-oriented people may often be risk-averse, but they help strengthen important team functions such as budgetary control. The detailers make sure that the team is still there each morning.

We may be predisposed to think one group of people is more important than the other. That is erroneous. They are all equally as important in their role and indispensable to the health of the team.

## Debunking a Myth

Diversity is not an unmitigated good, and there is a point at which diversity can stifle progress. Group diversity can certainly enhance performance and innovation by virtue of new perspectives, knowledge, and skills. However, in a diverse group, biases can stagnate progress and cohesion. People often stereotype each other, which blinds them to a more holistic picture of their teammates. Fortunately, leaders can militate against this. When they don't, bias invariably reduces effectiveness.

The point being that there are diversity costs. We should be aware of them and prepared to assuage them with objective and strategic thinking.

The science on neurodynamics suggests that diversity should be actively managed. Abandon any sense that a diverse team can entirely self-organize. You need someone on the outside, watching and committed, to cultivate healthy group dynamics and collaboration.

As diversity increases, so too do a number of well-studied threats, such as:

***Turnover***. When group members perceive each other as unchangeably different, or unwilling to coalesce differences, the compounded stress will drive some people to seek the safety of familiarity.

***Framing***, How the team leader presents the issues that arise from diversity will affect how people approach them. Here it is advisable to approach them dispassionately, and hopefully later on, more personally. For example, present the issues as problems for staying competitive and emerging victorious.

***Belief***. Research has found that teams with pro-diversity beliefs are better at harnessing the power of that diversity. That is, if they believe that their diversity is a competitive advantage, it will usually turn out to be so.

***Tenure***. The longer you keep a team together, the fewer the negative effects of its diversity. Teams with high degrees of familiarity are better able to take advantage of diverse experiences among team members.

Some antidotes to the perils of diversity are as follows:

***Groundwork***. The values instilled in a group at its formation permeate all its future interaction and performance. Set the groundwork for success and pro-diversity from the onset.

***Direction***. The team has a clear and compelling direction that everyone is aligned with.

***Strategic***. The team members were chosen strategically with clear purposes and intentions in mind.

***Supportive***. There are resources and assistance available to each team member in equal proportion, so that any needs or concerns do not go unaddressed at crucial moments.

***Mentoring***. There is a network of seasoned professionals and experts available to provide guidance and input when the team is unable to accord on a matter.

## Teams Are Not Cookie Cutter

There will be all sorts of dynamics within a team. Not everyone will relate in the same way or feel good about each other, but that doesn't mean that the team is dysfunctional. In fact, there are many teams that have orbited around pairs that disliked each other at heart yet recognized their ability to produce and create together.

There are teams that have antagonistic relationships. They can be strange to watch, look combative, and yet produce remarkable and surprising results.

There are teams of people who fundamentally dislike each other. These people would never be together outside of work, yet they recognize that for some reason their outputs are worth the strain.

There are teams of people that both like each other and produce wonderful work. It's difficult to cultivate these partnerships and not let the amiability transcend or damage the work relationship, but when it works, the yields can be wonderful.

The point to remember is that harmony isn't necessarily an indicator of success. There will be moments of disagreement and emotions will flare; but if the lines of communication are fluid and the beliefs and mission are true, teams tend to overcome and grow for the better.

# CHAPTER 14

## *The Best Leadership Literature. Ever.*

Most of us enjoy broadening our horizons by wallowing in a good book, thinking about its relevance to our lives, and changing that little bit inside after putting it down. There are few things more beneficial to the soul than reading, and I thought that I would dedicate an article to a few of the classics that have shaped my leadership views—just the tip of the iceberg, but you have to start somewhere.

Instead of giving you a brief overview, which cannot possibly do these great works justice, I thought that it would be fun to share a few short quotes. I have enjoyed writing this article and I hope that the quotes might tempt you to read (or re-read) a few of them.

### ***The Art of War* by Sun Tzu**

"Engage people with what they expect; it is what they are able to discern and confirms their projections. It settles them into predictable patterns of response, occupying their minds while you wait for the extraordinary moment—that which they cannot anticipate."

### ***The Prince* by Niccolo Machiavelli**

"Everyone sees what you appear to be, few experience what you really are."

"The first method for estimating the intelligence of a ruler is to look at the men he has around him."

## *Endurance: Shackleton's Incredible Voyage* by Alfred Lansing

"No matter what the odds, a man does not pin his last hope for survival on something and then expect that it will fail."

"Of all their enemies—the cold, the ice, the sea—he feared none more than demoralization."

## *Good to Great* by Jim Collins

"Letting the wrong people hang around is unfair to all the right people, as they inevitably find themselves compensating for the inadequacies of the wrong people. Strong performers are intrinsically motivated by performance, and when they see their efforts impeded by carrying extra weight, they eventually become frustrated."

## *Tribes* by Seth Godin

"In a battle between two ideas, the best one doesn't necessarily win. No, the idea that wins is the one with the most fearless heretic behind it."

"Change isn't made by asking permission. Change is made by asking forgiveness, later."

## *Delivering Happiness* by Tony Hsieh

"Happiness is really just about four things: perceived control, perceived progress, connectedness (number and depth of your relationships), and vision/meaning (being part of something bigger than yourself)."

### *How to Win Friends and Influence People* by Dale Carnegie

"When dealing with people, remember you are not dealing with creatures of logic, but with creatures bristling with prejudice and motivated by pride and vanity."

"Talk to someone about themselves, and they'll listen for hours."

### *Man's Search for Meaning* by Viktor Frankl

"Man does not simply exist, but always decides what his existence will be, what he will become the next moment. By the same token, every human being has the freedom to change at any instant."

### *The Tipping Point* by Malcolm Gladwell

"Look at the world around you. It may seem like an immovable, implacable place. It is not. With the slightest push—in just the right place—it can be tipped."

"There are exceptional people out there who are capable of starting epidemics. All you have to do is find them."

### *Emotional Intelligence* by Daniel Goleman

"Our emotional mind will harness the rational mind to its purposes, for our feelings and reactions—rationalizations—justifying them in terms of the present moment, without realizing the influence of our emotional memory."

### *In Search of Excellence* by Tom Peters

"Life is pretty simple: You do some stuff. Most fails. Some works. You do more of what works. If it works big, others quickly copy it. Then you do something else. The trick is the doing something else."

### *True North* by Bill George

"The reality is that no one can be authentic by trying to be like someone else. There is no doubt you can learn from their experiences, but there is no way you can be successful trying to be like them. People trust you when you are genuine and authentic, not an imitation."

### *Seven Habits of Highly Effective People* by Steven R. Covey

"Habit 1: Be Proactive. Habit 2: Begin with the End in Mind. Habit 3: Put First Things First. Habit 4: Think Win/Win. Habit 5: Seek First to Understand, Then to Be Understood. Habit 6: Synergize. Habit 7: Sharpen the Saw."

### *The Alchemist* by Paolo Coelho

"It's the possibility of having a dream come true that makes life interesting."

"Everyone seems to have a clear idea of how other people should lead their lives, but none about his or her own."

### *Meditations* by Marcus Aurelius

"You have power over your mind—not outside events. Realize this, and you will find strength."

"Everything we hear is an opinion, not a fact. Everything we see is a perspective, not the truth."

# CHAPTER 15

## *Are You an "Antifragile" Leader?*

In his books *The Black Swan* and *Antifragile,* Nassim Nicholas Taleb looks at the impact of "impossible" events on our lives, and how we might react differently in this age of disruption. These disruptive events are sometimes so random that they are virtually unpredictable, but he argues that the natural reaction is to yearn to analyze their origins, rather than go with the flow.

Maybe we need to stop gazing into the past and simply live a bit more in the present. Every day brings uncertainty, but why can't we learn to live with it and even benefit from it? We can thrive from volatility.

Within this idea, Taleb invented an interesting concept: antifragility.

The core meaning of this word is the ability to thrive on disruption. Leaders should stop cowering behind their defensive ramparts and go out to fight whatever comes around the corner, turning the tables of the battle in their favor. Uber, Airbnb and Tesla are only a few examples of companies that are taking this approach. With disruption becoming the norm for business, it is also cascading down onto a personal level.

It is no longer a case of standing out from your rivals and being the last man standing in a fight. It is no longer enough to be resilient and determined. You have to find an entirely new dimension for your response—to get stronger when you are under pressure, to be antifragile.

A submarine's glass dome is an interesting example. As it dives deeper, the water pressure increases, but the dome actually gets stronger with the increases in pressure. Antifragility isn't about crumbling, it is about growing with the difficulties.

Taleb likens antifragility to the Hydra from Greek mythology. The Hydra was a multi-headed dragon. Whenever the hero cut off one of the Hydra's heads, two would grow back in its place—the Hydra became stronger with adversity.

Leaders need to evolve their businesses in the face of external pressures. They learn, develop, then learn some more. The moment they are static, they will snap. They have to move with flexibility, but resist firmly when things threaten to overflow.

Antifragility is all about finding a new direction, rather than sustaining yourself in the status quo.

According to Taleb, stress is a source of growth to be welcomed rather than avoided. Growing pains are a natural part of any life worth living. This isn't exactly the reason that we go to work, but it is a reality that any leader needs to meet head on. The best businesses of the next 50 years will be the ones that will have thrived through adversity and turned disruptive influences to their advantage.

The antifragile will be the last ones standing, but they don't tend to stand in one place for very long.

# CHAPTER 16

## *How Leaders Use Comedy to Influence*

Using humor at the right time and in the right way can have a huge impact on the outcome of meetings, presentations, and discussions at work. A study by the Bell Leadership Institute found that, along with a good work ethic, humor was in the top two most desirable traits for a leader. We all intuitively feel that this makes sense – being around a comedian makes us all feel that little bit better, but what exactly makes it so powerful in a business setting?

Well, to start with, humor makes you likable. The "likable" revolution has gathered pace over the past few years, fueled by the likes of LinkedIn Influencer Dave Kerpen. You will go the extra mile for someone that you like, and humor is a great way to make friends and influence people, irrespective of rank or seniority.

Humor helps to break down barriers between people, and when the humor is natural (rather than forced jokes), it helps to create a common ground for everyone concerned. Many people feel compelled to wear this professional mask at work, but humor often reveals their authentic nature; understanding what makes someone tick is crucial for building deeper relationships.

It is also a weapon against one of the corporate enemies – stress. It evokes a positive emotional response in almost any situation, takes you away from stressors, and allows you to physically relax when you laugh. Having a laugh with colleagues is a great way to energize yourselves when a problem is getting you down. You might not feel able to crack a joke yourselves, but when the boss does it, it gives you the license to take things that little less seriously. Humor puts people at ease and reminds them that there is more to life.

Humor can also lead to some incredibly creative solutions. When you are brainstorming with a group of people, it is easy to have tunnel vision in your approach and thought process. Humor can help to see the situation in a different light, potentially discovering a novel perspective that you had not previously considered. Relaxation can provide a fertile ground for ideas as your mind switches mode for those crucial few seconds. The endorphins that laughing produces can often kick-start your brain to take a different tack.

Having your people looking forward to coming to work is the holy grail of any HR team, and creating a permissive workplace where humor is welcomed is often one of the first steps to take. Laughter provides crucial fuel for any working relationship, relationships that otherwise may be strained because of the unrelenting demands of the job. Giving your team a laugh on a regular basis is one of the most precious gifts that a leader can give.

Humor helps a leader to lower the barriers between relationships and may help them become more approachable. Often, bosses are put on a pedestal and don't always hear about potential issues until it is too late. The closer your relationships with your people, the more informed you will be. Cracking the odd joke breaks down these barriers, whether they are imagined or real.

Laughter also helps people to create lasting memories. If you want someone to internalize a certain message, you could do a lot worse than telling an amusing anecdote about it.

Laughter helps trigger endorphins in the brain, and this in turn helps to lock in memories. Storytelling is a great way of engaging your people, but funny stories will break through the noise that little bit easier.

Laughter makes people feel good. Surely, that has to be the goal of every leader.

# CHAPTER 17

## *Good Leadership Calls for Light and Shade*

Over the course of my career, I have thankfully met very few one-dimensional leaders.

You know the types: so certain of themselves that they don't feel they have to change their approach, and so thick-skinned that no criticism can touch them, and therefore, have the chance to change their sacred opinion. They surround themselves with "yes people" and choose to ignore everything that doesn't fit within their worldview. Their thinking is narrow-minded, and their behavior is utterly predictable—my way or the highway.

Happily, they are in the minority, and the law of averages is such that they get sent to the highway on a regular basis. Their careers suffer as a consequence, and they sulk off to join the rest of the self-entitled moaners, who think that the world owes them a living and that they have been dealt a bad hand. At no point do they think that they could have been a little bit more flexible in certain situations.

They tend to move from company to company on a regular basis.

In my experience, it is easiest to do business with leaders who are able to vary their behavior depending on the circumstances. If you have let a client down, you have to adopt a conciliatory tone. If you are trying to win business, you have to aim to listen more than you talk. If you are in a conflict, then a firm but fair approach is required. There is never a one-size-fits-all resolution when other people are involved, and if you take the situation and the people into account, you will have a much better chance of achieving your objective.

I find it especially interesting when you are taken out of the office setting. Maybe your spouse has got to know the spouse of a CXO in your industry, and you start socializing. The business façade drops, and you have the chance to truly get to know someone on a human level. It might be that this relationship is carried over into the business setting, and while relations will be more formal, there will still be a more relaxed element. Just because we go to work with the goal of making the most amount of money for our respective companies doesn't mean that we stop being "normal people" at a barbecue on a Sunday.

If you can find that balance of light and shade for yourself (in any setting), you will be a trusted colleague and, maybe in time, a trusted friend. If you try to fit in to accommodate others, you will find that they do the same for you, and your life will be made that little bit easier. Life is so much more fun with a bit more light and shade. It is also a given that business is equally more profitable—let's all try to be that little bit more flexible with our behavior.

# CHAPTER 18

## *Why Creative Leaders Last Longer*

Understanding what is going on in our own heads is difficult at the best of times.

However, if you have a diverse team reporting to you, you have to interpret their thoughts, translate them, and package them in a way that everyone will understand. Sometimes you will have to tailor the same message in different ways. For example, sales guys will have a different mindset than the operational team. They all need to internalize the ideas in their own way.

The thing about ideas is that they often come back significantly different than when they originally left your head. This is where the "creative leader" starts to come into their own. They are happy for their ideas to be interpreted and reworked by their teams, and they can piece together the technicolor jigsaw that is formed by a whole lot of people thinking freely.

It is not about the idea – it is about the sum of ideas that are spawned by their idea. Creativity is not about simply putting a great idea into the world, but rather cultivating that idea and letting it grow into something entirely different, something better.

Therefore, in my view, the role of a creative leader is to facilitate a culture where everyone can play with ideas and feel that their opinion is valued. It's much more about creating a climate in which people are not afraid to contribute and be themselves.

They give their teams the confidence of their convictions. Often people lack confidence because they can't do something and, consequently, assume that they're incapable of it. There's a very big difference between not having learned to do something and being incapable. Leaders encourage them to aim for the moonshots and help them to fill in the gaps along the way.

Employees enjoy being allowed to do things their way. They enjoy the freedom to make mistakes and collectively come up with solutions. When they try new things, they feel that they are growing. When they achieve the impossible, they will feel on top of the world. They understand that it would have been impossible without the guiding presence of their creative leader, and they will love them for it.

The minds of the many are better than the minds of the few. Leaders will still be able to pick the best threads from their team's thinking, but as long as they don't dismiss the less worthy ones, the flow of ideas will continue at pace. When leaders encourage creativity, the result will be owned by the collective rather than the individuals. Sometimes one person's idea will be adopted, at other times it will be another's idea, but the group will feel that they own the idea because they were all involved in its conception. This is so much more effective than a diktat from an authoritarian, "do what I say" type.

Creative leaders last longer because they take their teams with them on their journey towards success. This gives them both better ideas and more engaged employees. There is nothing more important in the fast-moving modern workplace than these two things.

# CHAPTER 19

## *Are You a Leader Who Pays Lip Service?*

Your words suggest one thing, but your actions do not match them.

In the fraught world of any leader, this scenario will come to pass daily. Sometimes they will promise things with the full intention of delivering, only for circumstances to conspire against them. At other times, they will find that lack of time causes them to only partially do what they said. However, the worst case is when they are so busy that they do not fully think through what they promised entails, and in reality, they have no chance of making it happen.

Leadership lip service is a slippery slope.

If you say to someone, "Yes, no problem. I'll do it," you have to leave them with a decent amount of certainty that it will happen. If you don't even get close to delivering on your promises on a few occasions, the next time you say this, they will start to doubt your understanding of the situation and your intentions to do it. This will cause them to micro-manage the situation, taking more time out of your day and adding more worries to their days.

Lip-service creates uncertainty, and uncertainty creates unnecessary activity.

Trust accumulates in a well that has to be topped up on a regular basis; if the well is depleted, people won't rely on its contents for much longer. If a leader is not trusted by their people, they will become redundant, and their people will look to other sources of inspiration and growth.

Leaders who practice lip-service are often primarily interested in themselves. They promise something, but it doesn't happen because it eventually doesn't tally with their self-interest. They live in a world that revolves around them, but with every broken promise, that world becomes ever smaller… until they are left on their own. Well, that would happen in an ideal world, because it would teach them a lesson, but the truth of the matter is that many of their staff have no choice but to put up with the uncertainty, and many of the lip-service leaders continue with their insincere ways.

For those (unfortunately rare) leaders who do care about others, they care more about what they promise. They may be more likely to say "no" more often, but at least that enables the requester to find a different route to accomplishing what they need. They can be relied on, and communication with them is simple and effective. Equally, others will feel the need to reciprocate their reliability, and in turn, their lives will be made easier. If you treat others right, others will treat you right, and a virtuous circle appears.

How many times have you not delivered on your promises recently? What were the circumstances? Did you have any intention of delivering on those promises in the first place? The best intentions don't count if there isn't a final product.

# CHAPTER 20

## *Leadership and Dealing with Workplace Adversity*

The workplace is a battlefield for all sorts of conflicts. It's a terrain unlike any other social environment in that it demands we put our roles and objectives before our emotions, recreation, and preferences. Well, it did at one point. Now we have come to realize that this balancing act is unsustainable and unhealthy. The workplace of today demands greater empathy and compassion from its employers, and greater flexibility so workers can mitigate personal and professional responsibilities.

This is a radical change. It's unfamiliar to us, which is why its fraught with confusion and uncertainty. We start and stop often. However, over time we've come to better understand what allowing space for our personal lives at work can look like, and how, in many ways, it can improve rather than impair productivity.

This poses a great challenge to all those invested in the process. It poses special challenges to leaders, who often bear the brunt of failure at any organizational level.

This article is aimed at those in a leadership role, be it formalized or tacit, because as we are all learning, leadership doesn't only flow from authority, it also flows from our self-determined relationship to those around us.

## Descend Toward Rock Bottom

A wise friend once told me that rock bottom is a solid place to put a building. It should be our baseline, our foundation, and a place that we default to when things are not going well because it's a place of self-reflection and growth. Especially so when we trust those around us. When there is trust, there is little need to second-guess intentions.

Rock bottom can be a devastating place. It can also teach us valuable lessons about ourselves and about others.

At an organizational level, it's crucial to attune ourselves to the sources of conflict that can drag us to that place. It's a precautionary measure where the growth of hitting rock bottom can be simulated without the damage of impact. So yes, my suggestion is that we constructively seek out those sources of conflict. To do so effectively, we need to identify them first.

Leigh Branham points to common hidden reasons why employees leave a workplace—aversion being a useful signal of deep discontent. The reasons include a basic lack of trust and integrity in leadership, belief that leadership is outdated and out of touch, sense that leadership is self-interested (greed and power being their main motivators), the perception that there is a lack of enthusiasm and commitment among coworkers, and observation that coworkers and leadership alike question the integrity, decision-making, and effectiveness of upper level workforce members.

Any one of these is enough to undermine our best efforts to love our workplace. The reality is that most workplaces grapple with one or more of these pitfalls. Branham suggests three antidotes to stave off these impressions and reverse the loss of trust, solidarity, and willingness that they cause.

## The Three Tenets of Sustainable and Healthy Leadership

A sustainable and healthy leadership style must do three things according to Branham:

1. They must inspire confidence with a clear vision, an actionable plan, and with the competence and resources to achieve it. People will only follow leaders they deem capable. They don't want to follow someone into ruin or work toward a goal they can't see clearly. When goals and leaders are brought into focus, directives and objectives are seen as progress rather than empty and purposeless.

2. Back up words with actions. Simply put, do what you say you will do. Leave lip service at the door. There is no easier way to subvert cynics and pessimists than with the confidence fostered by reliability. Don't talk about quality only to force unrealistic timelines on people, obligating them to produce less than their best. Don't talk about respect and then arrogate it all for yourself with little regard for the collective. That is poisonous hypocrisy.

3. To receive trust, you must give it. Show the people in your workforce that you trust them. Give them responsibility, ask for their opinions, don't micromanage, and generally believe that every person has untapped potential that can be unleashed through trust and healthy leadership. This attitude will permeate the work culture, where everyone will then lift each other up, empower each other to succeed, and assume trust, reliability, and confidence are givens.

The goal should be widespread, collective community building such that you foster an environment where everyone is unafraid about openness, collaboration, and motives. It isn't easy to do this. Our work culture and values are antithetical to it. But it's demonstrated that command-and-control workplaces fed by fear and power mongering rather than trust and collaboration are volatile and unstable. They plant the seeds of their own demise, and they sanction it at an institutional level.

## What Does Your Work Culture Allow for?

It isn't easy to view an organization objectively, either when you are within it or outside it. What's worse, many organizations operate secretly and possessively. This emanates from within, from the very people who make it up. Over time this encourages duplicitousness, furtive looks, and power dynamics that hamper progress and productivity.

How then do we avoid this, cultivate a culture of promise, trust, and productivity, while casting secrecy and possession in a bad light? Here are a few tips:

1. *Make the case.* Whether your team is new or old, instill the belief that teamwork and peer support promise greater returns than any other modality of work. Then, live it out.

2. *Raise the stakes.* Once you've established the idea of teamwork and peer support, devise tangible and clear-cut ways to materialize it.

3. *Bond over commonalities.* You all face the same oppositional forces as a work unit. Identify your competition and endeavor to create a unified front against it.

4. *Dial up the intimacy.* Don't be afraid to get personal at the right times and right places. A question that often gets people sharing is, "What struggle from your past has influenced you most?" It's our personal story of triumph.

5. *Don't be afraid to take on the role of mediator.* Sometimes the group will fall into detrimental habits of communication. Address those peaceably with the goal of moving beyond the surface.

6. *A safety net.* We speak about safety nets and support systems but don't quite know what they are, although we can often tell when they are there. For me, it's knowing that you can speak your mind without destroying a relationship or hurting your career. The attitude No One Fails is a solid starting point. No matter the situation, no one fails; they just gain opportunities to reflect and do better next time.

Remember that the person saying all this has an inextricable impact on how the message is received. Make sure that they have some credibility in the group. And if that isn't the case, then they should start by acknowledging whatever doubts and hesitancies the group may have about their credibility. This is not easy but necessary to dispel any noxious assumptions and beliefs.

## The Roots of Doubt and Hesitancy

Research on conflict has revealed that most conflict stems from at least one of three sources: lack of clarity, a relationship issue, and resistance. These are gratuitously vague, but they can provide an initial framework within which to assess others and ourselves in moments of conflict.

When you are in the midst of conflict, ask yourself the following questions to discern your position in the argument: Where am I unclear? What is the relationship at stake? What am I resisting?

When answering these questions, remember that self-denial is toxic for any dispute.

Start with a whole-hearted desire to introspect and recognize your position in the conflict so you can begin to glean a solution, be it a compromise, a new attitude, or a rupture.

Conflict, trust, credibility, peer support, and teamwork are all ingredients in the same milieu. They are social dimensions that coexist well if we learn how to balance them and address them each in proactive ways.

There is no reason that a situation should get out of hand if the people involved are truly focused on finding a solution that genuinely addresses the concerns of every person. In those moments, even if a solution is not found, trust and credibility can grow.

# CHAPTER 21

## *Leadership Style That Fosters Creativity or Stifles Innovation*

Remember paint-by-numbers, that most prescriptive of coloring books?

I'm not sure whether being led by numbers to color an image can be classified as art at all. The lines, the numbers, it all seems quite regimented and contrary to what I consider creativity. I suppose there is something to be said for granting the non-artists among us a taste of artistic triumph, but I'm sure that for those who craved a creative buzz, it left us absolutely sober.

What does this have to do with leadership? Everything.

### Yesterday's Management Is Today's Death Trap

When I read certain management textbooks, they seem prescriptive in a similar way to paint-by-numbers coloring books. The numbers look a little something like this, "If a certain person acts this way, you need to do the other," "If they adopt a certain body language, it means this," and "If they have failed at something, they need to do it this way."

We live in an age when management theories abound, and when the workforce is changing rapidly. People are motivated like never before to improve their personal prospects in search of self-actualization. As people migrate between companies early in their careers, they can encounter all sorts of managers. Unequivocally, the paint-by-numbers managers are anathema to today's workforce culture. Most people do not prefer structured, rigid, and authoritative work environments or managers; they prefer them to be collaborative, flexible, and flat.

## Trust Them to Mix Their Own Paint

When confronted with managers who tell you how you "should" do things, who opt to exert force rather than open their ears, who impose rules without consideration of individual differences, concerns, and complaints, today's workers tend to walk away. That is why mangers would be prudent to eschew the paint-by-numbers approach, whenever reasonable. Managers who accept that there is no hard-and-fast method for most things are in a good position to relate profitably to today's workforce. Surely some things are the way they are because there is little room for change given certain externalities, but when it comes to management styles, the affair is entirely subjective.

In addition, by adopting a paint-by-numbers approach, you are stifling creativity, and in a work environment, creativity is akin to innovation. How can you expect to disrupt an industry, increase efficiencies, absorb new technologies, or stem rates of attrition if you don't give your people enough leeway to make their own decisions? The moment you tell them, "You should do this," you suppress critical thinking and limit the applications of whatever skills, education, and experiences they may have.

If that's not enough, the perils go beyond workplace frustration and creative stagnation. The paint-by-numbers approach is a liability. When you dictate to an employee, you relieve them of responsibility. If something goes wrong, they can fall back on your directive. How will you reasonably tell that person they should have done something different? From their perspective, they were simply doing what they were told. If paint-by-numbers is the name of the game, that is what they will do. You, on the other hand, will be sure to suffer for it.

The prescriptive manager will never get the best out of his team because they will all be working within suffocating constraints. It is far better to leave them to their own devices (while keeping a watchful eye), so they can experience the glory and satisfaction of creating their own masterpieces.

*If you hire someone, you must trust them to mix their own paint.*

# CHAPTER 22

## *Leadership That Builds Synergy & Harmony in the Team*

The mantra that I have been toying with as of late is "Manage to make an impact."

I've come to realize that many companies still need to step away from traditional hierarchies and models of work distribution in order to promote happiness, passion, and community inside their institutions.

Recognition is vital to upending the power dynamics that encumber contemporary institutions. When recognition of value is practiced, it naturally leads to overall happiness in the workplace and merit-based team building, placing authority in each expert of the team rather than solely in a managerial figure.

In this article, I cover those topics and propose some ways that you can cultivate trust, reciprocity, and collective will inside institutions.

The short of it is that every employee's experience, feedback, and expectations matters. When an institution acknowledges this and candidly rehashes its time-old processes and hierarchies accordingly, great things can happen.

## Recognition Is the Key to Happiness

In the workplace, recognition can come from many sources, but it means more when it comes from a manager or a higher up. Power structures are being challenged and dismantled every day, but that doesn't mean that the perception of authority has vanished. Whether you are opposed to pre-established power dynamics, the fact remains that power is multiform. Power can flow from knowledge, experience, or material wealth. If someone who you perceive as more powerful recognizes your efforts or achievements, it will hold weight.

The research supports this.

In fact, the research has gone as far as to quantify the preferred distribution of recognition that employees prefer, based on self-report. On average, employees want recognition from three sources: managers, the organization as a whole, and their fellow employees. The preferred mix is 50-30-20, respectively.

Whether you adhere to the mix or not, today's work culture demands recognition as a prerequisite for market success. When an employee gives their loyalty to a company, they will champion it. It's happening more and more thanks to social media. Employees can grow to feel a kinship with their employer, but only when they judge that the company has their best interests in mind and authentically aims to maintain it. Institutions can foster this loyalty by upholding employee recognition as a value. It will help employees feel like members in a tribe or a community.

## Five Ways to Offer Recognition That Works

When deciding to give recognition, the goal shouldn't be to laud a person with pretty words and a plaque. The recognition must spring from a work relationship based in empathy, understanding, and clear expectations.

I have composed this list of five ways to help set the groundwork for meaningful recognition.

1. Provide clear expectations, validation, respect, loyalty, and trust based in a strong working relationship kept alive by open lines of communication.

2. Determine what each person has to offer and wants to offer so you can leverage both their strengths and their predispositions. In that manner, you can select challenges and opportunities that suit them.

3. Personalize recognition in terms that the person would use. This can only come from succeeding in the first point. It will show honest care and concern, and preclude the perception of ingratiation or pandering.

4. You can start a cultural movement wherein everyone more easily and sincerely recognizes each other. Encourage recognition and constructive criticism throughout the institution, amongst employees, at all levels of the hierarchy.

5. Go out and celebrate as a team. Move as a single unit, as a family. Recognition within a cultural unit can become a group activity.

Because these changes are meant to permeate every level of an organization and may run contrary to practices already in place, I suspect your head may be swimming in "yabbuts."

That's the term that innovation-strategy pioneer Larry Keeley invented to denote thoughts like, "Yeah, sure this all sounds good—but here's why this would never work in my organization."

## The Three Yabbuts of Innovation

Chris Artel and Lisa Kay Solomon explain in *Moments of Impact* the three main yabbuts that can upend attempts to innovate or modernize an institution. They are politics, near-termism, and the karaoke curse.

***Politics.*** All organizations are political in nature. Every person brings self-interest to the table. Since politics is a pejorative term, we can unfairly assume that all politics are bad politics. Well, no. Politics exist on a continuum. Bad politics is solely about self-interest, resource control, and empire building; good politics is about honest debate, values, and moving forward together.

***Takeaway.*** The four political pitfalls are refusal to declare whose propositions are better, feigned participation, diffidence, and agenda hijacks. Make sure you neither fall prey to them, nor let your team members succumb to these pitfalls when trying to change the status quo.

***Near-Termism.*** Individuals and companies alike need to learn how to balance short- and long-term goals. The difficulty is that human beings are notoriously bad at just that. There are a number of temporal biases that truncate our best attempts at planning. One extensively documented and studied temporal biases is temporal discounting.

Temporal discounting is best explained by a seminal study conducted in Stanford University back in the late 1960s by Walter Michel. Namely, the Stanford Marshmallow Experiment. Researchers found that the ability of children to delay gratification by choosing to take two marshmallows in 20 minutes rather than one marshmallow immediately had long-term predictive value. In follow-up studies, preschoolers who exercised self-restraint had greater self-control and success as adults.

***Takeaway.*** You would do well to take heed of this experiment. The desire for immediate or short-term gratification is strong in us all. When you are in the midst of sparking institution-wide change, make sure to keep a look out for this bias. A way of short fusing it is to setup incentives that would make the alterations worthwhile. For example, a Friday night outing as a group to highlight the week's good/bad moments can be sponsored by the company. Free drinks anyone?

***The Karaoke Curse.*** Imagine that you are in a Karaoke bar. You and your group step into the room, have a couple of drinks, make selections, and take turns signing. There is usually at least one person who can sing much better than everyone else. After enough drinks, the worst singer will think they are Frank Sinatra when singing alongside the better singers. A person's confidence can sometimes exceed their competence, particularly when they are in the company of more competent people.

You'd be surprised how damaging it can be when someone doesn't notice that they are not qualified to opine on a matter. That compounded by the belief that their ideas are golden—when they aren't—can tragically derail an otherwise fruitful conversation.

When you want to initiate institution-wide change that forces you to rail against entrenched power structures, this kind of person can inhibit progress. That is when strategic thinking becomes crucial.

***Takeaway.*** The advice of the Karaoke Curse cuts both way. Make sure that you can take a step back from a conversation to evaluate what your contributions are accomplishing, what it implicates for next steps, and how it would play out in a real-world scenario. When someone else is getting trigger happy, ground them the same way you'd ground yourself.

Beyond the Karaoke Curse, strategic thinking entails holistic analysis and process-oriented R&D. Any change within an institution will affect any number of moving parts. Apprehending what will change and how before you act will save you a lot of time and energy.

## A Few Tips from Successful Strategic Thinkers

Good strategic thinkers may not realize how good they are. When you see one in action, though, you can almost immediately recognize their talents, especially if you don't let your ego get in the way.

There are a few tips that have been handed down to me by strategic thinkers that I admire. I would like to share them with you now.

***Systems Thinking.*** Model and tinker with modes of thinking and organizations.

***Scan and Identify Patterns.*** Continually scan for new data and extrapolate insights from sources all around you.

***Challenge Assumptions.*** Encourage challenges to presuppositions, even your own. When you reveal underlying thinking processes, you reveal deeper meanings.

***Balance Long- and Short-term Goals.*** Keep an eye toward future and present goals simultaneously. They usually do not oppose each other, but rather beg to be balanced.

***Synthesis and Storytelling.*** Constantly observe people and operations in other industries to create a coherent story and find opportunities to merge their innovations with your own.

***Hypothesis Testing.*** Trial and error. Do not be afraid to try something new. You can learn from failed attempts.

Once you've done a lot of your initial information gathering and started thinking about strategy, remember that changes like these take team effort. Be sensitive to group dynamics. Find ways to pair people where they naturally intersect rather than where they differ. Identify who wants to support you in your venture and leverage them to meet your needs.

## Team and Process Build for High Performance

Putting together a team involves a number of complex maneuvers. You must coordinate individuals with a broader context and think about relationships, bottom lines, and productivity. I'll say it again. Work distribution is complex.

At the heart of it all, you must ensure that the individual people do not feel like cogs in a machine. Yes, they should feel part of the institution, and yes, they must feel integral to its success, but that cannot supersede their individuality.

Consider that every person in a team must feel a shared responsibility to their department, to each other, and to the company as a whole. When you move people around without inquiring about their expectations and goals, then they can feel unimportant, more like objects than people. That is not a good feeling.

If you manage to inculcate each person in a team with a sense of greater purpose that meets both the institution's needs and their own, then you can reap the rewards of a greater sense of purpose, passion, and commitment.

## Delineate Process from the Get-Go

That work experience is born when workflows are defined. Each person must know what their role is and what is expected of them. That can only happen when you plot out what teams you need and who you need on your teams.

Be strategic about it. Think about culture, work experience, and attitude. It will be hard for you to change the way the institution runs if you have people in it who don't value what you value. Not everyone will be a fit. That's okay. If someone is not a cultural fit, then they are a risk to the community you are trying to build. Do not feel compunction about letting someone like that go. The integrity of the institution is more important.

Another strategic maneuver for team building is the 80/20 principle, also known as Pareto's Principle. It has been observed in prestige companies around the world.

***Pareto's Principle.*** In some of the most successful companies, there exists a work distribution called 80/20, based on Pareto's Principle. Simply stated, the principle holds that 20% of a set is generally responsible for 80% of the related result.

For example, if you have a team of experts, then each expert can use 20% of their time to carry out 80% of the business needed. This is feasible when you undo traditional managerial schemas. Presumably, experts can administrate their own job function. You'd be surprised how much this increases job satisfaction, commitment, and productivity.

In practice, the idea is that the best leaders openly take control of their careers, their lives, and their time. From an employee's perspective, that means, "I know what I am doing. I know how to get it done." From the employer's perspective, that means, "When I see talent, I don't try to control it. I nurture it."

The takeaway is that power structures can be poisonous. To that extent, there are institutions founded on power dynamics that exploit power gaps. That may work in the military, for instance, but in the real-world, submission to authority in that manner is counter-productive and undesirable.

## Do Not Pay Deference to Power Structures

If you are on the fringes of a dominant culture, conventional wisdom may compel you to acclimate to the styles, values, and modes of communication prevalent in your social context. In the workplace, it would be no different. It's a way of relating and of closing whatever power gap is perceived.

Hierarchical cultures of this sort are usually unsustainable. The acclimations come at the expense of individual preferences, hopes, desires, and maybe dreams. In these situations, the sense of disproportion can be detrimental to all people, leading to frustrations on both sides.

As we delve into power-gap dynamics in an institutional context, we notice how hierarchies tend to dictate the way people live. In those cases, time and again, we have seen that people prefer an egalitarian management style, wherein the institutional structures are flat, open dialogue is encouraged, and managers are team members rather than overseers.

***Bridge the gap***. Bridging the gap and instituting overall egalitarian changes can have beneficial impacts on relationships, communication, and productivity. Remember the 80/20 principle. There are vast resources that are probably wasted on managers and administrators because the employees they oversee are reasonably more than capable of keeping an eye on themselves.

The goal here is to cultivate trust, empathy, and, increase productivity and innovation in the process. There are many ways to go about this. People are different and groups of people more so. When you embark on the journey of leveling power structures, promoting recognition, and building efficient and community-minded teams, you must identify the ways in which your employees want to be communicated with. The efficient way to do this is ask. Just ask.

Once you do that, you can start strategizing how to implement the changes mentioned above. It will be an incremental process but worthwhile in the long-term.

***Watch out for stumbling blocks***. There are five pervasive stumbling blacks that hinder attempts to create teams like I have described above.

1. Lack of trust.
2. Fear of conflict.
3. Lack of commitment.
4. Lack of accountability.
5. Inattention to results.

## Conclusion

It is so important in today's economy that institutions listen to their employees.

Institutional leaders need to consider employees' feedback, self-management potential, and desire for community-building. An institution that makes those central values can guarantee that employees stay and defend the institution.

Remember that employees have an insider's perspective and likely are willing to vocalize it. Do your best to ensure that what they say aligns with your true values.

# CHAPTER 23

## *Pride, Leadership, and Business Relationships*

Have you ever taken a position on an issue at work and refused to budge? You heard compelling evidence, considered it for a moment, but had your conviction rapt by a vague sense that "I will not back down." If all parties involved refuse to budge, paralysis sets in. Pride surges like a corrosive rain that melts away a relationship nurtured for years.

The ancients warned of the detriments of excessive pride. Religious texts and philosophical treatise are rife with examples of pride's havoc. Despite all forewarnings, even today pride plays a devilish role in our relationships. Pride burns hot, demanding attention and incensing the spirits. It places ego at the forefront of our interactions and holds onto its location steadfastly. It will not be moved. It need not be. Relationships will often crumble before one's pride. The tragedy beyond what is lost is the misperception that fuels pride.

We sometimes believe, implicitly or explicitly, that compromise or concession is synonymous with defeat. The antidote is intellectual humility. The belief that no one is always right, or beyond that, that right or wrong is simplistic.

If you start a conversation with intellectual humility, you will be more open to learning and changing your opinion. As you sit at the negotiation table, tensions rising, you'll reflect on that belief and seek common ground.

It'll keep you tempered in the face of piping hot exchanges. Don't allow yourself to walk away or turn your back on a negotiation just to be correct when so much can be gained from cooperation and compromise.

And in the business world, if you are pinned as a hot head, people won't want to deal with you. Their confidence in you will evaporate. You will be deemed volatile and unreasonable.

Pride claims many victims, even our success. Pride may wrap itself around our eyes and blind us to constructive criticisms and object lessons. Relationships may be lost obliviously, without any vindicating reflection. It's not easy to quiet our pride, but we should work against it. A good place to start is by looking to those we admire. Ask: What techniques do they use to calm their ego?

A broad horizon is an excellent perspective against the ego-centrism of pride. Remember that we are stronger as many than as one. It is the law of the wild we had the luxury to forget. That's precisely what unity can allow us. When we consider our actions as tied to greater purposes that affect the people around us, we ground our thinking in practical concerns, real consequences, and the collective good. Being right comes secondary to the benefits of compromise.

When we work together, we can accomplish so much more. Don't let pride confine you to yourself.

# CHAPTER 24

## *Leaders Are Experts at Recycling*

It makes me feel great when I take various household items to the recycling center. This is a cause that our family fervently believes in; if you can do your bit to help the environment, why wouldn't you do it?

The regimented part of me likes the routine. Plastics in this bag, paper in the other—everything in its place and then repeat the next day. When a routine is familiar, it almost becomes part of who you are.

Leaders are also expert recyclers, in their own way.

Whatever activity a leader is doing, the likelihood is that they have a pre-programmed instruction manual in their heads. They may have done something similar before, or they may be so observant that they have learned from when someone else did it. They reach deep into the recesses of their brains to find their "starting point," and the success of any venture is often dependent on where they started and in which direction they were pointing. This information is recycled from their past experiences.

I often find it interesting to look at someone's eyes directly after I ask them a question. It is a fairly well-accepted fact that if the average person looks to their left, then they are accessing visual and auditory memories (or having an internal dialogue). You can almost see them take a brief trip into the past for a split second. The less-thoughtful people look you straight in the eye and blurt out the first thing that comes into their heads. I would trust their judgment that little bit less.

Leaders can build on past events because they are utterly present in every moment of their lives. When you notice the smallest nuances in every situation, you choose to squirrel the memories away for use another day. If you get in the habit of being observant and inquisitive, you can subconsciously store an incredible amount of information to inform your future decisions. If you spend all day thinking about Taylor Swift's latest video (not speaking personally!), that probably won't be much use for the future.

"Shake it off, shake it off, ah ah…" No, don't think about Taylor Swift. Don't do it!

Easy to get distracted and lose your train of thought, isn't it? That's the trick in all this. Accessing memories and experiences isn't easy; you have to remain focused on the problem at hand and shut out all of the daily worries for a few minutes. It is important that you have something to recycle, but it is also vital that you can concentrate on mentally retrieving the memory and deciding how it would be useful to solve your current problem.

As our personal and professional lives increasingly start to blend and our lives become even more complicated (in a good way, mostly), it is becoming ever harder to internalize all these lessons as it all seems to blur into a great mass of activity. If we don't learn the concrete lessons today, we won't have anything to recycle in the future when we really need it. I personally enjoy a few minutes of "me time" at the end of each day to think about what has happened.

When I do this, recycling those memories is that little bit easier for the future.

# CHAPTER 25

## *What Type of a Leader Will You Be?*

There are many qualities which are required of the modern leader. Some may see themselves as a visionary, others achieve success by being detail-orientated, while yet others realize their success through their people.

Truth be told, there is no one characteristic of a leader that can be said to be "more important" than the others. The best leaders have a chameleon-like existence—changing their modus operandi to suit the situation. In this chapter, I would like to consider a few different leadership modes, which you might put into practice in the coming year.

I am sure that you will have a some "preferred styles," but there will also be a few that you know you need to work on. Which styles do you recognize in your immediate bosses?

***Conductors create cohesion through direction.*** When you have a large orchestra whose members have no reliable means of communicating with one another, there has to be someone standing in a visible position showing the way forward for all concerned. The conductor understands the impact of their every movement on each part of the collective, and they skillfully create a masterpiece.

***Thinkers analyze and suggest possibilities.*** Sometimes, a leader has to consider every angle of a problem and make their teams think about the bigger picture. Thinking on their own is not enough; they have to have the courage to suggest a way ahead and the belief that their convictions to follow through.

***Architects sketch out the options for the future.*** If there is no written business plan, there is no business. There is nothing better than looking at a logical and sensible plan, which doesn't only exist in the head of the leader. The architects can communicate their vision in simple terms on "paper" and this gives their team something to unite behind.

***Planners tell us how and when to achieve.*** A direction is a good start, but the planner helps to map out the milestones of how to get there. They are experienced in understanding the realities of making something happen, and people follow their pragmatic leadership "because it worked last time."

***Executors make things happen through people.*** They don't sit in their rooms and press a button, they get out into the office and cajole everyone into action. The executors realize that they can't get things done alone—they are the catalyst, the fire starter, the "gun" at the start of the race to get everyone moving. If people don't move when they should, they are also the ones to give a swift kick up the backside to get them going.

***Teachers are our mentors and coaches.*** No team can move forward without knowledge. Whether this knowledge is acquired externally, or whether it is realized by the individuals themselves, the leader's role is to move their team to understand what is required. Teams are never more motivated than when they are learning.

***Innovators come up with that vital spark.*** The last characteristic is one of the most important. So often, when a team comes to a standstill, it is innovative leadership that takes them out of it. Motivation plummets and stress rises if you are stuck in the muddy doldrums for too long.

# CHAPTER 26

## *How Do Leaders Manage the Room?*

The holiday season gives an opportunity to renew old friendships and strengthen family ties. We all feel blessed to have so many amazing people in our lives.

However, in these super-sized gatherings, there are always a few individuals who cause us to shudder with revulsion. They simply seem to "rub us the wrong way," and no matter how many months or years have passed, the effect never seems to diminish. The strange thing is that our partners never seem to think that they are that annoying. They just don't get it!

The thing is that interpersonal relationships are highly complex beasts. Everyone has their individual preferences, and it is rare that everyone in the room will be positively disposed towards you.

In the festive season, most people turn a blind eye with the solace that the discomfort is only temporary, but even this fragile harmony can be shattered by a misplaced phrase or smirk. We've all been there...

Moving to the office setting, any leader has a much more demanding job on their hands. They have to coax and motivate each member of their team every day of the year, whatever the business weather, and no matter how steep the climb. They have the same 5-25 people in a room on a regular basis, and they have to navigate their way through the potential minefields of discord.

For a leader to test (and regulate) the temperature of the group, they have to develop a radar system that can pick up on the slightest change in the team dynamic and then react accordingly.

Just as a family host might sense that the game of charades is starting to get a little boring or that the kids are starting to get slightly boisterous, a leader must sense changes in the reactions of his team to a certain situation and manage it before things grow out of control. There are many platitudes about this phenomenon, but maybe none better than "keeping their hand on the tiller." If there is an iceberg looming on the horizon, the sooner that you react, the better the chances of taking evasive action.

When a leader is "in tune" with the dynamics of the relationships within the room, they can anticipate and pre-empt discussions before they even occur. They might know that two individuals would have different views on a certain topic, so rather than give them the opportunity to make it personal, a good leader will "own" the issue themselves and sidestep the personal conflict.

A great leader should also be prepared to adapt. Rather than be the frog in gradually boiling water, they need to change their plans before it is too late. The key to this lies in their perception of who owns the "agenda." It they see any activity as their personal project, they will be more precious when it comes to changes. If they genuinely view every activity as a "team" activity, they will involve everyone that little bit more and be that bit more open to input from everyone. When the wider team is involved, they will be sure to pull a leader out of the rapidly-heating water before it gets too hot.

The last idea is that the best leaders sit back and, to an extent, let the room manage itself. Yes, they keep a hand on the tiller, but they save their interventions for crucial moments rather than actively steer the ship themselves. A high-functioning team can perform the "auto-pilot" function perfectly well, but only if they are given the chance to do so (and to make the occasional mistake). A room that manages itself is motivated by doing what is best for the group, and the leader can sit back (to an extent) and gain a dispassionate viewpoint.

So, I hope that your holidays have been enjoyable, and that if you had to "manage" a group of relatives, you were able to understand the undercurrents of the group, steer them toward the right activities and away from the sensitive topics. Above all, though, I hope that your guests were able to have fun amongst themselves—that, after all, is what the holidays are all about.

# CHAPTER 27

## *The Best Leaders Learn to Bite Their Tongues*

Sometimes, self-control can be the difference between a quiet parting of the ways and a raging argument that ends in a messy scuffle.

A lot of us carry resentment, annoyance, and even anger inside us at any given time. Polite society requires us to keep our mouths shut most of the time; why cause a scene and potentially damage a relationship when you can simply just let the anger slowly dissipate?

Yet sometimes, even those of us with the best self-control can let things bubble over. Maybe there have been one too many sarcastic comments from the same person. There may be a recurring issue with an operational process that is easily fixable, but a certain individual doesn't wish to address it. It may simply be that someone was thoughtless and offended you for no real reason.

When the volcano erupts, things can very quickly spiral out of control.

It is often the case that although the person reacting doesn't "start" the incident, they are often the ones to finish it. Emotions escalate and things get out of control faster than either party would rationally consider normal adult behavior.

Not knowing when someone might "explode" is a worry for colleagues, team members and bosses. It means that they are unreliable and actually fairly untrustworthy. Very few tasks in the workplace do not actively involve communicating with others, and if a certain individual is not always able to control their emotions, there is another risk factor added into the scenario.

It only needs to happen once, but word will get around, and there will be a question mark against your temperament for the foreseeable future. There are enough reasons to get a black mark against your name for a promotion, but this is one of the hardest to shake. Short of undergoing anger management therapy, people will know that this risk is always going to be there.

That is often why leaders are pictures of self-control (i.e., they can get angry, but by design, not because of an unplanned emotional outburst). Here you might disagree with me and say that you know many leaders who fly off the handle. I would question whether they are the most effective managers… I wouldn't say so myself, and I have met a few of those types in my career.

If you walk into a meeting with your boss and you see that a client is trying to wind you up, you want to be certain that your boss will keep a cool head. If someone from another department is causing trouble, you know that your boss will rationally and logically de-escalate the situation without collateral damage.

These sorts of bosses are great. They are like a rocky cliff face—no matter what sort of a pounding that they take from the sea, they will not budge.

Have you gotten angry recently when you could have bitten your tongue? How do you think it looked to others? Do you think similar episodes could harm your career chances?

# CHAPTER 28

## *Thoughts of a Scared Leader*

Leaders are not some mythical species, put on this earth to be a perfect example to the rest of us. They are as fallible as anyone else, but as the pressures of failure are that little bit higher, many tend to hide their true feelings behind a façade of strength and control.

It would be very interesting to explore which situations call for vulnerability and which call for resoluteness, but in this chapter, I would simply like to share some of the specific feelings in these leaders' heads. I am sure that you will be able to recognize hints of these feelings in your superiors every now and again, and the best thing that you can possibly do is offer support and reassurance. Everyone gets scared, and much of the time the solution lies in a gentle hand around the shoulder and, "It will all work out fine."

I have certainly had these five thoughts coursing around my head at various points in the past (and even right at this very moment!).

1. *I don't know what to do.* Everyone feels lost sometimes, but leaders feel like they are the ones who are supposed to be giving guidance rather than needing it. Impatience is often the root cause of this feeling – the route to take is not always immediately clear, and spending time collecting your thoughts and allowing the pieces of the puzzle to fall into place is often the solution. The three words "I don't know" are the

hallmark of the strongest leaders; they can't know everything, but you can be sure that they will find someone who does.

2. *I don't feel appreciated.* Leadership is a lonely mantle. The CEO has their head stuck in the strategic clouds, and most CEOs are not so given to everyday praise in any case. Some reports may be adept at giving feedback and showing appreciation, but mostly, leaders have to learn to motivate themselves through their results and the results of their team. Is no one saying thank you? Suck it up and get on with making the difference that you know you are making.

3. *I don't think I'll succeed.* Success seems like a constant journey. As soon as you have achieved one goal, then the next one takes its place. Failures are inevitable on the way to success, but the nature of the journey is that these failures will plague you until you do finally reach your goal. The ratio is probably "I don't think I'll succeed," 60% of the time; "Hey, maybe this might have a chance," 39% of the time; and "Yes, we've done it," 1% of the time. If you are always pushing yourself and your team to the limits, you will always feel that you are never quite there. Deep down, you do believe, but these fleeting doubts cannot be avoided.

4. *Do people listen to me?* One of the classic signs of insecurity. If a leader stops believing in themselves, they assume that others have stopped believing in them as well. They start to dilute their message as they are scared that it will not be accepted, and their effectiveness takes a dive because they are not speaking their mind. This sense of paranoia is then made worse by their employees' suggesting improvements about the second-rate suggestions. A vicious circle of doubt ensues, and they lose their confidence entirely.

5. *I want to give up.* Your employees probably think that you are the most determined and resolute person. They follow you and believe in you because you outwardly believe in yourself. Inwardly, you are screaming, "No more! That's it! I can't take any more. This isn't going to work. Why do I keep doing this?" No leader can reach the top without feeling

this, and most of us have indeed leaned on our colleagues and teams at some point. Reaching impossible goals is not a burden to shoulder on your own. As with all of these thoughts, that is the key to flourishing as a leader—no one is perfect, and we all get scared. Your team will rally around you if the self-doubt gets really tough.

# CHAPTER 29

## *Leaders Are Born in the Playground*

If you have kids you drop off or pick up at school or maybe just walk past a school once in a while, it is worth pausing for a minute or two and looking around. The dynamics of the playground have changed a little since we were at school, but it is still fascinating to observe.

The way that kids interact with each other has changed as parenting habits have changed. This isn't a blog about the merits of modern parenting, nor is it a discussion about wrapping our children up in cotton wool and policing their every move in the playground. I merely make one simple observation.

There are certain kids in any playground who have this aura about them. They are not the loudest, the tallest or the sportiest. They don't have the smartest coats, the most fashionable hairstyle, or the coolest shoes. They are, however, surrounded by other kids, drawn to them like insects to a bright light, keen to be a part of their gang.

It is this feeling of belonging that is the key aspect of any playground. You don't see too many children sitting down on their own, quietly reading a book or staring up at the sky. They are all busy exploring what it is to be sociable. There is the ball games gang, the skipping gang, the tag gang, the fighting gang, the girly gang, and the singing gang. Each age group divides itself up into these little cliques, and while some children will be able to flit from clique to clique (an admirable skill), many will identify themselves with a certain group.

"I play tag at lunch," or "I sing songs with my friends," might be two common responses that parents hear.

The thing that is most interesting is how these groups organize themselves. I believe that there are children who help to mold the group dynamic, resolve disputes, and integrate new members. They are not chosen as captains or leaders in a formal voting system, but their leadership credentials are nonetheless democratic. They lead because others follow them. It has always been this way. They don't have titles, they aren't differentiated by salary or status, they are just kids that you want to be around. Actually, to my mind, that is a pretty good definition of a leader, "someone I want to be around."

These kids are fair to those around them, they are compassionate, and they listen to the will of the masses. They are always enthusiastic, the glue that binds the group together and makes every member feel that they belong. This feeling of belonging is what gives (elementary school) kids that little warm feeling inside. It is why they go to school with a smile on their faces.

The leaders of the playground play a big role in ensuring they feel this way.

# CHAPTER 30

## *IQ Is Worthless Without These Three Qualities*

Some people would assert that there is no direct relationship between intellectual intelligence and "success" in life. That word means so many different things to different people, but we will leave that for another chapter.

This assertion has been proven by multiple studies, and, deep down, we know that there is a kernel of truth. A basic level of intelligence is certainly required to achieve most things, but whether your IQ is 90 or 130, there are a whole host of other factors to level the playing field or even give you an advantage over your more intellectually gifted peers.

If you are a chess grandmaster or a brain surgeon, then IQ probably makes a bit more of a difference, but for most of us normal folk, the mix of ingredients contributing to our success are far more diverse. We enter adulthood with an assortment of these ingredients, molded by our upbringing, but the moment we hit the "real world," it is entirely our choice which of them we wish to develop.

I could probably write a whole chapter with an exhaustive list of these ingredients, but for the purposes of clarity, I would simply like to share my top three. To my mind, IQ is not worth much without them.

***Passion.*** From the moment that we are asked, "What do you want to do when you grow up?", we spend our lives searching for our Reason (with a capital letter). Everything that leads to our Reason gives us that little extra frisson of excitement, but this search demands energy. That comes from our passion, that inextinguishable flame within us. No matter how hard, no matter how long it takes, we will live and breathe our dream until we achieve it. Then, we give the dream an upgrade and the process starts again. Realizing our potential is a journey where the destination is constantly moving that little bit further up the road—our passion pushes us to carry on past previously achieved goals. Passion says, "Let's go again."

***Knowledge.*** A higher IQ does indeed give us the capacity to assimilate more learning, but knowledge comes from time and energy invested in this learning. If you have the intellect, but don't invest the time, your knowledge will be inferior. If you invest the time on the "right" subject matter, your level of knowledge will make up for your lack of IQ every day of the week. High school dropouts can "know" more than MBA graduates from Harvard; they have simply chosen to invest in their knowledge in certain subjects. Make sure that you are putting your IQ to the best possible use—what knowledge is most useful to help you achieve your goals?

***Creativity.*** The ability to generate ideas and recognize alternative possibilities is crucial in solving problems, communicating with others and finding new avenues to fulfill our potential. The road to success is littered with failures, but we very rarely have to start from the beginning. Creativity means reinventing the road, taking a few shortcuts and building on your journey thus far to find a new direction. The "intellectual" giant will keep pounding away at the statistically "right" things to do—the creative genius will turn the facts on their head to create a new reality. The creativity "muscle" needs practice to keep it strong, but if it is a regular part of your life, it can greatly enhance any results that may have been achieved by intellect alone.

# CHAPTER 31

## What Sort of Leader Are You?

The best leaders adapt their leadership style according to the situation, but no matter how flexible their approach, every individual demonstrates dominant characteristics, which govern their relationships and dictate their success.

Being aware of your preferred styles and their impact on those around you is the hallmark of the most successful people. In this chapter I would like to contemplate seven different leadership behaviors Which ones do you relate to and which ones drive you up the wall?

***Autocratic.*** The lone wolf of the management world, the autocrat makes his decisions alone and imposes his will on his minions. They bulldoze through life unchallenged and are the passive-aggressive background noise of any meeting. They are effective in a crisis or when an employee requires supervision.

***Laissez-Faire.*** The opposite of the autocrat, the laissez-faire leader simply lets things fall into place of their own accord. They don't supervise or motivate, which is good if their people are professional enough not to need it, but not so good if more control is required. If there is a crisis, laissez-faire leaders tend to sink along with their team.

***Transactional.*** The carrot and stick approach is one of the most typical and objective management styles. Good behavior (and results) are "rewarded," bad behavior (and results) are "punished." They agree with their team to sign up to certain goals and norms, and positive or negative deviation from these norms brings the corresponding result. Transactional leaders need to be competent coaches – assisting their people to move towards their rewards.

***Democratic.*** So, what do we think? Consensus building lies at the heart of the democratic leader's philosophy, and they seek to gain buy-in from anyone they work with. This is particularly useful when there is uncertainty or when fresh ideas are needed. This style can be frustrating when there is a level of urgency or when the direction is genuinely cloudy.

***Pacesetting.*** Every now and again, people need to be shown the way forward. This is not telling someone how to do something, but allowing them to model their behavior on your actions. This works well when the leader already has a skilled team that simply needs help in their choice of which path to take. There is nothing more comforting than following someone's well-trodden route.

***Authoritative.*** The authoritative leader is different from the autocratic leader—rather than dictating to their team where to go, they get their team enthused about a common goal and then leave it up to them to decide how to get there. They might say, "Come with me," to their team, but they don't mind whether that's on foot, on a bike, or in a car. The destination is the most important thing, and the authoritative leader inspires people to shoot for it.

***Coaching.*** The coaching leader encourages people to step out of their comfort zone and expand their mindset in any given situation. This is a forward-looking management style that is best suited to building cohesive and robust teams. If people are less open to feedback or if the leader's knowledge is lacking, this works less well.

I asked a few of my colleagues which two styles best characterized me, and the various answers were revealing. Your self-perception is often different from how others see you. The interesting part is working out why!

# CHAPTER 32

## *The Triathlon of Leadership*

Multi-disciplinary sports often make me think of the challenges of leadership.

There are so many "events" that the most effective leaders should excel in, that their work week could well be compared to an Olympic decathlon. However, in a ten-event decathlon, as in business, there are often a couple of events where the athlete is not so strong – maybe they have a weak javelin throw or a stuttering long jump. Similarly, a leader may not be so proficient at public speaking or time management—but they get away with it because the rest of their "game" is so strong.

However, things change with a triathlon.

Here, there are only three events – swimming, cycling and running (in that order). To win races on a regular basis, you have to be at the top of your game in each discipline. There is no hiding a weak event behind the strengths of the others. It is one of the most brutal forms of competition out there – man and woman against the elements, against their competitors and, most importantly, against themselves.

So, what are those three types of activity for any leader? What are the crucial three elements of the work week that they simply can't do anything but excel at? There are many contenders for the "triathlon of leadership," and everyone will have a different view, but these are my top three leadership events:

1. *Empathy.* The true nature of leadership is putting yourself in the place of others. Unless your agenda is a shared agenda, you will fail. In order to reach a shared agenda, you have to understand the perspectives, hopes, and dreams of those around you. Listening and acting on what you hear (rather than what is in your own head) is one of the key skills for any leader. You could equate empathy to the breathing patterns of a long-distance swimmer; they turn their heads for a vital breath of air every couple of strokes—that gives them the strength for the next couple of strokes. Instead of air, a leader has to show empathy and understand the people on a regular basis—otherwise, they will sink.

2. *Self-Belief.* How can someone who doesn't believe in themselves inspire that belief in others? Many people talk of the importance of humility in leadership, but you can't afford to be so humble as to become invisible to those who follow you. When times are hard, you have to know that you will be able to take your team along with you, no matter what happens. When everyone else starts to doubt, your unshakable belief should be what they can cling to. In cycling, the bigger the front "cog" of the bike, the higher the gear and the faster the bike can go at full speed. How big is your "self-belief" cog?

3. *Vision.* The last leg of the leadership triathlon is the toughest—maintaining empathy and self-belief can be energy sapping, but the true fuel of a leader is their vision. Triathletes start the final run stage with a clear vision of them finishing the race, maybe catching the person ahead and passing them in the finishing straight. Vision is about believing that the seemingly impossible is possible. You don't know how you are going to get there, but as long as you know the final destination, a "work in progress" is good enough. A leader without vision is like a ship without a destination, floating aimlessly out on the sea.

Empathy, self-belief, and vision. These are my three leadership triathlon events.

# CHAPTER 33

## Predict the Leadership Weather

We have all walked into meetings expecting a stormy reception because the boss is having a bad day for whatever reason. We have also walked into meetings with skies seemingly set fair, only to be hit by flash floods of frustration and crashing waves of criticism.

The key to surviving any natural disaster is preparation. If you are prepared for the tornado, you can hunker down and wait it out. If you are caught out in the open with no safe haven when a storm hits, you are putting yourself at serious risk.

Navigating the emotional storms of your work environment as carefully as possible without putting yourself in danger is vital for the long-term health of your career. You often can't fight the storm, but there are many ways to come through unscathed.

So, here are a few humble suggestions for when the boss is in a stormy mood:

***Make sure it isn't you.*** It is crucial to understand what has provoked the mood, and your first starting point should be to rule yourself out! If you are unaware that you are persistently doing things to rile the boss, you may think that the constant moods are a coincidence, but your days will be numbered. Find a way to solicit feedback and act on any signals of discontent, no matter how subtle.

***Don't let it affect you.*** It is easy to take emotional outbursts to heart and let them ruin the rest of the day. This has a knock-on effect on your relationships and will undoubtedly shake your confidence. Sometimes you have to simply put up the palm of your hand, let other people deal with their issues and get on with your own life. Someone else's (often irrational) moodiness is not your problem.

***Clarify their gripes.*** If you have no choice but to deal with their mood, there is a useful technique that negotiators and guidance counselors use to defuse emotions and allow people to consider their feelings. It is sometimes useful to repeat back your boss' concerns and give them a chance to go into further detail. This shows them that you are listening to them and buys you a little more time to craft a suitable response.

***Time your interactions.*** No one chooses to walk into a war zone. Unless something is critically urgent, maybe it is best to wait until your boss is in a more favorable mood. They are trying to deal with whatever is bothering them, and the last thing they need is another "pull" on their attention. Bosses will value the sensitivity of those who "stay away." Employees without that radar should beware.

***Document events.*** If conflict escalates and things start to get nasty, make sure that you document everything that has been said, save your emails, and inform a trusted ally about what is going on. It might get to the stage that you need to involve HR, so don't let your career suffer because of a psychotic boss.

***Have an escape plan.*** On a more mundane level, think up a few ways of taking yourself away from conflict situations. Maybe you have an urgent client call or an email that simply can't wait. As long as it is a pressing business reason, you can usually get away and let your boss cool down. If you become a passive sponge for their rage, they will assume that this is acceptable, and these events will happen ever more regularly. Get away from the situation as soon as you can.

Whether a storm has been "predicted" or not, hopefully these simple ideas will ensure that you are suitably sheltered from the worst of it.

# CHAPTER 34

## *Do You Know a Machiavellian Leader?*

I am fully aware that the subject of the title is a prettwell-worn cliché, but to know your enemy is to be prepared, so I wanted to explore some of the traits that these unscrupulous operators might exhibit.

However, rather than come up with any original ideas (perish the thought), I thought that I would refer to the seminal work *The Prince* written in 1513 by Niccolo Machiavelli himself. Napoleon, Bismarck, and Hitler were all fans of the book – maybe a few people in your office have a copy stashed under their pillows?

Machiavelli's basic premise was that if you want to lead, you need power. If you want power, you have to do all you can to hold onto it. To start with, here are a few selected beliefs of a Machiavellian leader:

*I - Don't manage by consensus. Do it yourself.*

*II - When you win power, you need to show strong leadership immediately.*

*III - If you don't have a clue what's going on, just get your hands dirty.*

*IV - Unpopular decisions will bring hatred and resentment – it comes with the territory.*

*V - When you are under pressure, you have to defend only the important stuff.*

*VI - When you are in charge, being loved is optional, better to be respected.*

*VII - Deceit is usually easier than you think – if the people that you are lying to have an interest in being deceived.*

*VIII - Being in charge lets you tell the story your way and in your own time.*

*IX - When two people fight each other, the weaker one becomes your friend.*

*X - If you've had a setback, don't wait for someone else to make it right.*

The underlying thread here lies with the belief that consolidation of power lies in the hands of the leader and their hands only. They do not allow people to get close to them and closely control the messages that they communicate. Their autocratic style does not allow any space for individual expression and their "minions" are either compliant, or they are sidelined.

The Machiavellian leader is equally not concerned with being popular. Their agenda will be better served by being respected than loved, but this respect is often one of fear rather than admiration. They will not think twice about pitting people against each other, "dividing and conquering" potential future rivals, and building their power base with the masses of the losing side. If there are enough battles, there will be enough "losers" who fear for their lives (or their careers). If you feel like a loser, what is there left but to cozy up with the megalomaniac boss? He has you right where he wants you, but what other choice is there?

Machiavellian leaders are not afraid to let things fall off the table. If a project is deemed unimportant to them and they have other priorities, they will not hesitate to let it lie fallow. They don't care whose interests may be harmed—for them other interests do not exist outside their own. They are pragmatic about the cyclical nature of life (and business) and are ready to make the required decisions themselves before the decisions are forced upon them.

However, as with many things in life, there are two sides to every coin. A few of the ten traits listed above could equally be used by a benevolent leader. Machiavelli's leaders were driven by a selfish desire, but for the leader who is conscious of empowering his team to perform and winning by helping them to win, there are also a few nuggets of wisdom. Getting your hands dirty if you do not understand the situation and putting right potential mistakes yourself is management advice that would grace any textbook.

It is natural that each type of leader has a certain amount of power...

The question for Machiavelli was: do you use it or abuse it?

# CHAPTER 35

## *The One Word Leaders Never Use*

As soon as you introduce uncertainty into any relationship, the seeds of doubt quickly germinate and spread their roots. It is often the case that success is reliant on the actions and promises of others—so anyone that may be perceived as unreliable (fairly or unfairly) is often marginalized when the important tasks and projects come along. The ability to deliver on what you promise is one of the most valued attributes of a modern leader.

However, often a solid track record of delivery is not enough when you are seeking to gain and retain the trust of your colleagues and your customers.

You have to talk the part.

Persuasion and influencing skills are crucial in greasing the cogs of business. We all grasp the importance of how you look and how you act—much of influencing is non-verbal. What you said is purported to have less importance, but there is certainly one word that all good leaders (or aspiring leaders) should avoid like the plague.

### *Try.*

As the Jedi Master Yoda famously said to his trainee Luke Skywalker, "Do or do not. There is no try."

I could end the chapter here, as it is pretty self-explanatory (as is Yoda's custom), but these few words get to the crux of what makes someone successful, so it is worth a few more minutes of reflection.

## *Try is self-denigrating.*

It implies uncertainty about your ability to complete a task or, at best, a lack of self-confidence to make it happen. Too many undertakings have been doomed to failure right from the start by using the words, "I'll try." If you hardwire your brain to give you a potential way out, you are giving yourself an automatic excuse for failure.

By ridding your vocabulary of the word "try," you make up your mind whether you will do something or not. Everyone has the option of ignoring or rejecting most activities in life. We don't have to say "yes" to everything. However, if you do say "yes," you should do everything within your power to accomplish the task. Obstacles will come your way, but you will get around them. Circumstances might change, but you will persevere. Success might be postponed for whatever reason, but you will keep going until you have accomplished what you have set out to do.

This mentality is incredibly powerful, but it is also contagious.

When your colleagues know that you are the type of person to make every conceivable effort to be true to their word, they too will be more open with you. Your approach of uncovering every possible stone will encourage them to do the same. Your success in achieving where others have failed will prompt others to wonder why. Their conclusions will often boil down to the same thing.

## *He doesn't "try" to deliver. He does deliver.*

Here is where my article gets a little debatable… Can you change your actions by changing your attitude? Can one small change in your language introduce a ripple effect that affects many crucial areas of your life? Can you take time and circumstances out of the equation by committing to your promises?

I believe that you can. I have seen enough "light bulb" moments in the careers of colleagues and employees to understand that the absence of this smallest of words can make the biggest of differences.

I won't say, "Try it."

I'm sure that you understand why.

# CHAPTER 36

## "Soft Play" Is Not for Leaders

You might be aware of these "soft play" areas for kids that offer parents an opportunity to have a quiet coffee while their little ones let off steam in a safe environment. Many of them are veritable labyrinths of fun, with all sorts of slides, nets, obstacles and tunnels to navigate. The great thing for the parent is that every conceivable surface is covered in a bump-resistant foam that stops even the heftiest of collisions from causing a dent.

Of course, there will be far fewer kids visiting hospitals with broken limbs or seeping wounds, and that is a good thing. However, you don't learn to stand that little bit further away from the swing when you are pushing it until you have been knocked over a couple of times. Mistakes hurt, but you amend your behavior to avoid that mistake the next time.

Taking this chapter away from the realm of childhood, you could use the same comparison in the workplace. If you "play it safe" in your career, you are insulating yourself from your full potential. If you shield your team from difficult situations and tricky decisions, the moment that they are on their own, they may not be able to cope. The harder you fall, the higher you can bounce.

If you look at those people that you would call "leaders" at work, they likely haven't had an easy rise to the top. They will have made mistakes, let people down, and felt inadequate on many occasions. That is because they took the decision to step out of the "soft play" risk-free environment and meet the harsh realities of corporate life head on.

Those who played the political game by avoiding curve balls and not sticking their heads above the parapet may indeed have reached a certain level, but you can be sure that they did not realize their full potential. When you avoid the flak, it is inevitable that someone else on the team has to take it. Do this too often, and it gets noticed. No one likes slippery shoulders.

The same goes for those who seek perfection in their lives and their careers. Perfection is manufactured, and it never tells the whole story. You didn't explore certain avenues for fear of getting it wrong. You were afraid of getting hurt, so you lived life in second gear. You have an unblemished record, but what would your record have looked like if there were a few more blemishes along the way?

The great Steve Jobs said, "The greatest artists like Dylan, Picasso, and Netwon risked failure. And if we want to be great, we've got to risk it too."

Those who are imperfect have a certain magnetism about them. They have taken some knocks, but they have survived. They are not reckless in terms of assessing their risks, but they factor in the likelihood of a few bumps and bruises along the way. Like the magician who pulls off an amazing trick, the disbelievers want to understand how they have done it. Mistakes do not always equal demise (if you learn from them)—you pick yourself up and dust yourself off, but you are all the wiser for it.

Every now and again, I take stock of my life and try to ensure that it doesn't take the guise of that children's "soft play" area. Am I really making the most of the opportunities that come my way? Am I dodging certain issues in search of an easier life? Am I ready to bump my head on the metal bar without the protection of the cushioned padding?

The school of hard knocks is what makes us feel alive.

# CHAPTER 37

## A Leader's A-Z of Body Language

The best leaders are avid readers, and I am not only talking about books. They are masters at reading the non-verbal clues that we share.

This is such a vital topic for anyone who wants to move up the corporate ladder, and most of you will have read countless articles with suggested "Ten Vital Body Language Hacks," so I thought I'd offer a slightly different format.

Here is an A-Z to trigger some thoughts on the topic:

***Aggressive.*** The face gives it away with frowns, pursed lips, and even snarls. Space is invaded, the body is opened (inviting an attack) and fists may be clenched. Notice the aggressive body language and potentially avoid the fight.

***Barrier.*** Bad body language creates barriers to communication and building

relationships. Crossed arms and legs can indicate inflexibility and lack of interest.

***Congruence.*** When your words do not match up to your movements and expressions, people get the feeling that "something isn't quite right." The seeds of doubt are most often sown when there is incongruence between what you say and what you do.

***Defensive.*** You can't build rapport if you sense that someone is not open to your messages. It is important to recognize when they seek refuge from the conversation, and you can take measures to engage them.

***(Micro) Expression.*** These brief facial expressions last only a fraction of a second. They occur when a person either deliberately or unconsciously conceals a feeling. Seven emotions have these universal signals: anger, fear, sadness, disgust, contempt, surprise, and happiness.

***Fidgeting.*** If you are seemingly not in control of your bodily movements or making repetitive nervous movements, it could be hampering your attempts to communicate effectively. Some studies have championed fidgeting as a way to ease the cognitive load and streamline decision-making, but many view it as an annoyance.

***Gesture.*** We are hard-wired to be expressive, and our gestures are outward manifestations of our personality. No one can read our minds, but everyone can make their own interpretation of how we are acting.

**Handshake.** Touch is a key aspect of interpersonal relationships, and the first touch between strangers is often the handshake. Too firm, and you come across as being aggressive; too limp, and you will seem like a push over.

***Involuntary.*** Unless you make a conscious effort to understand the effect of your body language on others, it will remain a mystery. Much of how you react to situations is entirely involuntary – you need to make an effort to change.

***Joke time.*** Lifted eyebrows, rolling eyes and smirking mouths are some common signs of sarcasm. Detecting that twinkle in someone's eye is not a gift given to everyone. There is always one person who doesn't get it!

***Kinesics.*** The fancy word for the interpretation of body motion communication such as facial expressions and gestures, that is, nonverbal behavior related to movement of any part of the body or the body as a whole.

***Lying.*** Their demeanor changes, and they are restless for no reason. They might rub their nose or their eyes in the wake of an untrue admission. They'll probably keep eye contact for a little longer than usual. If they smile when they feel that their lie has been swallowed, this is a certain sign of duplicity.

***Mirroring.*** This is when one person subconsciously imitates the gestures, speech pattern, or attitude of another. People naturally use mirroring to build rapport, but it also forms the basis of influencing techniques such as NLP.

***Non-verbal.*** UCLA professor Albert Mehrabian developed one of the most well-known rules when it comes to non-verbal forms of communication. While 55% of messages received and processed by your brain are based on your body language, 38% of messages are processed based on your tone of voice, and only 7% of your received meaning will be based off the words you are saying.

***Oculesics.*** This is the study of eye movement, eye behavior, gaze, and eye-related nonverbal communication. It is said that the eyes offer a window to your soul – one quick gaze, and (theoretically) everything is clear.

***Power Pose.*** In her well-known TED talk, social psychologist Amy Cuddy shows how "power posing" —standing in a posture of confidence, even when we don't feel confident—can affect testosterone and cortisol levels in the brain, and might even have an impact on our chances for success.

***Quitting.*** If you aim your body towards the door, are you preparing for a quick getaway? If you look down or around the room, you might seem disinterested. Slouching looks as if you are disengaged, and playing with your hair looks like boredom.

***Repetition.*** If something happens often enough, we have a tendency to be persuaded. Repetition creates a pattern, which consequently and naturally grabs our attention at first and then creates the comfort of familiarity.

If you are trying to change the impact of your body language, repetition will work, but don't make it too obvious!

***Submissive.*** If someone is actively seeking to avoid conflict, they may act as if they are shrinking away from a confrontation. They make themselves less physically imposing, lower their heads and maybe even widen their eyes to make them seem more vulnerable.

***Territory.*** The regulation of physical distance is key with body language. Invade someone's personal space, and you may seem aggressive; stay too far away, and you might look disinterested.

***Underwhelmed.*** Bored people are given away by more than the stereotypical yawn. When a person is bored, they will either consciously or unconsciously look for ways to distract themselves or will show signs of wanting to get away from the situation.

***Visual Cue.*** Body language happens in the same way as a conversation. You give people verbal and non-verbal cues, and they will react to you. Effective communication entails adequately responding to these cues and ensuring that your cues are interpreted correctly.

***Worried.*** Fidgety, distracted, shaky, possibly moody, or reserved? All could be signs of worry. If there is any sense that your brain is not "in the room," then people might think that something is bothering you.

***Xxxxx.*** Show people some "love," and their body language will change for the better. The moment you let someone know that you care almost always helps to break down barriers. If you make them feel important, they will open up to you.

***YOLO.*** You only live once. There is only one chance to make a first impression. Make sure that your body language doesn't ruin it.

***Zzzzzzzz.*** If you aren't dynamic enough, you run the risk of your audience falling asleep. Your words and tone of voice aren't always enough to keep them hooked.

# CHAPTER 38

## *Why Simple Ideas Are Often Best*

The Color Run™ is a 5K race in Trento, Italy. Worldwide, there are over 300 such races each year.

I want to tell you about the race to illustrate the power of a simple idea.

Basically, you wear a white T-shirt, and—per their website—as you run the course, "You will see smiling faces along the course whose main goal is to douse you in colorful powder to ensure that you look like you ran through a beautiful rainbow by the time you cross the finish line."

That's it. That's the idea. Simple, right?

Founded in 2011 as a profit-making event, this program has grown into what the organizers claim is the single largest event series in the world.

In a world filled with 5K and 10K races, this one stands out for its focus less on fitness and more on fun. Participants share advice like, "Keep your arms down and twirl as you move through the color throws to get a more even color placement," and, "If you don't want to spend the next few days scrubbing colored powder out of your center part, wear a cap or a wig (in white of course!)"

In fairness, this isn't even an original idea. It's a commercialized version of the Hindu festival of Holi, which includes throwing colored powders on people as part of the festival.

But the commercial race shows what is possible when you brilliantly execute a simple idea. Too often in business, professionals—and entire companies—stagnate because they lack a "big idea" to change their circumstances. In reality, they don't need innovation; they need a good idea that people understand well enough that they can execute it brilliantly.

The race works because it is an incredibly simple idea. You can describe it in a few words, and have other people instantly grasp it. "That sounds like fun!" is almost certainly the response you'll get.

Once you arrive at such an idea, you can execute it again and again. My guess is that The Color Run™ in Brooklyn, New York is not much different from the one in Marseille, France.

The more complicated an idea, the less likely it is to survive and thrive. Complicated ideas have a tendency to fall apart, because people cannot describe them accurately or consistently.

So, if you want to do something innovative and unique, try a simple idea that you can execute brilliantly.

# SECTION 2 – SELF-IMPROVEMENT

# CHAPTER 39

## *Self-Interest Is Tied to Shared Success*

Recently I've noticed a dismal trend. Sometimes our best attempts at avoiding conflict and suffering are its primary causes. Mainly, we strive to avoid undesirable situations, yet our avoidance may be the very reason we undermine ourselves and others.

The culprit is our tendency to create personal narratives free of culpability. We like to believe that our motivations are noble, we are capable of selfless generosity, and we can accept contradictory viewpoints and see people as they are. And when someone comes our way who tells us otherwise, well then, they must be wrong. They must have an ulterior motive. They must be morally bankrupt in some way we aren't.

When you see it spelled out in this way, surely you recognize the irrationality in this line of thinking. How could someone believe such things about themselves? The truth is we hold these kinds of beliefs, and they play out in our day-to-day through our thoughts and actions. We seldom notice them because we compulsively reject any self-reflection that clashes with our beliefs about ourselves. It's human nature.

On a personal level, this is disastrous and disheartening. We are fond of the conviction that we know ourselves better than others do. Although that may be the case, it doesn't mean that all we know of ourselves is accurate.

What's more, on an interpersonal level, that disparity may be the underlying cause of endless conflicts and suffering.

In this chapter, I tie this delusion to a host of personal and interpersonal conflicts, and explain how our open acknowledgement of this irrational belief system can not only improve our individual lives, but also improve customer experience and business practices as a whole.

## We Are Our Own Roadblock

There are so many of us. The world has never been quite this populated. The degree of disconnect amongst people has also never been quite this pronounced.

You might have heard the battle cry against the disconnect, to see the world through another's eyes, to empathize. It resounds throughout every area of human activity. At the local, corporate, and governmental levels, we hear people demand it. But perhaps more than ever before, inequality is on the rise.

I think this shows that we are all far too wrapped up in ourselves. Even those people who demand empathy often lack the ability to empathize with the object of their exhortations. It's a zero-sum game.

Therein lies the self-delusion I think accounts for so much of the violence and discord we see today. Each of us is wrapped up in our lives, unable to view ourselves as part of a larger whole.

I believe that if we do so, then we can become better people, better leaders, more successful, and generally increase psychological well-being.

## The History of Being Wrapped Up in Ourselves

Self-interest is a primal drive. For much of our existence as a species, we evolved to protect our well-being and that of our families. The world was fraught with dangers, so selflessness was not an option. You were either hunter or hunted.

Currently, however, many of those dangers are gone, yet our primal drives are not. Our bodies haven't caught up to the state of contemporary life. Some situations we treat as life-or-death scenarios actually pose little threat to our existence. Think about traffic. How often do you berate other drivers disproportionately?

But that's just the surface. The real driver is not self-interest, but rather fear. Fear compels us to steal, attack, and lash out. We are afraid of much. A poignant example is the women's anti-aging industry. If fear doesn't keep it alive—fear of aging, fear of rejection, fear of a loss of social capital—I don't know what does.

Now, mollifying fear isn't a matter of having more guards around you. You can be in Fort Knox and gripped with fear about fictive impending doom. This explains why so many people can work themselves to death and never feel they have acquired enough. No matter how much we acquire, we may always feel impoverished, and that's because of a dominant and motivational fear.

In other words, fear and self-interest go hand in hand. It is fear that galvanizes our self-interest.

Now, you might expect me to give you ten ways to do away with fear and become a better person. But I won't. I don't think there is anything wrong with fear or self-interest.

## The Crown Jewel of Fear and Self-interest

Self-interest and fear are our connections to what truly matters. We only fervently guard those beliefs and connections that are part of our identity, those things that feel like life-or-death. They are our essence, if you will. And when we understand that this drives much of our decision-making—and that of others—we tap into the tools to engagement, innovation, and success.

Self-interest and fear are formalized within us as the Happiness Delusion. The delusion informs our behavior, and beyond that, it shapes our perception of it. We are deluded into ignoring anything we deem negative and accepting only what we perceive as positive.

In different contexts, the delusion takes on different forms, and therefore, different names. Economists have called it confirmation bias in some cases, and theory blindness in others. The point is, when we are deluded by formalized self-interest and fear, we are unable to see clearly.

The ten common denominators of the delusion observable in society at large are:

1. Stress and fear are bad.
2. We should focus only on the positives.
3. Heroes are successful by good deeds alone.
4. We operate rationally and morally.
5. It will all work out in the end.
6. The most important good is looking good.
7. Ignore your critics and detractors.
8. The universe is conspiring to help you.
9. Human beings are amazing.

**10.** Delusion beats reality.

These are the feel-good beliefs that serve our self-interest to keep us safe from suffering and harm, especially from the harm that arises from the realization we aren't as good as we thought. This belief system simultaneously blinds us to the damage we cause to ourselves and to others.

The antidote to the delusion that will permit us a more exact picture of ourselves and others is *recognition*. We must stop and recognize.

## Use the Delusion to Accomplish Your Goals

The key to wielding self-interest and fear in order to dispel the parts of the delusion that do not serve us is twofold.

First, we must recognize that everyone, including ourselves, acts in their self-interest out of fear. It is not a fault, but rather an innate attribute of humanity.

Second, we must recognize the self-interests of others and learn how to harmonize them with our own. This second point is crucial to our evolution as a species that no longer lives in the wild and treats every interaction as a life-or-death scenario.

A few techniques to change your perspective about others and their self-interests are as follows:

- Align your intention with the identity and values of those you wish to relate to.
- Frame what is important to you in terms of what is important to them.
- Link your success to the success of those you wish to influence.
- Demonstrate how you serve communities and networks as well as individuals.

- Acknowledge and offset the cost to them (they are aware of the cost even if you are not).
- Learn to accept the self-interest of asking, "What's in it for them?"

As you learn to rethink your relationship to others and to receive their self-interest differently, you'll become more familiar with the bonds that make up people's identities and your own.

For example, the bond between you and your immediate family may compel you to go hard on a business deal because your child wants to attend a top university, and you want to help them graduate debt-free. That's a consideration unknown to your negotiator but influences your mood, attitude, and persistence

## How to Build Familiarity for Business Success

A strategy to build familiarity with the unknown is to rehearse it until it feels known and familiar. This approach is used by salespeople and presenters often. When you establish connections to accepted truths and real-world, relatable examples, it brings your propositions into focus and reduces the appearance of risk.

You might be nervous about approaching a business situation and making it too personal, but actually you could empower yourself by being the only person in the room to ask rather than assume motivations.

So, the next time you are in a negotiation or in a position to persuade someone, ask them, "What is your expected outcome and why?" or ask them, "What is your concern about this transaction?"

Use this to enhance your brand experience as well. In a sense, that's what customer feedback is about. You want to glean a deeper understanding of why customers are using your product and why they aren't, to then modify your behavior and align your interests with theirs.

It's not counterintuitive, but it is hard to do, because we often assume that when we recognize the self-interest of another, we automatically subvert our own.

## When You Build Familiarity, You Make Choices Easier

The success of Apple is due in no small part to its driving ethos, "A computer for the rest of us." At a time when the world of computers was reserved for those who could read code and understand the secret language required, Apple launched a PC with a visual interface. It had a Trash icon into which you deposited your "trash" and folders you could put your files into. It was a revolution that democratized access to technology.

Apple's success can be traced back to that ethos, which essentially takes the familiarity principle to its maximal expression. By making everything familiar to us, Apple consequently made it easier.

They reduced the friction in the process of computer-use with an intuitive logic. They simplified erstwhile complex systems. They reduced time/energy investment by swapping out or consolidating processes rather than breaking them down into discreet yet myriad ones. They used marketing to let everyone know just how easy Apple products are and how customer's lives would improve from use. And in general, they were hard on results and flexible on processes.

## Unlock Human Potential by Being More Human

The problematic factor in all this is that to make things familiar we must first be familiar with ourselves and others. But we often fail to do so.

The happiness delusion blinds us to the undesirable characteristics of humanity. But when we acknowledge them, recognize our role in them, and learn how to target our innovations and our solutions toward them, we can create more human technology, infrastructure, processes, and honest approaches to real-world problems.

We cannot continue to operate under the impression that each of us is good and everyone else is bad. We are all flawed. We are all self-interested. We are all afraid of something. When we are honest about that, we can establish a culture of reciprocity and mutual benefit that uses self-interest as a guidepost rather than a weapon.

Once we do this, we will unlock tremendous human potential.

# CHAPTER 40

## *Life Lessons from the Rio Olympics 2016*

The Olympics tend to fill people with a motley mix of pride, disappointment, and awe. The athletes are inspirational and often force you to reflect on your own life, in some cases, with deprecation, and in others, with determination. It's important to remember that despite the ease with which Olympians perform (irrespective of winning or losing), there is a history of sweat, strain, and pain behind each of them. We should not ignore this. With great dedication often comes great sacrifice.

When we learn these athletes' grueling stories, we can uncover lifelong lessons that go beyond victory or defeat. Every athlete has a storied past that can inspire us to reevaluate our own past and move into the future with renewed conviction.

### Family Support Is Incomparable

US Gymnast Simone Biles made winning an Olympic gold medal look effortless. But behind her huge smile is the story of a troubled childhood.

Simone Biles never knew her father, and her mother struggled with drug addiction. To safeguard her from the consequences, Simone was adopted by her grandparents. They fostered her talent, and it quickly began to blossom.

Her grandparents sacrificed holidays to travel with Simone to competitions. They encouraged her to be the best she could be for herself, and they provided her with all the love and support a devoted family could. The story of Simone Biles is a shining example of how familial support early in life can put us on a path to success.

Simone says that her grandparent's words resound as her biggest sources of inspiration,

"Be the best Simone that you can be," and, "You don't have to compete against anybody. It's just you and yourself out there.".

## The Importance of Marginal Gains (Team GB)

As of 2010, no British cyclist had ever won the Tour de France. Dave Brailsford had a plan to change that.

Their secret weapon was the theory of marginal gains. The concept is simple. By improving in every area of cycling by at least 1%, they could cumulatively create a significant advantage over their competition.

They started with the main culprits of our failures: bad habits. They began by optimizing the riders' circadian cycles, ensuring they got sufficient sleep and nutrition every day, without fail. Then they focused on the ergonomics of the bike seat and the weight of the tires. In those cases, they sought a mere 1% improvement.

As the theory of marginal gains predicates, despite the increases being small independently, overall those tiny changes accounted for the difference between failure and success.

Can you imagine how much more productive your business would be with a similar approach?

## Success Is About Inspiring Others

While chasing personal success, we seldom stop to consider who we are affecting in the process or who we might be inspiring.

Back in 2008, Singapore's Joseph Schooling looked up to Michael Phelps as his hero. After meeting Michael Phelps, Schooling's conviction to be a better swimmer was solidified. Schooling wanted to follow in Phelps' footsteps. He trained hard to attain this dream.

Fast forward to Rio 2016.

A now 21-year-old Joseph Schooling beat Michael Phelps to the gold medal. The headlines concentrated on Phelps becoming the most decorated Olympian of all time. But the ensuring lesson here is that success is not solely about individual accomplishments, it's also about the effect you have on others.

## Never Give Up

Mo Farah made history this year by claiming his third Olympic title for Great Britain.

What makes his story even more inspirational is how the 33-year-old recovered heroically after being tripped by his training partner. Despite the peccadillo, Farah jumped back to his feet and secured a gold medal without even dusting himself off.

Maybe Babe Ruth was right when he said it's hard to beat a person who never gives up.

## Don't Take Yourself Too Seriously

Despite immense pressure to perform, three-time consecutive men's 100m gold medalist Usain Bolt gleefully reveled in the spotlight. By inviting Brazilian samba dancers to his press conference in Rio, he taught us all how to not take ourselves too seriously.

Success is meaningless unless we actually enjoy what we do.

## The Takeaway

The next time you say to a colleague, "What are your plans for the weekend?" remember that the Olympic champions we cheered over finish lines were asked the same question countless times, and usually they answered, "Training."

To achieve what you want in life, you need to set your goals and devote yourself to making them a reality. It won't be easy. You will need extra supplies along the way and support from family and friends. You'll need to fall down and get back up again; you'll probably need to identify some idols; and just like the Olympics, not everyone will walk away with a gold medal.

If we learned anything from Rio 2016, it's that winning isn't everything, because even the losers can walk away proud that all their perseverance brought them to the Olympics.

And four years from now, they'll have another opportunity to claim the gold.

# CHAPTER 41

## *Finding Your Inner Balance in Life*

What do you want to do in life? It's a daunting question that serves to remind us how unsure we can be any given day about our destination or our purpose. It's as if someone were demanding, "Tell me your future!"

The problem isn't the question: The problem is our understanding of it. The question is merely asking you your end-goal. An end can take many forms. You may not know what career you want to have, where you want to live, or what you want your salary to be, but there are many things you do know. You know the kind of person you want to be and the principles you want to uphold. In other words, you know your character and ethics.

With those two axes, you can plot your achievements and contributions.

At any given time, I believe there are aspects of your character and principles that you may alter. You are fixed and in flux. It's a matter of consciously deciding who you want to be.

### You Are Fixed and in Flux

Our character and principles at any given moment should be fixed. We should have a clear sense of what they are—like a personal mission statement. A mission statement is a set of core standards for behavior that steel us against the winds of change that blow daily.

They grant us security, guidance, wisdom, and power.

See how I made it sound easy until I unloaded those broad and seemingly intractable concepts? Let's unpack them briefly.

***Security***. Your sense of worth, identity, emotional anchor, self-esteem, and basic personal strength or lack thereof.

***Guidance***. Your source of direction in life, an internal frame of reference that includes standards, principles, or implicit criteria that govern moment-by-moment decision-making and actions.

***Wisdom***. Your perspective on life, sense of balance, judgment, discernment and comprehension.

***Power***. The faculty or capacity to act and the strength and potency to accomplish.

These attributes flow from your core, your center of identity. You might not realize it, but even now you have a center from whence flow these attributes in varying degrees; and not always to your benefit. The great thing about our identity is that it can feel fixed but is actually in constant flux.

At any given time, I believe there are aspects of your character and principles that you may alter. It's a matter of consciously deciding who you want to be. By identifying your center, you can choose to shift it or amplify it.

When you pinpoint a true center, you then grant yourself another benefit. You can establish your true end, and from that point, crafting a mission statement is much simpler.

## Identify Your True Center

There are ten common centers in people's lives. Only you can truly identify your own; no one else can do it for you. Granted, we often think we know the true intentions or purposes of others, but that's a fallacy. You and only you can know yourself best (it's purely a matter of access to information, i.e., no one else is in your head).

So, what do you think your center is?

***Spouse***. Your life perspective surrounds things that may positively or negatively influence your spouse or relationship.

***Family***. Your decision-making criteria are what is good for the family and its derivatives.

***Money***. Moneymaking is your end-goal; by any means necessary is your motivation.

***Work***. You see your life as work.

***Possessions***. You make decisions based on what will protect, increase, or better display your possessions.

***Pleasure***. You see the world in terms of maximizing enjoyment.

***Friend***. You see the world through a social lens.

***Enemy***. You are counter-dependently guided by your enemy's actions and base decisions on what will thwart your enemy.

***Church***. You see the world in terms of "believers" and "non-believers" and "in" or "out."

***Self***. You view the world by how decisions, events, or circumstances will affect you.

Your center may not be one single center. We often have a combination of centers, motivating us in different directions. The problem is that you can't appease the demands of all centers at once. At some point, you will need to say, "What is my priority?"

When you pinpoint a true center, you then grant yourself another benefit. You can establish your true end, and from that point, crafting a mission statement is much simpler. That mission statement will give you security, guidance, wisdom, and power, bolstered by the knowledge that it serves your true center.

Still unclear about where to begin with your mission statement?

Self-knowledge is instrumental to this entire process. The better you know yourself, the more successful you will be.

## A Mission Statement Appetizer

I am very fond of questions. In fact, I don't think we ask enough questions. We assume to know too much. Plus, when we were younger, impatient adults probably squelched our curiosity and inquisitiveness.

Take a good look at yourself and ask the following questions. The answers will reveal much about yourself.

1. What are my boundaries? How far am I willing to go? How far am I willing to let others go? This information is vital.
2. How will I ground myself? What is my battle plan for when life gets tumultuous? It's crucial as well
3. What impassions me? What makes me happy? There is nothing more potent than self-fulfillment. When you target your main sources of passion, you are imbued with energy, conviction, and strength.

If you follow the guidelines I've laid out here, you might also find your core mission statement. From that point you cannot be shaken, and your resolve cannot be broken.

## The Final Frontier Is Oneself

We spend our entire lives with ourselves and yet we cannot answer the most essential questions about ourselves. That is why self-knowledge is powerful. It allows you to be inner-directed and sensitive to your relationship with others. When you embark on this path of self-knowledge, you eventually find stability.

If you follow the guidelines I've laid out here, you might also find your core mission statement. From that point you cannot be shaken and your resolve cannot be broken.

# CHAPTER 42

## *The ROI of Caring for Others*

Ever wonder why so many people don't care about what you do or have to say? Ever envy that other guy everybody cares about?

When you peer down the rabbit hole, you decide to let whatever you see into your life. You might even decide to jump in. You would if you cared enough.

It is so much easier to live a superficial life, walking past everyone else's troubles pretending that you don't notice. Contemplating your own worries is perfectly scary enough, thank you very much, and you proceed to ignore many of those as well. Out of sight, out of mind, so let's go watch a sports game and drink some beer.

The stresses of modern life have made many people view this as a coping strategy. Personally, I don't blame them. The last couple of decades have brought all sorts of existential threats to our doorsteps—global terrorism, worldwide economic fluctuation, natural and humanitarian disasters, to name but a few. It is enough to make anyone want to "shut up shop" and think about themselves for a while.

But it doesn't need to be this way.

The thing about caring about others is that they start to care about you. If you take the time to look beneath the surface and do something about what you find, they are likely to take more of an interest in what is going on in your life. You do have to "give" first, but if you give enough, it is assured that lots of people will give back. No matter what is going on in the world around them, the caring people in the world (whether they are bosses or employees, mums or children) will always be insulated from all the stuff because they know that they are not going through it alone.

Caring about what lies beneath isn't hard. You don't have to lay someone down on your psychologist's couch and insist that they reveal their deepest fears. It all starts with a question, a question that demonstrates that you care about them. Don't be too specific; leave it open enough for them to talk about what is truly on their mind, and don't talk at them too much—giving them time to think is the first step to true understanding.

Sometimes there might be a long gap between the first exploratory conversation and the second, but that's okay, you can't expect someone to turn on the emotional tap and let everything pour out. Make yourself available for them, listen attentively to the subtext, and try your hardest not to be judgmental. "If I were you, I would do this" is the last thing that they want to hear. Just being there for them will be enough.

In our manic business world, I don't think that we care enough about each other. It works both ways—leaders with their people and also employees with their bosses. The boss is human, too, and they might feel that they can't talk about their problems for fear of seeming weak. That is a horrible situation to be in, and they will equally appreciate it when their employees show that they care.

When did you last put someone else's life and feelings first? I know that I could do it a little more—just writing this chapter is making me think of all the times when I could have been a better listener and taken that little bit more time for other people.

When you care, people will care about you.

# CHAPTER 43

## *How to be Truly Innovative & Creative at Work and in Life*

### Creativity

It's a feel-good term that has gotten a lot of traction recently. Like a song on the radio, it has gotten a little too much play and is now obscured by usage. What is creativity? And on that note, what is innovation? What is creative innovation?

Many organizations use these terms to describe their practice, their approach, their philosophy, but do they actually have a clear sense of what each or both mean?

I have a hunch that many of them don't, and if they do, then it's a narrow conception of creativity that doesn't begin to cover the manifold experiences and perspectives that one might consider creative.

This isn't just a matter of semantics. Not being clear on what creativity and innovation are has practical consequences on business structures, product and service offerings, and the very people we bring into our teams.

I wrote this article to address the ambiguity latent in present day usage, and to specify how we can incorporate creativity into our teams and organizations.

## What Is Creativity and Innovation?

Teresa Amabile is the Edsel Bryant Ford professor of business administration in the entrepreneurial management unit at Harvard Business School and a director of research there. According to Amabile, creativity is not necessarily an eccentric personality or a lover of art, nor is it a sign of intelligence. And even if it were, she infers, it isn't necessarily good either.

To some this might be controversial, but it highlights an important point. There are myriad opinions about what creativity is, and not all of them are good. In fact, some may be conspicuously pernicious misperceptions that could lead organizations in the wrong direction or prevent you from integrating creativity into your organization altogether.

The point is that misperceptions abound, and they might be hampering our betterment in some way.

Let's plot out common misperceptions to start with.

***Perception***: You have to be born with creativity.

***Reality***: Most creators and innovators have learned how to be creative.

***Perception***: Creative ideas come from eureka moments.

***Reality***: Creative moments are usually the culmination of a creative problem-solving progression.

***Perception***: You have to work in a heralded innovative organization in order to be creative.

***Reality***: Any organization can adopt innovative practices, and any individual can use creative methods independently.

***Perception***: Creativity doesn't apply to business.

***Reality***: Creativity wins a lot more than it loses.

***Perception***: Creativity is creativity; it's all the same.

***Reality***: All creativity is not created equal.

The demystification doesn't clear up a crucial point though. What is creativity? Part of the problem is the question. Creativity isn't a single thing. There are types of creativity.

There is artistic creativity, functional creativity, linguistic creativity, spatial creativity, etc. The idea that there is a creative disposition is also fraught. Many people are capable of operating within rigid constraints and still exercise their creativity. For some, this runs contrary to what creativity is. I think that has more to do with your stereotypes about creative personalities than anything else.

In the case of innovation, learning to work within constraints to then remake or break them is important. You can't have at it *ad hoc*. You should at least be targeted. Lawyers are familiar with this kind of creativity. They need to think openly about the law, working within constraints by looking for alternatives, be that interpretations, clauses, language, possibilities, etc. That's creativity right here. And in a business context, this kind of creativity is key.

For some, this kind of constraint creativity makes sense. For others, it might seem like a paradox.

I have six principles that might bring the conversation down to Earth for the skeptics.

## Six Principles of Business Creativity

***Pattern***. Look for patterns in your life, your projects, and your tasks. Start with the most obvious patterns and expand from there. Often we want to see big, overarching trends, but that isn't the best way to get your mind accustomed to this sort of thinking.

***Solution***. A solution can take many forms. There doesn't even need to be a problem to provide a solution. A solution can be alternative, pure and simple. Someone wants options, possibilities, and each possibility you conceive is a solution to that desire. This is a mindset. Be solution-oriented. Believe that there are alternatives all around you. It'll free your mind to play.

***Trial-and-Error***. One major downfall of large companies with defined and rigid work distribution is the near impossibility of trial-and-error. You may recognize that an alternative exists based on a pattern you've identified, but have no means of testing it.

That's a problem. Nevertheless, you won't know if something truly works until you try it and that's okay. We can't anticipate everything.

***Combine***. A stonewall to innovation is specialization. I know this is polemical. Some would say the opposite. I believe a sure-fire path to innovation is learning to think liberally about how ideas can coalesce to create new alternatives based on existing patterns, and it helps us create bridges where they didn't exist. Bridges are good.

***Variety***. Keep your repository of ideas varied. Explore different fields and different perspectives. It is possible for our minds to stagnate. Stagnation impedes our ability to combine, find solutions, test ideas, and find patterns other than those that predominate in our mind. When you expose yourself to a variety of ideas, you can truly flourish and innovate.

***Idea Generation***. Your ideas don't need to be complete when you pump them out. It's okay to toss around just words, images, potential plans, and other such fragments. An idea board or the like will help you visualize your ideas and perform the abovementioned techniques more easily. Just generate ideas and as you go, they will surely take shape.

***Remove***. Once you've let your mind fly with all these possibilities, associations, and analogies, start paring away at the idea board. Remove the non-essential, the impractical, and the farfetched. Don't toss them in the trash, though. Just set those ideas aside for future reference. What doesn't work within current constraints may fit perfectly within future ones.

***Unity***. Ultimately, what you seek is unity or harmony, not perfection. Nothing will be perfect, but it can be unified and harmonious even if varied and imperfect. Make sure that your ideas flow logically, align feasibly, and propose a different—albeit possibly unfinished solution—to a present dilemma or uncertainty.

## Roadblocks to Creativity in the Workplace

All this is wonderful to consider and imagine in a vacuum, but some of our jobs don't allow for all the approaches I outlined above. That's precisely why innovation is extolled as such a virtue and why creativity has been regarded as revolutionary. It forces us to rail against established power structure, institutionalized practices, and ornery people. If you decide to embark on that journey in a context that demands obedience, it'll take you down a road of self-exploration and tribulation.

Some roadblocks to creativity in a workplace are

***Lack of collective will.*** A lack of purpose in the group can hinder movement, creativity, and productivity.

***Individual and group bias.*** Be aware of the assumptions and stereotypes that predominate in your workplace. They may be difficult to navigate, but not doing so can seriously stymie your efforts toward innovation.

***Self-fulfilling prophecy.*** The worst thing you can do is to hold yourself back. If you assume you will fail from the get-go, then you are dooming yourself to failure. To innovate or rail against habit, you must recognize your ability to do so by galvanizing the people around you.

***Operational practices and procedural practices.*** There is a big difference. Operational practices are those that ensure and direct the overall function of a department or company. Procedural practices dictate protocol within a specific department and at the individual level. Identify which one you want to approach creatively. It can make presenting your ideas easier, so you don't scare people away or make them nervous about backlash.

***Accepted truths.*** There must be accepted truths for things to work. Some are less favorable than others, though. Identify what the accepted truths are, whether they need to be revised or eliminated, to what end, and why. In a business, revision geared toward the bottom-line and productivity tends to gain more traction and acceptance.

***Lack of time.*** You are just too busy. Then get a group of people to help you. In fact, whenever possible you should start a team effort. Solidarity is the wellspring of motivation when times get tough. By identifying and delegating tasks, you can make great things happen.

***Intolerance to questions.*** Some people do not like being questioned or having questions lodged at them about work related to them. In other words, they take it personally. A way around this is to frame questions impersonally or to specify that questions about operations and procedures hinge less so on the individual and more so on systemic functions.

## Circumvent the Roadblocks

In general, the way you present the products of your creative scrutiny has an impact on reception. A way around the roadblocks I described is to be clear, concrete, and systematic about the problem you'd like to approach creatively.

***Define the challenge***. Spend a considerable amount of time identifying what, exactly, you want to reconsider or analyze. The more concrete, clear, and systematic you can be, the more likely you are to garner support and hold attention.

***Brainstorm.*** Open up to brainstorming with other people. You can be the catalyst for change and not necessarily have to lead it. Often times, good ideas gain momentum independent of the originator because they resonate with enough people that unify.

***Discovery***. If you realize you feel lost after brainstorming, that's a good sign. It probably means that there are real questions that don't have answers which represent holes in your operations, procedures, or business model. The disorientation is a good thing in the long run.

***Broader context.*** This is one way to get past the discovery phase. When you realize that you don't have the answers or that the resources at your disposal are insufficient to resolve the emergent uncertainties, seek out pieces to cobble together the bigger picture. Customers, industry trends, new experts, history, speculation, etc., can all help you glean the bigger picture.

## In Sum

Creativity in a business context can bring up all sorts of issues, but it can also be conducive to wide-scale innovation that can skyrocket a company. The Internet has shown us the benefits of open collaboration, being receptive to the ideas of others, trial-and-error, collective will and brainstorming, and being uncertain yet willing to try. In an organization, those practices can yield great value.

Google and Apple have premised their business models on this creative exploration. No matter the business, you can too.

# CHAPTER 44

## *The Key to Great Business Relationships is to Understand a Person's Past*

Whether you are joining a new company or managing a newcomer on your team, gaining an understanding of the back story is crucial in your dealings with other people.

We are all a product of our experiences, so if you simply treat someone's words and actions at face value, you will be missing out on a whole lot of valuable context. If you understand someone's past a little bit, you won't need a crystal ball to predict their future.

However, the Spanish Inquisition notwithstanding, delving into the past is rarely a simple task. Unless the "journey" back has relevance to here and now, very few people will be happy to open up and spill their deepest secrets. If, however, they can understand the context of the questions and their value in building your relationship at that moment in time, they will be much more obliging. Therefore, understanding someone's past is an opportunistic pursuit—you have to take the chances when they present themselves. Alternatively, you could go to a bar and have a few drinks, but it's possible you may not remember much the next day. Being selective about when you ask the searching questions is crucial to building up a picture of what has made someone tick.

People like to talk about themselves, so if you get the chance to ask someone about their past, especially in a relevant way, let them talk. If you are too direct with your questioning, it can quickly bring the conversation to a halt, but if you let the conversations flow freely, it can often lead to valuable insights that you can add to your mental picture of the person in question. It is interesting that people will often tell the stories that they think you want to hear, but there are so many subtle details surrounding each story that you will be able to infer much more than the direct message of the story itself.

If you can listen to the hidden messages, a rich picture will soon materialize.

Digging into the past is like connecting the dots. If you understand why a person was compelled to make certain decisions, and how those decisions worked out, you will have a fair guide as to their reaction in a similar situation today. You also need to understand the wider context of their actions—forging ahead with a business in a booming economy is very different from a foolhardy sprint into the jaws of an oncoming recession. How did they rise to the various challenges? How did they treat the people around them? How did they react to failure? What would they do differently now?

Finally, as any relationship is about forging a mutual understanding, you should be equally happy to share details of your own past. Don't bore people with the details, but it is often worth telling the odd story to give some context to your current actions. When you tell stories, people will often find things to relate to, and your relationships will become that little bit stronger.

Digging into the past may sometimes seem irrelevant, but you never know when the knowledge that you acquire could come in useful.

# CHAPTER 45

## *Does Authenticity on Social Media Matter?*

I have written hundreds of articles and books over the years, and I must admit that it can be slightly addictive when one goes viral. People empathize with you, you get an avalanche of likes, and suddenly the sun seems to shine a little brighter in the sky. It's especially the case if you wrote the post from the heart, about a topic that is important to you, and you genuinely value the discussion that is generated. In fact, if a blog is congruent with who you are and what you do, it doesn't matter if it gets ten likes or 1,000 likes, it is still adding cement to your personal brand.

As long as you are putting out content that builds on who you are, you can't go wrong. However, the moment you start to chase a hollow popularity, an entirely different picture can arise.

Trying to concoct a formula for online stardom is a sure-fire way to confuse your followers, colleagues, and friends. One minute you are posting stupidly easy math puzzles, the next you are asking a mindless multiple-choice question, and then you might post a provocative political quote. All these things will garner "likes" from a certain section of the online community, but will they be the right people that you want to reach?

I can almost guarantee that the answer will be no.

Selling out on social media is the same as selling out in life. The litmus test for whether you are selling out is a simple question. If you were sitting in a restaurant with your friends, would you say half of the things that you say on social media? This is the ultimate authenticity test. If you would hesitate to say a certain thing in real life, for fear of a strange reaction from those around you, why is it somehow acceptable to say it online? In fact, your online footprint is far more permanent than anything that you ever said in a restaurant once, so it is truly worth thinking twice about that controversial post that you hope will "go viral."

With social media, you never quite know who is reading. The likes and shares are visible, but they constitute a vast, shadowy realm of observers, who are never going to reveal themselves. Your network is tighter than you think; there is a high probability that your posts could be showing up on the timelines of a future boss or investor. Is fleeting viral popularity worth alienating those who truly matter? It is very easy to press the un-follow button, and the moment that this is done, there is no way back.

It is all too easy to create a pseudo-personality on social media since the checks and balances of a "normal" social setting is not as present. And in a country where freedom of speech still prevails, there is great risk. Although we are mostly free to say what we wish, that doesn't mean that it is a good idea to do so.

If you sell out on social media, you never quite know who will buy the story.

# CHAPTER 46

## Does Anger Have a Role in the Workplace?

I saw a trailer for the *Angry Birds* movie the other day. It recounts the story of how the birds of the hugely popular cell phone game came to be so angry with the pigs, and it shares the motivations behind their self-sacrificial desires for death and destruction.

For those of you who are unaware of the game, the player can fire birds from a catapult at various structures containing the enemy pigs. The birds have many special abilities that help to destroy these structures (and the pigs within them). Some birds explode, some carve straight through the building, and others act like bouncing bombs. Their many means of destruction have one thing in common. They are angry.

But why are they angry? What possible justification is there for their aggression? Well, without any spoilers, the film explains that the pigs have stolen the birds' eggs, and that the birds simply want to get their children back. It gets them mad. Any five-year-old can understand that, surely. Before the pigs stole the birds' eggs, they were pacifists, and anger was very much frowned upon.

Do they have the right to get angry and go on a catapult-fueled rampage? Is there ever any excuse to lose your temper and express that pent up anger of yours? What does it achieve?

Let's consider this situation in the workplace.

## Does Anger Have a Place?

If a colleague stole your child, you would have every reason to be upset. But, that probably wouldn't happen. The pertinent question is whether the expression of anger has a place at work at all.

The stereotypical image of the boss thumping his fist on the table and demanding a reaction from his people in a fit of anger is no urban myth. It happens on Monday mornings or Friday afternoons in conference rooms across the world, and it usually does produce a reaction. People get scared, they redouble their efforts, and talk poorly about their boss. Is it the right way to motivate others?

When a colleague persistently lets you down, ignores your needs, and rides roughshod over your feelings, sometimes your own feelings well up to the point of explosion. In that moment, we may feel a sense of relief, but the outburst is often disproportionate to the cause. Why? Because we vent two years of bottled-up annoyance over the most trivial matters. "Surely, we can't just sit passively by and let them take advantage of us," you might think. Lashing out once in a while sets things straight, doesn't it?

No, it doesn't. The expression of anger is a one-way street.

When expressed, anger can be fatal. It doesn't allow for conversation. It doesn't facilitate a dialogue. It is a one-way avalanche of emotion designed to overwhelm the target and make them think differently. However, because it often makes someone back off, they don't get the opportunity to understand exactly why the person is angry in the first place. A repeat of any given situation is, therefore, highly likely—the expression of anger doesn't create an opportunity to learn.

I don't think that it is ever worthwhile to express anger. There are plenty of other ways that you can solve your problems.

# CHAPTER 47

## *How to Be More Productive Than Everyone Else*

For all the talk about our differences and unique experiences, there are some things that everyone shares. Time, for one, is a common denominator that underpins all human life.

Gary Keller and Jay Papasan pose a simple question in *The One Thing* that gets at the heart of the time and energy conundrum, "If everyone has the same number of hours in a day, why do some people seem to get so much more done than others?"

The answer is simple yet densely packed. Those people get at the heart of things by going small.

### Going Small to Make the Most

Going small is ignoring all the things you could do and doing what you should do. It's a matter of values and priorities. Your priorities should align with your values, which in turn determine how you spend your time. When you plug tasks into this formula, you begin to realize that some tasks don't make the cut. Slowly it'll become evident that not all things matter equally, and that the things that matter more are easier to focus on and yield the most returns.

One challenge to this is comparing seemingly incomparable things. How do you compare spending time with your family and spending an extra hour on a work-related task? Intuitively you may know that spending time with your family is important, but that doesn't necessarily diminish the urgency of completing your task. Life is complicated that way. Yet a fatal flaw in those comparisons stymies our thinking; they are far too broad.

Every day you should reassess your tasks, not your values. Your values are guiding stars and important to keep in mind, but not every task is an instance of existential reflection.

When you start a new day, reassess your tasks in order of priority.

Remember, success is built sequentially, not simultaneously. By staying vigilant and organized, you can carefully piece together your successes without compromising your values or feeling like you've run out of time.

## There is No Competition

Tasks, your family, your work—none of those should compete for your time. True, they are all vying for finite resources, but ultimately, you are in control of how your time is allotted and the quality of that time. When you relinquish that power, you forgo a nature-given control.

We should use our control to find balance wherever possible. When you try to attend to everything all at once and with equal effort, you will eventually careen out of control. In the long run, nothing gets done, and whatever does get done is subpar. In any case, something will be left to the wayside. You can't do everything. That's human. Just make sure what gets sideswiped isn't a value.

## No More Philosophy—Give Me the Practical Steps

As it goes with many things, the key to success is about changing perspectives. Once you do that, avenues and courses of action open before you. It isn't magic. It's basically turning around to face a new direction.

***Counterbalance work.*** View work as skill-based or knowledge to be mastered. This will force you to give more attention to *one* thing over another. That doesn't mean ignoring one thing for another, just giving it less of your time. What that thing *is* should be contingent upon what you want out of your work life or career. Professional success requires this kind of cost-benefit analysis.

Your life has multiple areas, and each requires a minimum amount of attention for you to feel that your sanity is intact. Identifying that minimum requires constant awareness. Spend too much or too little time in one area, and you will feel the negative effects. Strive to keep each area active enough.

***Seek results.*** Results should be concrete, tangible, and perceptible. In work it is essential; in life, it's grounding. What are results? Goals that you set for yourself that in aggregate amount to success. "I want to learn programming." Create a curriculum, a schedule, and follow it. When you complete that curriculum, you achieve success; every milestone on that path is a result. That's what I mean.

***Don't sweat the small stuff.*** When something you have identified as low on your priority scale is incomplete or low quality, don't stress yourself. It was low on the scale for a reason. You can't micromanage everything. You can, however, give your all to the high-priority tasks with the foreknowledge that success there is a far better investment of your time and energy. And one pro-tip is to handle the low priority stuff as quickly as possible. It's easy to get a backlog of low priority tasks; and when that happens, it's nightmarish.

***Manage your energy.*** Think about your energy and your life as an all-encompassing whole, not as segmented into discrete areas. We sometimes over-compartmentalize, which creates the illusory divisions between world life, home life, and leisure. The reality is that these all interpenetrate at some point; time is one common denominator, and energy is another.

The energy that you store within must last to fulfill all your commitments in each work area. Unlike batteries, we don't have dedicated stores for each area of life. Make sure to evaluate each commitment you make as part of the greater whole and how it will drain both your time and your energy. That can help you prune away new sprouts that sap energy from the wise old trunks that need it most.

Again, these considerations boil down to values, and the priorities that flow from those values, which should inform the time and energy you spend on each. It may sound convoluted, but it's actually quite simple.

# CHAPTER 48

## *Six Simple Ways to Create Balance*

What is the difference between work and home? For some of us this question is harder to answer than we would like to admit. We are always on, always connected, and always at the beck-and-call of our employers, partners, clients, etc. And since we have all grown accustomed to faster technology and faster responses, we have concurrently grown intolerant of delays—patience is a virtue lost on contemporary society.

That impatience is blurring personal boundaries that once separated each area of our lives. Ask someone the difference between free time and work, or home life and recreation. In the abstract they will have an answer, but follow up with whether they live those differences, and the conversation takes a tragic turn.

For these boundaries to hold up, they must be grounded in physical space and real activity. The time itself blends uncontrollably if what you do with the time is virtually indistinct. So, you are at home, but checking your work emails; you are at the park, but thinking about your home décor or bills. That's what I mean.

The problem is that work, leisure, and home are no longer defined and protracted places. They are states of mind. We no longer have three distinct segments of time allotted to each space, but rather some confluence of behaviors that converge in any of those spaces at any time, based on necessity, urgency, or stress. We can't expect to respect boundaries when we don't train our minds to make definite distinctions in time, space, and activity.

I don't think this is easy to accomplish. I personally struggled with making these distinctions and respecting them. However, I believe I've managed to reach a balance, and every day I strive to maintain it. My first piece of advice: keep it simple.

## Why Simplify Your Life?

Simplicity is a beautiful thing. In art, in design, in mathematics, simplicity is the mark of rigor, comprehension, and mastery. Life, however, is a complex and complicated affair that sometime spits in the face of our best attempts to simplify or organize it.

The best way to simplify life is on a timescale. Our time is fluid, whether or not it seems so. Aside from the sleep/wake cycle, there isn't much that constrains how we use our time. I am referring purely to time itself when I say this; surely there are all sorts of externalities that constrain our time, but those aren't common to all so I am putting them aside. The fluidity of time should help us simplify, not complicate, our lives.

When we add the dimension of value to our time, it makes organizing our duties, responsibilities, and commitments simpler. You can plot your priorities on the timescale and decide how much time should be allotted to each, based on the value you assign. And remember, how you choose to spend your time says a lot about what you value and who you are.

So, when we think about ourselves as existing on these two dimensions, the definitions of work, home, and leisure change. The boundaries limit our behavior such that we do not impinge on our values. When you are at home, you are at home because there are values that determine why you are there and how you spend your time there; when you are at work, your values inform your behavior in the same way; and so on.

"But I have so much to do! I can't possibly sideline my responsibilities based on my values."

Well that gets at a deeper question of how much you value your work over your home life. That's far too existential for this chapter. Anyway, each person has subtly unique value systems and factors to influence that question. There just won't be a general consensus.

Fortunately, whatever the mélange of values, responsibilities, and factors on your plate, there are six methods you can use to reorganize and restructure your life that are designed to simplify your activities, get more done, and enjoy more personal time either with others or alone.

## Six Methods for Simplifying Your Life

***Determine your values.*** Determine what is most important to you—just you—not necessarily egocentric values, but sincere and genuine values. One of the most important questions that can set you in this direction is, "What do I really want to do with my life?" Answering this question will grant you peace of mind and fortitude.

***Decide what you want.*** Write a list of exactly ten concrete goals that you want to accomplish in the next year. Once that is down, reread the list, and ask yourself this, "If I accomplished one of these goals in the next 24-hours, which one would have the greatest positive impact on my life?"

***Identify your major purpose.*** After completing the previous step, you can baptize the answer as your "major purpose." It doesn't need to be your ultimate purpose for the rest of your life, just your immediate, most beneficial purpose. Once you have that in hand, make a list that contains the other goals in order of priority subordinate to that major purpose. Think in concrete steps.

***Balance your life***. Align your values with your activities. It is often incongruence there that causes profound unrest. A sense of joy, calm, and motivation washes over someone who believes that their values, what they do, and the way they spend their time are all in alignment.

***Emphasize your relationships.*** Put the most important people in your life at the top of your list. Always. Everything else comes secondary.

***Promote your physical health.*** A healthy body is a healthy mind. There are countless studies on the connection between physical activity and mental well-being. Just a brief jaunt can stimulate your creativity, reduce stress, and increase your sense of freedom. Take care of yourself and you'll feel better all around.

## Don't Put Off Betterment

We all have the ability to change our lives. Never forget that you always have a choice, despite the limitations in your life. When you grant yourself the time and space to reflect on where you are, how you got there, and how you feel about it, you empower yourself to make a change.

Some changes are easier than others. Those changes that affect the people we love or involve difficult conversations, or risk, can seem especially intractable. Nonetheless, that's an illusion. As long as you avail yourself of courage and conviction, you can change your life—or in this case, simplify it.

# CHAPTER 49

## *The Art of Winning People with Words*

The way we speak is arguably more important than what we say. Even an inarticulate person can charm, sway, and move others with the tone of their voice, the cadence of their words, and the charisma they exude. As the refrain goes, "It isn't what you say but how you say it." I've learned this lesson over years sprinkled with miscommunication, misunderstanding, and missed opportunities.

In my experience, there are at least three noteworthy features of effective communication. They are self-awareness, trust building, and a willingness to navigate difficult conversations.

### Give Your Mind Time to Catch Up with Your Mouth

Our brains process at a fast rate, but sometimes can be outrun by our mouths. This is acceptable when you are not concerned about how you are speaking, or just not speaking. But, when you are in an interview, a meeting, a high-stakes conversation, or any other situation that demands you both think and speak accurately, efficiently, and intelligently, this disparity can cause serious hazards.

***Mind your mouth.*** Speak slowly. We tend to speak faster and faster when we are nervous. That can cause major slip-ups and can prevent you from catching errors of thought or inappropriate speech on the fly. When you reduce your speaking speed, you allot your brain time to catch up with what you are saying, which allows you to redact, revisit, or retract any slip-ups.

***Breathing.*** Breathing deeply or refocusing on your breath can help. It does wonders for me. When I am in a meeting, I like to keep tabs on my body, because it informs me what is going on subconsciously. If I notice that my breath has quickened or that my heart has sped up, just bringing attention to it will relax my body and give my mind time to settle. Almost simultaneously, my respiration calms, my muscles release, and my mouth reencounters my mind.

***Recording.*** One nifty and slightly invasive trick is to record yourself. I know that sounds masochistic, but like many things about oneself, how we speak and come off to others is nearly impossible to discern accurately unless we see ourselves from the outside in.

***Mixing it up.*** Your pace doesn't have to be consistent throughout a conversation. You can deliver familiar subjects slightly faster and slow down to drive home important points. It's easier to fly through familiar subjects, and that's fine, so long as they aren't obscure or dense.

***Talk cleanly***. The idea is simple. Just because what you are saying is complex doesn't mean it needs to be said complexly. The notion that jargon, fillers, bombast, and flowery language are impressive is misguided. I believe I am among many who appreciate simplicity and cleanliness in oratory.

***When in doubt, stop talking***. If you are uncertain or have confused yourself, just stop talking. It is better to pause for a moment and regroup than to waste time, energy, and someone's patience while you audibly sort through your own thinking.

***Focus on yourself.*** The traditional advice when speaking is to read your audience. That is certainly good advice, but it can sometimes cripple one's communication. Our brains can do a lot and yet only so much. Don't waste precious brain space harping on what your audience might be thinking about you. I suggest putting more stock in your point, your delivery, and your body language. Let the pieces fall where they may.

***Listen more and talk less.*** Listening is a compliment, not just to the speaker but also to oneself. It validates what your interlocutor is saying, makes them feel supported, and allows you the opportunity to respond completely to their point. Unfortunately, attentive listening has become a rare commodity. For that reason, a good listener stands out and makes a lasting impression.

## Say Only What You Can Abide By

In other words, mean what you say. Shari Halley writes in *How to Say Anything to Anyone*, that we all want to work with people that we can trust. If you want others to hear your suggestions and take them as you intend them, you must have a trust-based relationship. If you don't mean every word that you say, then you foment uncertainty and instability, which is infertile ground for trust-building.

When someone trusts you, they give you the benefit of the doubt, and that's hugely important for effective group dynamics.

However, there are a few behaviors that can stop trust dead in its tracks.

***Gossip.*** This is a far more complicated topic than I would care to admit. I suppose the most potent antidote against gossip is that if you have something to say about someone, then say it to that person. The extreme iteration of this would be that if you can't, then don't say it at all. I think that's impractical. Plus, not all instances of indirect criticism are material for gossip. The risk, however, is that what you say can be taken out of context when retold. The more you say, the greater the risk, so proceed with caution.

***Breaking your word.*** Do what you say you will do. If you can't, then inform the affected party as quickly as possible—the more forewarning the better. People who always show up late, people who don't do what they say they will, and people who miss deadlines are all ineligible for the kind of trust I aspire to here. Unreliability is a trust killer.

***Lying.*** We have all felt the compulsion to lie for different reasons. Adults and children are not so dissimilar in that they find it difficult to accept accountability. Displacing blame is a default defense mechanism: "But I didn't do it!" or "She started it!" Although it may not be lying in the fullest sense, it is tantamount to deception.

Denial is yet another lie tactic, and it's largely ineffective. Be honest, be self-aware, and put aside notions of culpability. Take responsibility for your part in an error, provide a solution, and move on. That way you maintain your integrity and get credit for being forthcoming. We value it in children, and so too in adults.

## Happily Jump into Crucial Conversations

A crucial conversation is a discussion between two or more people where stakes are high, opinions vary, emotions run strong, and the repercussions could be far-reaching.

Kerry Patterson, Joseph Grenny, Ron McMillan, and Al Switzler explain in *Crucial Conversations* that communities, relationships, careers, and organizations alike all draw from the same source of power, the ability to talk openly about high-stakes, emotional, and controversial topics. Some people are more adept at it than others.

These people tend to dissociate themselves from their egos by recognizing that each person has unique pools of meaning from which their thoughts, beliefs, and behaviors flow. By dissociating themselves, they make it safe for each person to share without the fear of judgment; even if what's expressed is controversial or at odds with their beliefs. In this way, they create a free flow of meaning, whereon dialogue can travel. Ideally—and more often than we know—this results in compromises and solutions that seem fair to the people involved.

It's elemental in these conversations that every person be fully committed to finding a solution that resonates with them. If someone sits back passively and doesn't share, then they will never be totally committed to a final decision. Those people generally end up quietly resisting and furtively critical.

A few tips for navigating crucial conversation are:

***Start with heart.*** Know what you want, and identify what others want. If they aren't sure, help them work it out. Once each person has a true north, they can steer properly.

***No either/or.*** People who believe in the power of dialogue usually abhor either/or distinctions. Few things in life are so cut and dry, and when it comes to mitigating differences between people, there exists much grey area. If you feel an either/or reaction coming on, reexamine your motives and ask yourself the following questions.

- What do I really want for myself?
- What do I really want for others?
- What do I really want for the relationship?
- How would I feel if I achieved what I want?

As tensions rise in crucial conversation, it becomes easier to slip into precisely the kinds of behaviors that hamper trust, vitiate compromise, and distract from self-awareness. In those moments, people tend to oscillate between holding back too much and becoming too forceful. By reflecting on your propensities in high-stakes situations, you can make a special effort to fill in your own pitfalls. That way, when a situation arises, you know what to look for.

Also, learn to step out of content. We can become mired in what is being said and entirely miss the underlying message. You can make a space safe and create room for perspective by pausing a conversation or stepping out temporarily. It may sound awkward, but it's preferable to letting your emotions hijack your brain and mouth, which can leave serious damage in their wake.

And perhaps, most importantly, don't fall captive to your ego.

A monologue is the ultimate expression of ego. It shows others that you only care about what you are saying.

Through it all, however, don't back off your belief. For all the good that can come from making these efforts, you don't have to lose yourself in the process.

# CHAPTER 50

## *Why Do We Work Best When We Have No Time?*

The clock is ticking. That deadline stalks you. It creeps nearer and nearer. You try to focus but you just get ambushed with images of all the things you did other than the task at hand. Existential crisis sets in. "Of all the pressures of life," you think to yourself, "the pressure of time must be the most merciless."

The stress detaches you from the moment and you dwell on what you are sacrificing. You thought you had it all planned out. You gave yourself an hour to finish writing your presentation. You know that if you don't finish, that'll mean less time with the kids in the evening. It'll mean hours of "15 more minutes, I promise!"

Time spent and time wasted have their repercussions, and if you don't navigate them properly, your life will be held for ransom.

For all the self-made tragedy of this scenario, it's precisely the bitter medicine that we sometimes need.

### A Thimbleful of External Pressure

From an early age, we learn the importance of pace for relatively simple tasks, like walking, and for relatively complex tasks, like writing an essay. Some people grow attuned to their pace at different tasks and more adept at planning accordingly. Others struggle to plan even in light of past experience. In any case, we learn to recognize our capabilities and to anticipate whether we will hit our targets—whether we act prudently is a different story.

When we start to fall behind, there are two common reactions. We either chagrin fatalistically, prepared to rearrange our lives accordingly, or we redouble our efforts and push through.

In the latter case, the stress can activate deep stores of mental focus and conviction that carry us through. In my experience, that is when miracles happen. True, we often want to avoid those cases because they are somewhat unpleasant, but they are also the stuff of inspiration.

You have probably seen the video of a mother demonstrating extra-human strength to rescue her son from beneath a burning car? I think high-stress situations are akin to that.

We hear stories of songwriters penning their greatest hits on a paper napkin in between activities. Dostoevsky wrote *The Idiot* under duress from debt collectors, and doctors save lives under incredibly high-stakes conditions. This isn't to say that high-stress is preferable. It is to say that once in a while it can bring out the best in us.

The key ingredient is external pressure.

When I go through periods of stress-induced productivity, the stressors aren't self-motivation and coffee; they're often frantic yet concerted reactions to impending meetings or social events. In those moments, I realize that there is so much I can accomplish in half-an-hour or in five-minutes. I simply need a thimbleful of external pressure.

Ready, steady, go!

## Don't Fool Yourself. Stress Can Be Addicting

Intense focus under pressure can feel great! Time stands still. Our mental acuity skyrockets. Ideas flows unfettered. The world around us dissolves. Time itself loses its primacy. All that exists is you and your task.

Some people call this flow, others focus, others the zone. Call it what you want, it's addicting. Once we come back to, we can't believe how much we've accomplished! "I never usually work like that. Why can't we work like that all the time?"

Often athletes cite "the zone" as a spiritual state of being. The mind shifts into automatic, coordinating every stroke, every step, every breath in holistic synchronicity. Monks and meditators describe this feeling as oneness. Whatever the nomenclature, it is pleasurable, and we often crave it. Our minds channel all of our latent experience, skill, and knowledge into a bottom-up cognitive harmony that frees us of the shackles of conscious deliberation.

It's nice. But, it's also exhausting, and the collateral damage can be grave. I acknowledge that. *That isn't a reason to eschew it, though*, nor bemoan the opportunity to tap into that primitive brain of ours. Like I said, once in a while, it's a source of inspiration.

Evolution granted us that gift—that superpower—however draining it might be.

Don't despise stress. Learn to exploit it.

# CHAPTER 51

## *How to Focus Under Pressure*

Stress is a myth.

According to Al Siebert, the widespread belief that jobs generate harmful stress is an "artificial consensus" reality, fed by the tidal wave of books, articles, movies, shows, anecdotes, and workshops that amplify work-related pressures. The intention is good, but as the adage goes, "The road to hell is paved with good intentions,"—and for those of you who feel afflicted by stress, I'm sure you will agree that "hell" is a fine synonym.

The myth is about the origin of stress and the place it is felt. In Al Siebert's view, strain is the bodily experience of stress, which often manifests in a physical experience of unwanted anxiety or tension. The problem is that people tend to conflate stress and strain: stress is external, while strain is internal. The impact of this conflation is not merely a matter of semantics. It influences how we treat it, how we treat ourselves, and what we change in our lives to cope with it.

In this chapter, I explore some strategies to cope with stress and reduce strain, in addition to highlighting the importance of focus for managing the two and learning new things about ourselves in the process.

## A Simple Plan for a Complex Problem

Sometimes we are caught in the midst of strong emotions, and we get tunnel vision. We are unable to stop, ask ourselves questions, and reassess our position. Being prepared with strategic questions beforehand can make that process easier when emotions flare.

Make a list of six or seven things that you feel irritated, upset, or distressed about. For each one, ask yourself the following questions:

- What pressures am I feeling?
- How are my work and my life different than they were a year ago?
- What is difficult for me now, and what difficulties am I expecting?
- What feels distressing to me?

The key is to take your time with each question and be thorough. Descriptive phrases work best—show then tell. Once you've done that, write about your general feeling regarding what you wrote down.

It is important to remember that you can't make feelings go away by sheer will power, but you can move through them, recast them, reinterpret them, and modify your reactions to them. The feelings are not the enemies, so don't chastise yourself for having them.

## Create Balance with Positivity

Going through the process of charting the negative factors in our lives can be draining and often cloud purview. That's why it's equally as important to do the same as above for all the positives in your life.

Think back and make a list of the positive activities that invigorate and revitalize you. Then, ask yourself the following questions:

- What do I have fun doing?
- What do I get enthusiastic about?
- What would I like to do that I keep putting off?
- Who do I enjoy sharing good experiences with?
- When do I sleep best at night?
- What positive aspects of my life am I ignoring?

Armed with these two lists, you are in a crucial position to make decisions about how to remove stress, reduce strain, increase the energy-increasing activities in your life, and find more moments of pleasure throughout the day.

## Hatch a Plan

University of Chicago Professor Salvatore Maddi's research conducted in the 1970s suggests that there are three qualities that increased resilience and job satisfaction among managers at AT&T.

The **first** was emotional commitment. They felt responsible to the people they led and wanted to help them succeed.

The **second** was the belief that they could influence outcomes. They would determine specific goals, devise plans, make lists, and decide what steps should be taken to attain said goals.

The **third** was a desire to problem solve. They were energized by challenges and enjoyed seeking alternatives to resolve issues that arose.

You can apply this three-step approach to any of the negative instances you detailed in the first list. The positive list can supplement this process. You can intersperse activities that grant you pleasure, relief, or vitality.

## Some Pro-tips for Personal Care

To some, especially males, this all may sound silly or effeminate. Talking about feelings? Listing the reasons I am strained or what stresses me? Maybe you believe the best method is to pile-drive through the hard times. That approach is bound to fail, and the reason is that it forces you to suppress your daily experience under a mountain of will that is actually rubble, which can easily be shaken to dust. In other words, you'll lose control, and when that happens, you'll wish you had dealt with your stress and strain earlier.

Here are my pro-tips for personal care:

***Awareness***. The process of creating these lists and hatching a plan will generate awareness. You may learn new things about yourself; about why you think the way you do; and about how it affects the people around you.

***Mind-body connection***. The distinction between mind and body is completely arbitrary. It's mainly a matter of perception. Indeed, our minds and our bodies are inextricably linked and in constant communication. Learning to interpret your bodily responses as communications from the mind and mental states as informed by your body allows you to view yourself more holistically.

***Social support***. Relying on others can be difficult, embarrassing, and awkward, but that's normal, especially when you are unaccustomed to open communication. Finding confidants and people whose advice and input you respect can help you gain new insights and feel supported, which can mollify strain and stress.

Please take these suggestions seriously. People who ignore their emotions, refuse to communicate, and opt for the bulldozer approach tend to be more fragile than those who listen to themselves, ask for support, and accept their weaknesses.

And the fact is that pressure from work, family, and responsibilities, is not easy to manage. It may appear that some people are immune to strain from external pressures, but that's a misconception. The difference is that some people have better strategies to cope. Now you have one too!

## The Secret Ingredient

All of this is nearly impossible to accomplish without focus. From the get-go, you must make a clear decision to center your mind on the task of finding alternatives, devising a plan, and staying the course.

It's important to note that focus is not the same as concentration. Focus conjures up something deeper than concentration, and that's strength. According to our dictionary definition, strength is "an extremely valuable or useful ability, asset, or quality." Strength subsumes our learned skills and innate talents, which means they operate both intuitively and deliberately. However, to activate our strengths, we must focus, such that the strengths get channeled into what we are doing.

In the context of managing pressure, strain, and stress, focus is necessary because it summons the best of yourself, and lets you to glean alternatives you wouldn't have otherwise. When faced with adversity, this kind of focus bring you closer to a resolution.

## Focus on Finding Yourself

Ultimately this post is about finding yourself. I don't mean that in a transcendental or spiritual way, but rather in a lived and practical sense.

When you take the time to focus on what surrounds you, how you feel about it, why you react to it the way you do, and the steps you can take to remedy inefficiencies, pain-points, and stress, then you will be in a better position to control outcomes and direct the course of your life.

# CHAPTER 52

## *Are Vacations an Opportunity for Business Development?*

In a world where increasing numbers of people are working for themselves, offering their services in a global market, I would like to ask whether random acquaintances on vacations could prove to be beneficial contacts for someone's business.

Imagine a guy named Ted. He runs his own small-scale digital marketing business out of New Jersey, but he has clients all over the world. Ted reckons that he and his family deserve a break, so they go on a Caribbean cruise for ten days. They are in the company of a few thousand other passengers, and given the close proximity and the packed calendar of events, they get to know a wide range of people. Ted doesn't want to talk about business, and the last thing that he wants is to view these nice people as prospects. When you try to sell to people, they resent it, right? So, apart from a tan and loads of great memories, Ted leaves the cruise ship on the last day and goes back to his desk exactly as he left it.

Is there a missed opportunity here?

Well, maybe, but these sorts of situations have to be handled in the right way.

If you are on a cruise ship for days on end with the same people, you cannot help but get to know them a little. You let them into your lives, and they become your "friends" for the time that you are together. In the ultra-connected world of social media, why would you not want to continue to allow those nascent relationships to flourish? You shouldn't hit them up to forward your sales pitches to their networks immediately, but you can support whatever activity they have on social media, and then they will be much happier to reciprocate.

If you have an agenda, give first, and your chances of success will be much higher.

The world of sales has been transformed in recent years and a huge percentage of sales decisions are made and negotiated online or over email. There may be a phone or Skype call, but few sales deals are entirely concluded face to face. That is the beauty of taking advantage of all these random meetings—you size someone up, you look them in the eye, and work out what sort of a person they are. It may even be the case that they are in some of your vacation photos, to be remembered forever. What an amazing opportunity to not just be remembered, but for your business to be remembered. They may be having lunch with a friend who needs your skills. They will be only too happy to recommend you, you can be sure of that.

Maybe this is a little cynical. Maybe holidays should be for relaxing and forgetting about anything to do with your business. However, as the gig economy heats up, and everyone becomes a boss, can people really afford to miss out on these opportunities?

This doesn't just apply to solopreneurs and freelancers. Even corporate folks can reap "shop" benefits from vacations if done the right way. I for one have had family vacations that have turned into great opportunities from a subtle chat with a fellow vacationer after that long day of fishing on the ocean.

# CHAPTER 53

## *Will You Keep Coming Back?*

We all need a bit of recognition every now and again, but very few of us have gone to such lengths to get it as Leonardo DiCaprio.

The guy has drowned on the most famous boat in history, played a mentally disturbed Aviation pioneer, and of course, reveled in the debauchery of Wall Street, but he had never been given the most coveted of prizes—the award for "Best Actor" at the Oscars. Until yesterday.

In the most grueling of conditions, through bitter snow and freezing icy water, he literally dragged himself to the winner's stage. Winning three Oscars, *The Revenant* was the worthy stand-out film of the last year, and its central premise, "he who returns from the dead," is pretty fitting for an actor who has been denied so many times before. Fully deserved in my view, it's a standing ovation from me, Leo. Well done.

We've all been there. There was the "close but not quite" promotion, the horrific redundancy process that nearly brought you to tears, and the failing at the last hurdle to get a vital budget approved. We give it our all, but sometimes our best is not good enough.

Slipping away from Kate Winslet's hands into a freezing and unforgiving Atlantic Ocean is a feeling that many of us have experienced. So near, but yet so far.

But most of us keep coming. We might stop for a while, take stock of the situation and find the energy to carry on, but generally we are mostly a determined and resolute bunch. Evolution made us that way. Our ancestors will have taken a good few maulings from bears and various other beasts in our pre-history, and they dragged themselves back onto their feet and kept living.

Thus, as the economy threatens to take a cyclical downturn (again), where do we think that we will all be in ten years? Will it have sapped our will to live? Will our endless thirst for self-improvement have been tempered? Will Richard Branson be taking us on trips to Mars?

We might be knocked down for a while, but we will get up again. Everyone's career has highlights and lowlights—if it were all vanilla, we could be accused of not trying hard enough. Fulfilling our potential is all about putting ourselves out there and being ready to not quite make the grade. If we don't hit the heights, never mind, but we will have developed nonetheless.

DiCaprio is a formidable actor, but there has to be a part of him that wanted this Oscar pretty badly. He kept enthralling his audiences, and while an Oscar is rarely the sole motivation for an actor, it is certainly a benchmark by which they can measure themselves. He came back and came back, time and again, and he has finally done what he has been dreaming about.

Next time you don't quite achieve what you aimed for, remember him on that stage, and remember him immobile under that bear. Sometimes life can feel like you have been mauled, but it is nearly always possible to drag yourself back into the reckoning.

# CHAPTER 54

## Talking Your Way to Success

There has been a lot of talk about comprehending your EQ or Emotional Quotient but hardly any that correlates effective communication to success in business and in life. I call this CQ, or comprehending your Communication Quotient. Maybe the two (EQ and CQ) are related in some manner, I don't know. What I do know, having worked tirelessly in building a business and convincing employees, staff, clients, customers, partners, and investors, is that communication matters a lot.

In line with my recent thinking about success and mindset, I started wondering if there was a way to understand the art and science of communication. In just about every context, communication is emphasized as not only a virtue, but as a practical tool. I wanted to know what makes communication potent and enriching, both at the individual and the organizational levels.

This chapter is a detailed discussion on the subject [2900 words] inspired by the books *Rainmaking Conversation* by John E. Doerr & Mike Schultz; *Crucial Conversations* by Joseph Grenny, Al Switzler, Ron McMillan and Kerry Patterson; and *Fierce Conversation* by Susan Scott.

We have been inculcated with the belief that discussions are just about sharing information, giving directives, resolving differences, and voicing our thoughts. Although they are all of those things, they are also so much more. This couldn't be more false.

Discussions are robust and living things that change as we do. Yes, they allow us to transfer ideas, but they also allow us to sow trust. It is with trust, vision, and collaboration that great things can happen. And all this must start with effective communication.

Businesspeople will tell you to grasp the nuances of language and that discussion is indispensable to business success. Some people do this intuitively. The subtleties of how to start a discussion, how to build it, and use it to shape thinking. Those people experience discussions as living entities with independent personalities.

For others, discussions are much like shooting at moving targets—hit or miss.

By breaking down what happens in discussion more generally, we can hone in on some important takeaways that can help us communicate purposefully and nurture cultures of success.

## The Three Types of Discussion

There are three types of discussion in business. They can be easily characterized by their intended goals, which you should keep in mind from the onset of any discussion.

The first is **transactional.** This involves exchanges of information.

The second is **positional.** This involves exchanges of power and influence.

The third is **transformational.** This involves exchanges about collaboration and moving forward together.

Of course, discussions go beyond your intended goal. They are multifaceted linguistic interactions with great complexity brewing below the surface. That's because communication happens at various levels simultaneously, and often, much of what we convey to another person is non-verbal.

## Communication Vs. Discussion

Our bodies send us innumerable cues that we respond to both consciously and unconsciously. When we are in the presence of another person, those cues are ignited and amplified, especially when the person is unknown to us. These underlying forces influence, if not dictate, the outcomes and progressions of discussions. We communicate with people at multiple levels, and sometimes, those levels don't harmonize.

If we detect our interlocutor as a threat, our ability to converse will suffer, and the discussion will stagger. As our heartrate increases and our brains fire all sorts of signals urging us to flee, the discussion won't deepen. This can be good at times; it can also be detrimental.

This reaction can occur whether or not you want it to. It's one of the beauties and curses of our biology. At any given time, the amygdala and the prefrontal cortex can be in concert or in disharmony. Although we do not have full-control over our primitive or instinctual brain processes, we can quell, guide, and habituate them.

## Blame the Primitive Brain

For fruitful discussion, a balancing act must be performed. When the amygdala overreacts, it can cause us to adopt a point of view narrower than we would have were we to reflect. However, in the heat and anxiety of an exchange, it can be difficult to conjure up that awareness. It is difficult, yet not impossible.

When we enter a discussion, our primitive brain begins to map out and categorize in an attempt to make sense of the stimuli and increase predictability. This process is sometimes misguided. We must rein it in with sheer willpower and conscious force. Failure to do this can have all sorts of unintended negative consequences.

Awareness consists of recognizing the viewpoints of others and finding ways to coalesce our own with theirs. This happens in every discussion. You test the waters, compare expectations, and identify whether views align—all this to build common ground.

## Business Mindfulness

In a business context, this can cause discussion-lockdown. If we perceive the other person as hostile, we communicate that to them non-verbally. Their bodies will react and direct them accordingly. Whether or not the perceived threat is accurate, the mutually experienced reactions will prohibit trust building.

This is undesirable because trust is the seed of any productive relationship. When our bodies overreact or get it entirely wrong, trust wilts and renewing it can take time. A personal goal should be to identify our bodily signals of flight. Sweaty palms, racing heart, nervous scanning, fast paces, all these are signals of our fear response. If we can identify them and activate higher-level brain functions to ground ourselves, our discussions can proceed smoothly and with ease. If we can't, we are subject to amygdala hijack, which is when our brain floods with cortisol, a neurotransmitter that forces you into survival mode; executive functions are scaled back, autopilot kicks in, and pulling out of that state takes a lot more effort than staying in it.

A few mental habits that have helped me in moments of amygdala hijack are labeling my reaction as normal; noticing whether I tend toward the same reaction (flight, fight, freeze, appease) every time I engage in particular levels of discussion; choosing an alternate course of action after recognizing my own instinctive reaction; and making a decision to acknowledge my emotions but not let them dominate me. For someone unfamiliar with meditation and mindfulness, this may all sound fanciful. It isn't. There is hard science to back up the benefits of mindfulness.

Mindfulness in a discussion with one person presents its own unique set of stumbling blocks and concerns. What about group discussions? What about organizational discussions?

## Thinking Big

People think and receive information differently when they are in groups or not personally addressed. Groups tend to raise the stakes and expect more from their speaker.

A few ways to build substantial connections to groups of people is through forthrightness, interpersonal connections, empathy, giving, and reducing uncertainty. These apply to one-on-one discussion also, but the stakes are higher with groups because you have fewer opportunities to get it right.

I will paint a picture.

You are sure to build trust when you tell people what is on your mind, show them that you are not so different from them, acknowledge what you think they might be thinking and give it importance, offer ways that you can help to further their interests, and reduce any uncertainty about your intentions or the feasibility of what you are saying.

In business and in life, communicating effectively with groups of people is essential. When you find yourself in a leadership role, this is even more crucial. To get your message across and mobilize masses, you need to cultivate trust.

With trust, all sorts of innovations can happen. Without it, people and ideas stagnate. Fear of judgment and failure are the two banes of innovation.

Leaders can instill these fears unconsciously by becoming mired in one type of discourse. I have noticed that many leaders can't get past the transactional and positional levels of discussion because they construe their relationships as power bargaining. These leaders use their authority to command, leverage, and yell at people until those people act satisfactorily. This may accomplish some short-terms ends, but it will never lead to the transformational level of discussion that changes lives and companies.

When we reach the transformational level of discussion with a person all sorts of feel-good hormones, like oxytocin, surge inside the brain. That hormone and others strengthen our connections to people. They are addictive. We grow to love the feeling of sharing, exchanging, and collaborating and that fuels innovation. Leaders can get addicted to power and being right. When that happens, their pleasure is derived from exerting dominance and squelching others. This "alpha dominance" is fatal. In an alpha-dominated environment, discussion can never reach the transformational level. Trust can never grow.

## Leaders Must Listen to Be Heard

When we picture a leader, perhaps we envision someone who yells or commands, someone with a peremptory demeanor, someone who never loses their north. These are visions of leadership that fit into an older—dare I say archaic—framework.

Leaders need not be dictatorial to lead. Confidence, vision, clarity, and strong listening abilities are the stuff of strong leadership. Today, in business and elsewhere, leaders are viewed as people just like anyone else, except that they sprang into action and brought other people along for the ride.

Some would say that strong communication skills and the ability to persuade individuals and masses at all the levels of discussion (transactional, positional, and transformational) are inherent qualities of a strong leader. Whether or not that's the case, I believe that strong leadership can be learned by understanding how to enact business mindfulness, forthrightness, interpersonal connectivity, empathy, giving, and uncertainty reduction.

When you strive to enact the attributes mentioned above, accessing the three levels of discussion is simple. The reason is that trust is present. Effective leaders, above all else, have the trust of their followers. You can lead with fear, sure, but that kind of leadership is volatile and corrosive. Leadership based in trust is resilient.

## From Dictator to Director

Shifting from the dictatorial perception of leadership to the relationship-building perception of leadership is somewhat counterintuitive. It must start with the realization that you do not have to be in control. Strong leadership comes from setting direction and harnessing the skills and talents of your teammates to move together toward a common goal. A strong leader doesn't need to be right all the time, overweening, micromanaging, know all the answers, or administrate group dynamics.

The members of your group have gotten where they are in life without you. Throughout that time, they have garnered experience, information, and skills that you probably do not have. That is an unlimited source of innovation. It is potential energy that can be left untapped by reverence to archaic power structures. The way to tap into that body of human resources can be broken down into five simple priorities:

1. *Transparency.* Be vocal about perceived threats and hostilities. When you encourage discussions that promote transparency and openness about topics that we tend to veil, trust can reveal itself.

2. *Relationships.* Relationships tend to revolve around core values. Good relationships are based in shared values or mutually respected ones. When you jointly decide on your core values, unity is easier to cultivate.

3. *Understanding.* When you are uncertain about something or you don't understand, don't be afraid to ask. Asking questions is an art. Ask for and listen to feedback from peers, employees, vendors, and customers. The people who don't agree with you can provide tremendous value so long as you're willing to listen.

4. *Flexible.* You don't have to be right. To acknowledge error or ignorance is not a sign of weakness. It is not a sign of incompetence. It is a sign of curiosity and strong leadership.

5. *We.* When you create a team that wants to help each other grow and succeed, you need not worry so much about yourself. Thinking in collective terms means that others will look out to ensure your best interest and you theirs.

## Leadership Toolkit 101

Reframe. Redirect. Refocus. Redistribute.

Remember those words because they are conversational anchors. I have often found myself in the midst of group conversations that have spiraled out of control and needed to deploy one or more of those strategies to reorient us all.

***Reframing*** consists of paraphrasing. This takes great listening skills. People can get hung out or blinded by words, so learning to rephrase things in terms that someone else can understand is a tremendous skill.

***Redirecting*** consists of getting back on track. This takes a list, at the very least. In meeting and group discussions, getting off track is inevitable. You can save time and mental energy by nudging people in the right direction.

***Refocusing*** consists of shifting perspectives. This takes the combined efforts of reframing and redirecting. There are all sorts of hang-ups and distractions in groups. As a leader or otherwise, keeping an objective perspective can allow you to pull others out of narrow-minded ruts.

***Redistributing*** consists of power displacement. This takes courage and willpower. In groups, some people tend to fall to the wayside while others dominate the discussion. Whether you are steering the discussion or not, redistributing power can foster openness, mindfulness, and non-oppositional collaboration.

A few more notes on strategy.

Remember to think in terms of shared success. Remember to ask questions and make sure you understand viewpoints before rejecting or modifying them. Remember to not aim at being right (it's foolish, self-centered, and counterproductive). Remember to use "we," "us," and other collective pronouns.

## Let's Think Together

To some, this next section will seem hackneyed. To others, it will seem commonplace. To me, I think it's neither because I don't see it happening enough. It's one of those things that people think they should do, but never actually do, like going to the gym or eating more nutritious food.

Go around the room and take the temperature. Ask people how they feel about the progress made. Invitations to contribute that spur from genuine interest are the stuff of collective spirit.

A useful heuristic to employ when closing out a group discussion is LEARN

L = What did you **like** about this meeting?

E = What were you **excited** about?

A = What produced the most **anxiety**?

R = What should we **celebrate** or **reward** about this meeting?

N = What next steps do we **need** to take?

You may think this is all cheesy or banal, but it makes a huge difference. The new workforce demands this kind of bonding and sees it as healthy.

All this goes a long way toward inculcating companies with a culture of shared success, teamwork, transparency, honesty, and trust. These values and norms give rise to trust and ease discussions at every level.

When you do this, new levels of discussion can arise that all stem from the transformational level. Of course, you can't get to these levels without some turbulence, usually known as the storming phase. All groups must go through it. Once you storm, clash, then you norm. Once norms are established, then you can perform. That is the Tuckerman Model of group dynamics. What I appreciate about this model is the healthy acceptance of conflict as necessary for success.

Below are listed the new levels of transformational discussion that emerge after the storming and norming phases:

***Fostering discussions.*** These discussions orbit around teamwork aimed at building a better culture with an organization.

***Humanizing discussions.*** These discussions orbit around embracing new perspectives. Othering is a common occurrence. We put distance between ourselves and the unknown, perhaps to remove self-guilt about othering. It's a vicious cycle.

***Aspiring discussions.*** These discussions orbit around shooting at possibilities and thinking ahead together. The word that best describes this level is expanding.

***Navigating discussions.*** These discussions orbit around practical knowledge sharing. Information exchange, best practices, and pioneering are all examples of navigating discussions. This largely involves moving away from withholding information to sharing it.

***Generating discussions.*** These discussions orbit around creating, producing, and leading, rather than relying on convention. It's risky business.

***Expressing discussions.*** These discussions orbit around the heart. They involve getting people to speak up, hear their voices, challenge authorities, and push brands and people toward interpersonal growth.

***Synchronizing discussions.*** These discussions orbit around getting people to align and move in unison. In the context of enterprise, synchronizing takes more concrete forms. Protocols, procedures, groups meetings, and the like should aim to synchronize people and resources.

## Conclusion

Some people may need to learn how to speak in new ways. It isn't natural for everyone to share their feelings, oppose ideas, or test new theories. As a leader or as an individual just trying to build strong connections to the people around you, there are ways you can enrich the quality of your discussions.

I have listed a few here. However, there are many more.

Take a step back and observe yourself and others. You will find new ways to build trust that relate to your context. You don't have to be stilted in conversation. You don't need to sound like a human resources robot. Just listen, respond, ask questions, build trust, and watch yourself and the people around you grow.

# CHAPTER 55

## *Developing the Mental Resolve for Success*

Failure and adversity are inherent parts of life. We will often strive for success and encounter the dark abyss of despair that is falling short of our goals. All people have failed at one point or another; people are failing as I write these words. What matters, ultimately, is your attitude toward success. You can either be self-defeating and fatalistic, or you can be optimistic and resilient.

Endurance is one's ability to recover from failure, the ability to get up, brush-off, and find a new path toward productivity and accomplishment, despite the unintended failure. Personal endurance is immunity from embarrassment, humiliation, and disappointment. It contributes to quality and fast decision-making.

It has been shown that successful people possess five factors that make up their endurance. These five factors are their armor, both mental and emotional. They enable them to take difficult and seemingly intractable situations, and turn them into opportunities for growth.

### The Five Factors of Personal Endurance

Off the bat, I'll just list them all. Before you dive into my description of them, I invite you to consider what they may mean to you.

1. Positive Attitude
2. Conclusive Choice
3. Ethical Compass
4. Uncompromising Resolve
5. Social Backing

***Positive attitude***. A positive attitude is not fanciful, but rather a driving force. It is the desire to move forward, to persevere when others are retreating in the face of change and hardship. This mandate is a self-fulfilling prophecy that foreshadows success when paired with conclusive choice.

***Conclusive choice.*** In most cases, success does not come from passivity. You must choose a course and stick to it, despite any apparent unlikelihood. Decisive action requires mettle. It requires the mettle to make difficult decisions when the convenience of an easier choice entices us from beyond. Better still are choices that are guided by an ethical compass.

***Ethical compass.*** Whatever the values that you conceive as imperative, use them as guiding stars when making decisions because they fill you with the conviction of moral certainty and belief. Once you have made a decision and begun to carry it out, you must stick to it, and this requires uncompromising resolve.

***Uncompromising resolve.*** Determination and persistence can be likened to omnipotence for mortals. Persist until you recognize that the best option is to quit, because sometimes it will be. The point here is to recognize when stopping is rational or reasonable rather than convenient or easy. Sometimes a little bit of help from others is necessary to identify that moment. That's when social backing is crucial.

***Social backing.*** Who can you count on to have your back?

## The Power of Positive Attitude – Optimism

Attitude is more than a sunny outlook on life. It is the true belief that good things will come in spite of bad things. There are two types of optimism: passive and active.

The passive optimist assumes the world operates on the brighter side and expects positive effects will follow negative circumstances, no matter what. They believe in the benevolence of people and of themselves.

The active optimist is more resilient, in that they are emboldened against negative circumstances. It helps them make decisions confidently with the assumption that they will prevail and triumph, irrespective of apparent difficulty. This can be aptly described as the expectation of personal success.

Even better still, the active optimist inadvertently sets the stage for a potent self-fulfilling prophecy. The expectation of personal success, bolstered and vindicated by moments of success, can affect real world outcomes.

Mental attitude toward an action correlates closely with the consequence of that outcome. Some call it manifestation, others call it destiny, and I prefer the less metaphysical term, self-fulfilling prophecy.

The potency of the self-fulfilling prophecy lies in certain features of the active optimist's mental attitude. The active optimist is less likely to accept failure, desist from a chosen course of action, flounder in determination, and accept rejection or failure.

## Optimism is Not Just Mental

The active optimist's mental attitude toward adversity and failure is the key to success. However, it alone cannot guarantee success. There are four ways to harness optimism and use it to secure real-world results.

1. *Incremental planning.* Break down large tasks into smaller and more manageable steps. When the task is too large and it cannot be broken down into manageable steps, ask for assistance.

2. *Vicarious optimism-building.* Observe others succeeding, and analyze their trajectory. The goal here is to recognize that there are no fundamental differences between you and successful people. You can acquire whatever they do or have that helps them succeed.

3. *Collective optimism.* Interpersonal support and connectedness have been shown as two central determinants of success. In the military, unit cohesion is pivotal to success.

4. *Self-control.* Oh yes, the dreaded cousin of willpower. The ability to control your actions, thoughts, and bodily reactions conveys self-confidence and cultivates active optimism. When you are not a victim of your whims and temptations, you are more likely to assume that you can conjure the oneness of mind to succeed.

All of this amounts to nothing if it doesn't materialize into action. Decisive action requires not only optimism, but also determination, endurance, and collaboration.

## Decisive Action Doesn't Mean Being Right, Just Sure

Decision-making is not easy. Selecting from one of the myriad options before us at any given moment is challenging. Often, the information available to us is insufficient to confer certainty in any one particular outcome, so we largely operate in the dark. This is where being decisive comes into play.

Decisiveness doesn't necessarily come from being right, just sure. When you are sure about a particular outcome, you act confidently. That alone can significantly increase your chances of success.

Decisive action is also about timeliness. Opportunities arise and disappear every second. Some are grander than others. Some go to the lucky. Frequently they are snatched up by quicker competitors. To recognize an opportunity is the first step; to act quickly is the second.

## Turning a Negative into a Positive

Interestingly, decisive action has been shown to reduce stress and empower people to rebound from adversity. Steve Jobs is an exemplary of this feature of active optimism. He resisted avoidance and paralysis when others may have succumbed. Take as an illustrative example his removal from Apple.

For some, that would have been an irrecoverable blow. Yet, Steve Jobs described it as an opportunity, "The heaviness of being successful was replaced by the lightness of being a beginner again, less sure about everything," he said. "It freed me to enter one of the most creative periods of my life."

Jobs went on to say he was "pretty sure none of this would have happened if I hadn't been fired from Apple. It was awful-tasting medicine, but I guess the patient needed it."

Steve Jobs did not exhibit some extra-human quality here. He was actively optimistic, made a decision, and was resilient against his turn of fortune. He rebounded and turned that failure into an opportunity for growth. This catalyzed a turning point for Apple and took a tremendous amount of personal responsibility.

## Personal Responsibility

Quite simply, if you do not take ownership of your actions, you will feel detached from them and never be fully invested. Endurance, active optimism, decisiveness, all require the sense that your actions emanate from you and no one else. It is natural to displace responsibility, especially when things get tough. In these cases, we should stave off our natural inclinations and opt for self-reflection.

Failure and adversity are fertile conditions for self-reflection. This is impossible if you do not feel personally responsible for your actions. You won't be prompted to self-reflect and grow. It takes great courage, but it should be done.

## It's Not All About You

Success is contingent upon your personal attributes, but it is also contingent upon others. Without the trust of others, you are less likely to build the interpersonal support vital to success. Trust is engendered by honesty, integrity, fidelity, and ethical behavior. These are the four parts that make up one's moral compass.

The moral compass tends to remove risk from business and personal relationships and confer predictability, which grants safety and fosters trustworthiness. If the situation is right, the trust and support of others can be crucial to success because life will present you with opportunities that you will not be able to tackle alone. This is especially true because so many outcomes and opportunities are dependent on the decisions of other people, who, most of the time, have no stake in our achievements.

The amazing thing about having a clear moral compass is that it aids decision-making and concurrently gains you greater degrees of responsibility and confidence from the people around you. These two factors perpetuate further success. Success begets success.

## Stay the Course

Thus far we have talked about the centrality of active optimism, decision-making, and morality to success. We have used a few terms that I think warrant further discussion. Terms like "tenacity," "persevere," and "endurance."

I take these terms to stem from the notion that steady persistence in a purposeful course of action, especially in spite of difficulties, adversity, or discouragement is vital. The steadiness of your persistence is largely dependent on your motivations for the chosen course of action. I find that actions motivated by and in alignment with your moral compass generate the most confidence.

When I speak of persistence, therefore, I see it as not only a state of mind, but also a mental, emotional, and moral attitude in the face of a challenge. This is key because we sometimes need to remind ourselves of our motivations. The closer they align with our values, the easier it will be to draw courage from them.

## Abandon Ship!

Steady persistence and relentless tenacity can look much like defiance. It is the conviction to say, "I will not give in," when opposed by people or circumstances. There is a caveat, however. Persistence and tenacity can verge on rashness and stubbornness. We must sometimes desist from our chosen course, despite sunken costs or effort.

When should we choose to do this? When a goal becomes more of a liability than an asset and when resources dedicated to one goal are better allocated to another. The inability to recognize that success can take the form of holding back or stopping could result in self-defeat. It takes great courage to do this, too.

## We Are All in this Together

Interpersonal support is considered the single most predictive factor of success. Simply put, there is strength in numbers. Interpersonal support is born out of shared identity with group members, shared values, and prior experiences of aid in times of distress.

When you initiate an action, interpersonal support to help guarantee an end result. When you are making a comeback, interpersonal support becomes even more instrumental. It can help you avoid a descent into the abyss of psychological or physical self-defeat.

To create the kinds of bonds that make for a good interpersonal support system, a few things should be kept in mind.

***Direct reciprocity.*** This is *quid pro quo*, pure and simple. I give you this; you give me that.

***Spatial selection.*** The likelihood of support increases with proximity. If you are physically acquainted with the person who you want support from, they are far more likely to help.

***Genetic selection***. Blood is thicker than water. If we are related, I will probably help you.

***Indirect reciprocity.*** This is where unintended gains come into play. Indirect reciprocity refers to self-interest and the potential benefits one person can receive from helping another.

***Group selection.*** Some social and cultural norms will prompt me to help you, even if I don't know you. Reference to a greater good or a moral obligation, for example.

It can be helpful to mind these types of social bonds; however, it can overcomplicate a very simple and intuitive fact.

When you are with people who share your values and goals, treat them with respect, show appreciation, listen to them, don't attribute to malice what can be adequately explained by stupidity, and, last but not least, think before you speak, great things can happen.

## Do Not Walk This Road Alone

Sharing our success is sometimes difficult, but all of these values, attitudes, and motivations are much easier to foster when you collaborate with others. Other people are sources of inspiration. They bear us up when we slacken. They can keep us on track.

All of that notwithstanding, the locus of success is still you. You are in control of your attitude, your decisive action, your moral compass, your relentless tenacity, and the value of your interpersonal relationships.

There's a proverb that I like to keep in mind when thinking about success. "If you want to go fast, walk alone. If you want to go far, take a friend."

# CHAPTER 56

## *Understanding Human Behavior for Success*

The study of human behavior and decision-making is endlessly fascinating to me. As a businessman and executive, I am grateful to experts who spend their time unraveling the mysteries of the human mind. I am particularly drawn to studies on the effects of context, emotions, expectations, money, and power on decision-making.

These questions span the gamut how we act as consumers, as business-people, and as policy-makers. In particular, the emphasis in these studies tends to be on our systematically irrational behavior. Life in general is quite complex, so there are a number of factors at play in every decision-making environment, whether or not we recognize them.

The exploration of those factors through careful research has revealed some fascinating and predictable results about the systematic ways in which we behave irrationally. Aside from being fascinating, these results can positively influence the way we live our lives.

By shining light on the general principles of mind that seem to dictate our decision-making and our behavior, we can reevaluate our own thought processes and those of the people around us.

## What's Going on Under the Hood?

There are a few general principles from the social sciences that have significantly affected the way I think about people.

I will work through a few of them here.

My hope is that some of these resonate with you, and possibly, make a positive difference to the way you live, do business, and think about decision-making.

## Problem of Relativity

In behavioral economics, there are two titans who explored the Problem of Relativity in a simple study, Amos Tversky and Daniel Kahneman. They posed the following thought experiment:

Suppose that you have two errands to run today. You need to purchase a pen and a suit. You go to an office supply store and find the pen that you were looking for. The pen costs $25. You decide to purchase it, but then you remember that the same pen is on sale for $18 at another store about 15 minutes away. Would you take the 15-minute trip to save $7? Most people reasoned that they would take the trip.

Now, suppose that you move on to your second task. You find the perfect suit for $455, and you decide to purchase it. Then, a customer whispers in your ear that the same suit is on sale for only $448 at another store just 15-minutes away. Would you take the 15-minute trip to save $7? Most people reasoned that they would not take the trip.

This should seem odd. $7 is $7, no question. However, the experiment elucidates that the value of a dollar amount can be perceived differently relative to the comparative reference point.

This general principle helps us understand upsells, for example. It is easy to understand why someone would be willing to add an extra $200 to a $5,000 catering bill when the same person would clip coupons to save 25 cents on a $1 can of evaporated milk.

The moral is that we should consider the value amounts objectively rather than relatively. A broader perspective on this could save us a lot of money in the long run.

## Free Is the Best Price

I think we can all agree that few things are superior to free. Part of the reason seems to be that zero, or free, has deep ties to our emotions. We often overreact when we hear something is free, assuming that that must be the logical alternative.

Assume that you had to choose between two products. One product is free and the other isn't. Studies show that people irrationally opt for the free one, even if it means greater expenses in the long-term.

Let's say that you had to choose between two checking accounts. One is advertised as free with no monthly rates or minimums; the other is $5 per month but includes free travelers checks, online banking, and possible cash rewards. Most people will choose the free account.

Zero, therefore, is not just a mere discount; it is a powerful decision-making factor. If you are in business, you may know this already. Zero can be used to draw in large crowds and guide decision-making toward long-term revenue.

It can also be a way to promote positive social norms. If healthcare providers want to decrease the incidence of disease and illness with preventative care and early-detection, they should make the tests critical to those goals free. People will be far more likely to take advantage of them. In the long-term, this may save healthcare providers millions of dollars in medical costs.

## Money Is Not the Best Motivator

Corporate loyalty is a slight oxymoron today. Most people move from job to job searching for better pay, better benefits, better amenities, and greater degrees of upward mobility. Loyalty to the company doesn't play into the decision usually. Loyalty to select co-workers, however, still has great impact.

That is why companies should start thinking about employee retention in terms of social norms. The productivity of employees is largely dependent on their talents and their willingness to do the work. More and more, willingness and happiness are key considerations for employment. Salary alone does not motivate people to risk their lives, for example.

Public servants who put themselves in harm's way won't cite their paychecks as strong motivators. It is the social norms of job satisfaction, professional pride, and duty that motivate them to potentially give up their lives and health.

The general principle to consider here is that we are not rational machines, but feeling entities. In fact, we very well may base many of life's more important decisions on emotional intuition rather than pure reasoning.

To recognize this can help us reconsider the way we think about decision-making, institutions, and our lives.

## Commitments Make Us Accountable

We all have temptations, vices, and habits that we want to undo or avoid. Some of us have alternatives that we'd rather replace those negative behaviors with. We will tell ourselves that we must change, but sometimes fall short. It may even seem like we have multiple personalities.

When we identify the negative behaviors, we tend to catalogue them in broad categories and then decide that the things in those categories will be eradicated from our lives by sheer willpower. Although this is a step in the right direction, it is irrational to assume that we can simply uproot negative behaviors by sheer willpower. We often need external incentives.

One way to help us keep from procrastinating when it comes to our self-improvement is with commitments. A commitment to other people means accountability. Yes, if your negative behaviors are emotionally charged enough, that alone may not keep you from them. However, it can bolster your efforts.

This general principle applies in other contexts too. Companies often use dictatorial measures to motivate their employees. This can be damaging in the long run. We all have some degree of self-control. It may wane sometimes, but being forced to do things won't fortify our self-control.

Making a commitment, however, can. It demands personal accountability, which can increase self-control through forward thinking and external pressure on our willpower.

## The Fallacy of Ownership

Ownership, as a psychological experience, is quite strange. We can feel and believe that we own all sorts of things that we reasonably cannot own. For example, there is a sharp distinction between owning an iPhone and owning an idea.

Peculiarly, we can feel that we own something before we even have it in our possession. Virtual ownership is a mainstay of marketing. The experience can be best described as wishful thinking.

Imagine that you see a couple riding along the California coast in their BMW, or you receive a Patagonia catalog with hikers scaling up a mountainside. Your desire for that experience, that clothing, or some part in that activity, is virtual ownership. Marketing thrives on this almost irrational desire for the things other people have or seem to have.

The general principle is that we often claim ownership of things that truly cannot be ours. Often, this can lead to bad decision-making and in a number of contexts.

In politics, the apparent ownership of an ideology, and our stake in its survival, is fallacious, yet we see in-fighting and large-scale policy decisions that seem to hinge on that illusion.

The moral is that we should put some distance between ourselves and objects of ownership. To whatever extent we can muster, we should seek to view all transactions involving things we truly cannot own, as transactions of pre-ownership.

## You Can't Keep Every Door Open

This is a big one. We often prefer to hold onto things that damage us for the fear that losing them would be a far greater damage. Doors are possibilities, and we need to learn how to close some of them. Some doors are bigger than others. The size has less to do with the potential outcomes and more to do with the difficulty of closing them.

Some doors might lead to a new career or a better job. Some doors are tied to dreams and hopes. Some doors lead to relationships with people. Wherever a door may lead, keeping them all open can be exhausting. It can deplete your time, energy, and sometimes, even your finances.

The general principle here is that we have an irrational compulsion to keep our options open. This doesn't mean there is something irrational about keeping our options open, but not every option is worth preserving. We must learn when to close doors, despite the uncertainty.

## Expectations Shape Our Perception

It is no surprise that our beliefs influence our thinking. The surprising thing is that our expectations influence our perception. We do not have to believe that something is the case, but rather we merely need to assume that something might be the case for it to infiltrate our perception of physical or imaginary events.

Have you ever had the experience of receiving an alphabet soup of a text message and still been able to decipher what the person intended to write? That is an instance of expectation infiltrating reality.

Have you ever had the experience of assuming what someone's personality will be like based on their attire? That is an instance of expectation infiltrating reality.

Are you familiar with the concept of placebo effect? That's an instance of expectation infiltrating reality.

This is unavoidable. The brain is not a blank slate, and as you live more, your repository of experience, whether real or perceived, grows. So too then does your ability to expect outcomes, irrespective of their plausibility or accuracy.

This isn't to say that our expectations are always wrong. It is to say that they aren't always right. When expectations enter the realm of human activity, as in inter-personal interactions, they escalate to the level of biases.

At that stage, it is critical that we acknowledge our personal biases and expectations so that we can safeguard against them when we make decisions.

The general principle is that our expectations can strongly influence our perception and attitudes toward real-world events.

The moral of the story is that we are not victims of those expectations. If we purposefully cultivate a healthy mindfulness about our own expectations and biases, we can assess them in the moment to determine whether they are applicable or inapplicable given present circumstances.

## Morality with a Price Tag

Honesty is the best policy, or so they say.

From an evolutionary perspective, honesty is rewarded highly. Honesty is connected to acts of altruism, reciprocity, fairness, all cornerstones of human civilization. From a historical perspective, cultures the world over have edified norms to promote honesty, including punitive measures to punish those who betray it.

When it comes to money, however, it seems that our perceptions of honesty can bend a little. When we find ourselves in situations that involve our financial benefit, we tend to see the world in terms compatible with our self-interest and less so with moral standards. This distortion can lead us to justify dishonest actions.

In a now classic experiment, students were asked to predict if people would cheat more for tokens that could later be converted for money than with cash. The students predicted that the rate of cheating would be the same, given that both the cash and the tokens represented money.

Their predictions were entirely wrong.

The participants who dealt with tokens were far quicker to rationalize cheating with a token than with cash. Their blindness to this human weakness is ours too.

Legal libraries are riddled with cases of corporate theft. People up and down the corporate ladder have committed also sorts of acts of dishonesty, cheating wherever possible, just to increase their wealth.

The general principle is that the more distanced we are from the cash itself, the more likely we are to commit acts of financial dishonesty.

Think about times when you or someone you know has stolen from the office, taken a glass from a bar, or maybe taken someone's lunch. The point is that we can be dishonest without thinking ourselves so.

It is difficult to say how exactly we can undercut this tendency. Hopefully being aware of our lax judgment when it comes to non-monetary objects will wake up our consciences somewhat.

## Pawns of the Mind

There are two takeaways from the lessons of social science regarding human behavior and decision-making.

The first one is that we are pawns in a game of mind that goes one below the surface of our awareness. We like to think of ourselves as drivers, fully in control of our decisions, but the truth is that free will is an illusion. Our wills are not free, nor are they unbounded. They are influenced by our emotions, relativity, social norms, context, expectations, and many other factors. These factors exert power over our decision-making every day.

The second is that we are not powerless against them. We must learn what our irrational tendencies are, learn about our biases, and learn about our weakness. That is the only way we can ward away their ill effects.

It is through vigilance that we can overcome our inherent shortcomings. This attitude is critical for all people, but especially for those in positions of power. Their decisions have an incalculably far-reaching scope.

If they do not heed the warnings of the social sciences, we may all be the worse for it.

# CHAPTER 57

## *The Social Media Marshmallow Test*

In the 1960s at Stanford University, psychologist Walter Mischel carried out an iconic test to understand the impact of self-control and delayed gratification on our lives.

Mischel and his grad students carried out research with 4-5 year-old preschool kids in the Stanford University Bing Nursery School. The premise of the research was simple. They gave the children a choice between one reward (a marshmallow) that they could have immediately and a larger reward (maybe two marshmallows) for which they would have to wait, alone, for 20 minutes. If they waited patiently without eating the first "available" marshmallow, they would earn the greater reward.

This provided a fascinating lesson in self-control, and Mischel's book *The Marshmallow Test* explores the findings in great detail. In a nutshell, those children who delayed their gratification went on to enjoy fuller and richer lives. Willpower, it seems, is a crucial ingredient for a successful life.

Marshmallows, hmmm, very interesting you might say, but what does this have to do with social media? Well, everything, in my view.

We are at the mercy of notifications buzzing from our phone. We feel that we have to reply immediately to every instant message. If we don't comment on that funny photo as soon as we see it, we feel like a traitor. Social media is everywhere, it is immediate, and it can be all-consuming.

What social media isn't, however, is our life.

Before our lives got consumed by our device screens, life was very different. Some people can make space for the "old ways" of life in their families and the workplace, but increasingly more of us are simply being swallowed up by the immediacy of the medium.

As someone who works in digital publishing, I understand the addiction all too well. You always want to read another story, analyze every comment, and click on one of those "you might be interested in this" links. Yes, you will probably be interested, but should you be interested, right at this very moment? Probably not.

It comes back to delayed gratification. Those people who have a healthy relationship with social media will be able to put their activity into a little "box," only to be opened when the time is right. They will have the willpower to wait until lunchtime to glance at their Facebook page, they will scroll Twitter on the train, but close it as soon as they get to the office. They might read (or write) a few blogs in the evening, but only when the kids are safely tucked up in bed.

If you can delay the gratification of social media, your life will be all the fuller for it. If you guzzle the marshmallow immediately, you will never be able to stop "eating." That isn't so healthy, and with social media (really) being in its infancy in the grand scheme of things, the temptations will get even more significant in the future.

# CHAPTER 58

## *You Buy from People You Like. Really?*

I have had some hugely rewarding relationships with complete jerks over the course of my career. I have also had relationships that delivered very little with some of the nicest people on the planet.

This may be why many of us have come to distrust the charming salespeople with their perma-smiles. We have learned by painful experience that, while it is a nice attribute, liking someone is not essential for doing business with them. I would much rather buy from an unpleasant salesperson, who delivered what they promised, than purchase from a lovely individual, where that certainty was never quite there.

In any business decision, the fewer the factors limiting the decision, the better. So much has been written about the importance of "likeability," but it is a simple fact of life that there will be many people out there with whom you will never see eye to eye. The fact that you don't get along will make business more difficult, but if they are (reliably) delivering the best value for you and your employer, should you really be dismissing them simply because you don't like them?

It is a complex question.

Some may say that life is too short to do business with people that you don't like. I have certainly curtailed relationships in the past where the emotional distaste simply wasn't worth it. Others may argue the opposite:

that life is too short to chance business opportunities on whether or not you like someone

I suppose it all comes down to your personal priorities. You can find someone unlikeable for a number of reasons. However, not each of those reasons will be justified. With some self-reflection, you can determine whether your reasons correlate with an informed, corollary character trait that in the past has indicated a major personal deficiency, or is simply you being picky. Certainly not all our irrational dislikes are entirely baseless; but some of them are. We should be leery of not casting side an excellent business opportunity because someone speaks in a tone we dislike or chews with their mouth open.

Also, it is crucial to note that relationships can change. Once you get close to someone and let them into your life, the cold-shoulder can often turn into a shoulder to cry on. Very few relationships will stay strained forever, and if both of you have a common goal, learning to work harmoniously together makes perfect sense.

So, yes, by all means buy from people who you don't like. Just because you don't get along now, doesn't you won't ever.

# CHAPTER 59

## *You and Santa Need the Same Thing*

Santa would be redundant if little children didn't believe in him… He stops coming if you don't believe; that's the way it works.

The elves would be laid off, the reindeer would be put out to pasture, and the Big Man would probably retire to a beach in the Maldives. If your product or service doesn't have a market, you won't last long. According to a 2012 survey, Santa has a potential global market of 526,000,000 Christian children under the age of 14. That market size is impressive, but how many are true Believers? 100 million? Maybe…. That is still more than enough to justify his strict fitness regime every autumn.

Santa runs a hugely impressive operation, making use of modern day technology wherever possible, and using cutting edge market research to slice and dice the wishes of the children. However, with the accumulated wisdom passed down from the Santas before him, there is only one number that truly matters:

The number of Believers (yes, with a capital letter).

Ok, enough of the sugary Christmas metaphors, but this example is valid for any business, no matter what size. Do you know how many Believers your business has? How many Believers do you need to break even? How do you go about collecting and retaining your Believers? Are you delivering something unique and compelling that makes their life that little bit more worth living?

Santa has a great feel for all of this, but do you?

How many times have you done something thinking that it is a great idea, only for the reaction to be lukewarm? Did you approach the idea from your customer's perspective or your own? It is so easy to "talk up" an idea in your head (and in the heads of your colleagues) and before you know it, it morphs into something totally different from what the market actually needs.

How many times have you talked up a project to your superiors, knowing full well that the basic numbers didn't support it? Getting a feel for the potential support from a certain initiative isn't always so tricky. Get close to a representative selection of your customers and a small "straw poll" will often suffice. Why don't we do this more often?

On the flip side, how many times have you tried to dictate the "rules of the game" to your Believers? They have free will, they can choose to stop believing at any time, and the moment you attach some strings to the relationship or go back on previous promises, they will be more likely to drift away. If Apple products suddenly become cumbersome to use, they will lose their believers overnight.

In my opinion, the biggest aspect of retaining your believers is offering them a value-added service that they understand, saying sorry when the service isn't up to scratch and acting on their feedback to delight them even more. Believers are your ideal marketing team—they will spread the word if you deliver what you promise.

I'd like one of those hoverboards please, Santa. I do believe, honest.

# CHAPTER 60

## *Ten Phrases to Motivate Anyone*

Sometimes the right collection of the right words at the right moment can cause a tidal wave of emotion, setting into motion seemingly "impossible" events.

The key to unlocking our potential lies in opening the floodgates of our emotions, rather than appealing to our more rational sides. We can read hundreds of well-researched opinion pieces about the migration crisis in Europe without raising an eyebrow, but we can see a heart-wrenchingly sad photo of a lifeless little toddler washed up on a beach, and our opinion is transformed. Our attention spans are getting ever shorter, and in the age of Snapchat, Periscope, and Twitter, the messages have to be short and powerful to get through to us.

It is the same in the workplace. Long meetings explaining the details of certain projects are being replaced by dynamic and collaborative ways of working in real time. Why talk for a long time about a project if you can get on with it and iterate as you go along? Theory is so twentieth century. Let's get into the thick of the action.

For all the power of an image (this is undeniable), there is still a lot to be said for a well-placed phrase. As with everything, the phrase will only be effective if uttered at an appropriate time and delivered in the right way by the right person. Our "oral tradition" has ensured that the pithy phrases have survived through the generations, and many a grandparent has passed the accumulated wisdom onto their grandchildren. Although they are much-maligned, the most popular "phrases" of some of the most amazing people in our history find their rightful place on social media. You never know who might find themselves at the right place in life to be touched by them.

For me, these ten quotes are ones that I will be passing onto my (hopefully future) grandchildren when I feel that they need an injection of motivation. Encouraging people is one of the richest of life's pursuits, and the following words have kept many a life on the right track or even taken it to a better place:

> *What lies behind us and what lies before us are tiny matters compared to what lies within us.* --Ralph Waldo Emerson

> *The tragedy in life doesn't lie in not reaching your goal. The tragedy lies in having no goal to reach.* —Benjamin Mays

> *Excellence is not an exception, it is a prevailing attitude.* —Charles R. Swindoll

> *Knowing trees, I understand the meaning of patience. Knowing grass, I can appreciate persistence.* —Hal Borland

> *Be patient with yourself. Self-growth is tender; it's holy ground. There's no greater investment.* —Stephen Covey

> *Success consists of going from failure to failure without loss of enthusiasm.* —Winston Churchill

*Successful and unsuccessful people do not vary greatly in their abilities. They vary in their desires to reach their potential. —* John Maxwell

*Out of clutter, find Simplicity. From discord, find Harmony. In the middle of difficulty lies Opportunity.* —Albert Einstein

*You miss 100% of the shots you don't take.* —Wayne Gretzky

*A comfort zone is a beautiful place, but nothing ever grows there.* —Unknown

These few short sentences make me feel warm inside. Words can be truly magical things, but it is what we do with the feelings that they evoke that is the mark of who we are.

# CHAPTER 61

## What to Do When Your Best Isn't Good Enough

You can't be good at everything.

"Why not? Surely if I try hard enough and practice long enough, I can set my mind to achieving anything. I wasn't able to hit a tennis ball a few years back, but now I can play a pretty respectable game. Surely proficiency is born from that magical mix of application and belief. If I try harder and believe in myself more than the other man, why can't I aim for the stars in everything I do?"

I won't often write many cynical blogs, but when I come across these unrealistic dreamers, I often feel an urge to shake them ever so slightly. Shooting for the moon in everything that you do is a sure-fire route to burnout and bitterness. Sometimes in life it is wise to pick your battles, and sometimes it is worth leaving the field for those, who are slightly more accomplished.

May I say it again? You can't be good at everything.

In his book *Outliers*, Malcolm Gladwell writes that it takes 10,000 hours to master any given skill. That is a couple of months more than a year of solid activity. If that is the case (and it feels pretty right to me), you have to be fairly single-minded in what you want to master. Trying to be good at everything will lead you down the garden path of mediocrity, and you will never truly excel at anything. However, when you dedicate your time to become brilliant at something, there will inevitably be other areas where you are less practiced. Lots of other areas, actually…

I would like to say that this is okay with me.

When I come up short in a certain activity, as long as I have completed it to the best of my ability, I don't let any failure bother me. It won't stop me from trying again, and next time my chances of success will be that little bit higher, but I don't jump up and turn my life upside down in an attempt to become brilliant after every failure. Sometimes you need to let the less significant failures wash over you and make sure that you remain standing for the tests that really do matter to you.

Life has so many opportunities to knock you off your course, but in my view, you should only let it get to you when the occasion really matters.

To give a simple example, there are some people who don't excel at public speaking. Please, believe me, I would much rather listen to someone coherently reading from cards than listen to someone's bumbling attempt at off-the-cuff storytelling that often leads nowhere fast. If you are one of these nervous public speakers, simply make sure that you do the basics and get the message across. Spend your time practicing whatever you are passionate about—maybe you enjoy coaching people. The more hours you spend doing that, the more impact you will have on everyone around you. The return on the public speaking "practice" is less clear.

So, when your best isn't good enough, don't sweat it. Go and do something where your best can get even better!

# CHAPTER 62

## *Business Lessons from Black Friday*

The concept of scarcity and the fear of "missing out" can drive the most amazing behaviors. Retailers have exploited this promotional tactic for decades, and it reaches its zenith in the annual Black Friday and Cyber Monday sales.

As a passionate Technophile, I must admit to checking out the savings on the latest gadgets, and as soon as my interest is piqued, the slippery slope beckons. There have been years where both my wife and I have joined the "unwashed masses" and battled elbow to elbow for the best bargains. We have also left stores wondering why exactly we purchased certain items.

The mania of scarcity is all-consuming. If you accept it as a truth, you will be forever in its power. In retail, there is a tangible benefit to this scarcity; there are only 1,000 discounted TVs, and, therefore, they are 50% of the normal price. It made me think of the other applications for "scarcity" in the wider business world.

The classic use that springs to mind is scarcity of time. The moment that you say to someone, "I've only got a minute," it focuses their thoughts so they can get to the point as succinctly as possible. If you say, "Go on, tell me the story," they will likely ramble on for five times longer, ultimately to deliver the same message. The most productive people "chunk" their days into manageable intervals and deliver the maximum number of tasks possible. If you feel that you have five minutes to finish something, it concentrates the mind. If you feel like you have all day, most of the morning will be wasted before you start to worry.

The second (and more insidious) concept at play in the workplace is the scarcity of knowledge. We all feel that knowledge is this mythical power—the more that we know, the more powerful we are. We go to meetings that are nothing to do with our daily activity, we read every single CC email that comes into our inbox, and we feel lost when a round of gossip passes without our participation. We don't need to know 90% of this stuff, but, just like walking past that tempting "pick up line" in the store, we are compelled to gorge ourselves on it. When we chase knowledge that we do not need, we are not only wasting our time, we are wasting the time of those who are kind enough to impart that knowledge.

A third concept could be seen as a scarcity of influence. There are certain people who want to stick their noses into every possible situation, determined to impart their valuable opinion. They feel that if they are involved in every possible decision, they will be able to make the best out of any situation. The opposite situation is where someone quietly sits at their desk, doing the job that they are paid to do; they aren't the "movers and shakers" of the office, but they do not want to be. The best companies are filled to the brim with these "steady eddies." Influence is only useful if you can make a difference with it.

So, in conclusion, use the scarcity of time to drive your productivity, don't worry about your perceived scarcity of (mostly useless) knowledge and finally don't worry if you don't have total control on events around you.

Have fun on Friday and try not to give into the urge too readily.

# CHAPTER 63

## *The Five-Step Mechanics of Creativity*

They are only five words that matter in this chapter, and they are fairly common words at that. For such an inspirational subject as creativity, you might be slightly disappointed. Surely, I could have come up with something a little different.

Well, my friends, the magic of these five words comes in their interpretation, as creativity is a uniquely individual pursuit.

Our brains have been wired by every single action that we have performed since our births; the vast majority of those acts could be seen as a creative choice. How do babies work out how to get Mum to pick them up? How do kids persuade their parents to buy them that ice cream? How does the teenage girl think up excuses to sneak off and see her boyfriend? How does the self-conscious guy pick up the courage to chat up the cute girl at the bar? They learn to be creative in their thinking, they learn from experiences, and they are always open to new ways of doing things.

In all four of these examples above, you could apply the following loop of five words to their thought process: Inspiration, Research, Production, Evaluation, and Incubation.

See, I told you, at first sight pretty boring, right? However, this is exactly how some of the most creative minds in the world came up with some of the most revolutionary concepts.

An apple fell in Newton's mother's garden (there is no evidence to suggest that it fell on his head), and he was inspired to consider the possibility of gravity. Edison famously researched 6,000 materials for the filament of his light bulb at his New Jersey facility before finally settling on carbonized bamboo. Although Ford did not invent the motor car, he did create the first mass production line that made Karl Benz's dream a reality for the masses. Coming into the modern world, I have to mention the *Dragon's Den* television series, which brings the evaluation of various "creations" into our living rooms.

As for the last word, incubation, well, that word is the most important of the lot. It happens through the process and through our lives. It is that moment of calm when nothing else is happening, and everything suddenly falls into place. Take a lunchtime walk through a park in any major global city, and you will see various creative types "getting away from things" and leaving some head space for their next big idea to solidify.

Creativity is indeed a process. It doesn't just happen in the shower—that is mainly for the incubation stage and could prove tricky for producing anything. It tends to follow the four first stages, with bouts of incubation sprinkled throughout. Research is difficult if the initial idea is not suitably inspiring, and production will be stuttering at best if the proper research has not been done.

Having said this, the most creative people are so creative that this all comes as second nature. They have hundreds of creative thoughts in their heads at any one time, and each thought is at one of the five stages of development (roughly speaking). You might still just be able to discern a mechanical process, but if you were able to read every thought inside their heads, it would all blend into a blur of brilliance.

When someone is in the creative "zone," all sorts of wonderful things can happen. Creativity is a habit, the more you do it, the easier it will come. Next time inspiration hits you, don't resist the urge.

You never know where it might take you.

# CHAPTER 64

## *Time for a Hackathon in Your Head*

Contrary to popular belief, we are not hard-wired to do anything. There is no genetic blueprint that insists that we must act in a certain way all our lives. We may have certain personality tendencies, but nothing is truly set in stone. With fertile ground, nurture wins over nature every time.

Disrupting the "wiring" in your brain is also not as hard as it sounds. Tech companies famously let their most talented employees loose in Hackathons, where they disregard the accepted norms, forget their day jobs and raise the bar past what they previously thought possible.

That is what a Hackathon in your head might look like: moving a certain thought process from impossible to possible.

Easy to say, but how do you go about doing it?

Let's start with a concrete example. You are having a tough time in life, and everything seems to be shrouded in shades of black and grey. We've all been there at one point or another. How is it possible to hack into these negative thoughts and usher them in a more positive direction?

In order to consider this properly, we have to go a level deeper, as there are lots of different types of negative thinking. Let's say that you consistently see yourself in a negative light. You feel like a failure inside and that if people knew the "real you" that they wouldn't like you. This is one of the most debilitating thoughts in our heads, and it pops up more often than we would all like to admit.

There is a thought process that might be helpful in this situation, and it can also be used to "hack" all sorts of other obstacles to leading a contented life. In every hack, you have to understand and accept the reality, take it apart and then put together a new and improved solution.

The situation: I made a mistake, and I blame myself.

Split-second thought. Here we go again; people must hate me for this.

Origin of thought. My childhood was filled with the fear of letting people down.

Challenge yourself. No one is perfect. Everyone makes mistakes. Maybe the key is to learn from it rather than wallowing in it. Maybe I'm too hard on myself.

Consequences? If I keep thinking negatively about myself, I will damage my relationships and even my health.

Positive thoughts. A mistake is not a failure—I am successful in many ways.

Take action. The next time I make a mistake, I will focus on the practical aspects of what I can learn from it rather than languish in self-recrimination.

This thought process happens in our heads hundreds of times each day. It may skip some of the steps, but essentially, our lives are full of situations, thoughts, challenges, consequences, and actions. It is absolutely in our power to change our thinking (and the results) within each of these steps, and under no circumstances should we feel that we are stuck in a self-fulfilling prophecy of behavior.

A (musical) record that is never broken gets that little harder to break every time you play it. If you have a habit of breaking and then re-recording records, then the boundaries of your potential will stretch that little bit further every time.

Think about having a Hackathon in your head every now and again. Your life will be all the richer for it.

# CHAPTER 65

## *Don't Take Things So Personally*

Once emotions are let loose, they are open to interpretation.

Many of us (myself included) have a tendency to overthink things. We see ourselves at the center of our own little universe and tend to assume that things revolve around us a little more than they do. I'm not sure that I would call it paranoia, but to a small extent that is what I am talking about. When someone gets angry, we wonder if we have contributed to it. If someone is disappointed, we hope that we haven't let them down. I am sure that you can think of some other examples.

The emotionally charged office is not an easy place for the insecure minds amongst us—and let's face it, that is most of us at some time or another. For some of us, it takes a superhuman effort not to get involved in all the emotional games. It is all too easy to fall victim to emotional Chinese whispers in a competitive office environment. The moment you show that you are prone to caring about what other people say and think (even if it doesn't concern you directly), you become a pawn for the manipulative politicians of the office. When you take things like this personally, that is when the bullies have a field day.

However, it is not only the bullies that can get under your skin. In the heat of the moment, it is so easy for even the most innocent of comments to be taken the wrong way. This is when you have to listen to the words and seek the meaning underneath the emotions.

Your boss may be having a tough day, but when he fixes his gaze on you in that meeting and says that some people need to pull their socks up, don't automatically assume that he is talking about you. If there are no grounds for him to think that, you don't have anything to worry about. Even so, he looked at you, he seemed upset—maybe you have misread things.

You also need to see the bigger picture. If your boss does this on a regular basis and seems to "pick on" people indiscriminately, then you can look at the situation a little more dispassionately. It's not you, it's them. So simple, so true, but so hard to tell yourself when your skin is so thin.

There is much more to this issue than telling someone to "ignore" the emotional messages that they don't agree with, but actually the trick to a thicker skin is relatively simple. When you feel "under attack" for whatever reason, try to understand what they are saying rather than how they are saying it. Ignore the tone of their voice, their facial expressions and their clenched fists. Don't overanalyze why they seem emotional. Just think about the message rather than the way that it is being delivered. That way, you'll get the information that you need, but will be able to filter out the (sometimes) unhelpful emotions.

In conclusion, yes, leaders can get emotional, but only when the emotions are consistent with the message that they are trying to get across. Otherwise, emotions have a tendency to cloud the issue.

# CHAPTER 66

## *Look in a Mirror Before You Judge*

This is simple common sense, drummed into us from our childhood, but it is nonetheless sometimes forgotten in the relentless dog-eat-dog business world.

Everyone is on a journey in their respective careers. Everyone will be traveling to different destinations at different speeds, and you can be sure that each of them will have their own unique set of obstacles in their head to overcome before they get there.

We have all criticized people for things that we were once criticized for. We have all made the same mistakes and learned the same lessons. Experience is often the key factor in top performance, and mistakes are the currency of eventual success. On the sixth attempt to reach a given goal, your journey is crucially informed by the wrong turns of the past.

You will rarely get anywhere without making mistakes.

Therefore, it is particularly disappointing when a "know-it-all" colleague or superior takes pleasure in pointing them out. These people think that they are helping the individual concerned, but more often than not, they are perfectly aware of their errors and what they need to do to rectify them. They will then make every effort not to repeat things next time. However, these self-righteous types insist on rubbing it in: "I wouldn't have done that if I were you," or "Are you aware of the consequences of what you have just done?"

The thing is, you can bet that these people made the same mistakes themselves at an earlier point and were handed the same critical treatment from above. They improved in the job and somehow came to see the criticism as a part of their growth, and, therefore, didn't have a problem with judging and criticizing others further along the line.

This circle of judgment can be broken.

We should all try to put ourselves in other people's shoes that little bit more, looking in the mirror and imagining ourselves in their situation. If we are honest with ourselves, much of the time we would have done the same thing. What, therefore, gives us a right to criticize them? Would empathy and a supportive word not be a more useful solution? When you make people feel better about their mistakes, they will be open to risking other mistakes. When you vilify and criticize them, they will be far more careful in the future.

When we judge and criticize people, we knock one more little nail into their armor of self-confidence. As that armor weakens, they will attempt fewer and fewer difficult things and, as a consequence, their personal growth will grind to a halt. If you believe that constant criticism is helpful for someone, just think how you would react if you were subjected to a barrage of advice and opinions all the time.

You would go into your shell and not venture out for a while.

All this is pretty easy to write down on this page, but far harder to accomplish in practice. Everyone has targets, everyone's performance is closely linked with the performance of others, but if we all were just to look in that mirror a bit more often before we judged someone, maybe, just maybe, we would be giving someone the space to grow.

# CHAPTER 67

## *The Ten Keys to Unlocking Inspiration*

When momentum starts to wane, inspiration is often the last hope to get you over that last hurdle. So many projects are consigned to the scrap heap because they lacked that final killer idea. Careers falter because people become disillusioned, unable to see a way out of the monotony. The jigsaw of life is often fatally incomplete without that final piece.

Inspiration is that intangible spark that comes from nowhere and can transform our thinking and light the way for our actions. It is not something that you can seek out, as it has no "permanent residence," but I do believe that you can do certain things to unlock your mind and welcome it with open arms when it does appear. Here are a few things that work for me when I need that extra shot in the arm:

***Write it down.*** When you write something down, it assumes extra significance, and I find that it helps me connect the dots and visualize what is missing. The mere process of writing something down forces you to slow down to the pace of your typing, and in those gaps between pen strokes (or key presses), useful thoughts can often materialize.

***Think like a genius.*** This is a creative thinking tool to get you out of your "way of thinking" and into the brain of someone else. Go and read an autobiography of someone that you admire. It may be Steve Jobs, Richard Branson, or Sheryl Sandberg—anyone whose thinking you admire. Get into their heads, imagine why they made certain decisions, and then think about your problems through their eyes. Different perspectives can work wonders.

***Phone a friend.*** Sometimes, you need the help of someone who knows you to get out of a "broken record" mindset. It is easy to overthink problems and convince yourself of certain "truths" about a situation when actually the reality is a little different. A friend who understands your personality might be able to guide you towards a different solution.

***Get moving.*** The links between brain function and physical exercise have been well documented. Many studies have suggested that the parts of the brain that control thinking and memory (the prefrontal cortex and medial temporal cortex) have greater volume in people who exercise versus people who don't. The mere act of exercising can help clear your mind and assist you to make better decisions.

***Distance yourself.*** Hard as it might be, spend a few days away from the problem. Go and do something entirely different, and you will often come back with a new perspective. This helps you to press the reset button inside your head and lets you view the issue with fresh eyes.

***Doodle.*** Doodling unlocks your creativity, enhances your memory and lights up neural networks that allow for cognitive breakthroughs that otherwise would have been lost in a daydream. It gives the mind a "white noise" background to the problem and can allow you to visualize complex ideas. Steve Jobs was an avid doodler—I don't think you require any more persuasion. Here is how Wikipedia describes doodling:

*A doodle is a drawing made while a person's attention is otherwise occupied. Doodles are simple drawings that can have concrete representational meaning or may just be abstract shapes. Stereotypical examples of doodling are found in school notebooks, often in the margins, drawn by students daydreaming or losing interest during class. Other common examples of doodling are produced during long telephone conversations if a pen and paper are available.*

***Forget perfect.*** Shooting for the moon is a worthy occupation, but if you aren't realistic about your goals, you will always fall short. Inspiration for something that is impossible will be impossible to come by and could end up disillusioning you to such an extent that you don't even achieve what may have been possible.

***Find a quiet place.*** Meditation provides a sense of calm, peace, and balance—crucial when preparing yourself to work through a difficult problem. Finding a quiet place to think through problems is important, but creating a quiet place inside your brain is even more important. It reduces the stress that you are feeling and helps you control those thoughts that are running around your head.

***Start afresh.*** When you have invested so much time and mental energy into a problem, it is hard to crumple up the piece of paper and throw it in the trash. It is often the case, however, that this is the only way forward. If you learn from the failure, you are never going to start with an entirely blank piece of paper. You will start with your past lessons in the back of your mind.

***Question everything.*** Who? What? Where? Why? When? Working out why you are taking the direction that you are taking can often provide side roads to other potential destinations. Living an unquestioned life will never allow you to fulfill your potential. If nothing is worrying you, you are not pushing your limits.

These ten things work for me. How do you get past your own road-blocks and find your inspiration?

# CHAPTER 68

## *Productivity Hacks from Cheeseburgers*

I had a friend in college who was rather proficient at eating cheeseburgers. Lots of cheeseburgers. And boy, could he get them down quickly. I think that he did it to impress the girls, although I'm not sure how attractive it actually was in retrospect. But, to give him his dues, he had a talent.

He is now a successful management consultant, juggling various projects, priorities, and demands like those proverbial cheeseburgers back in the day. We met up the other day, had a beer and popped into a local diner for "old times sake."

He then let me into the secret…

No, his old party trick does not impress his clients, but there is a lesson that he learned from his cheeseburger eating that helps him to this day.

You have to take small and manageable bites, eat quickly, and the process will flow. If you take large bites, your saliva will take over, and your mouth will become a sticky mess of meat, cheese, and bread. Chewing a small amount and swallowing little and often was the key to success.

It is the same when he manages his project work. When you are faced with a complex project, the best method is to break it into chunks and tackle each aspect until you have reached a satisfactory outcome (or next step). Then you can move onto the next part.

This also goes for the time that he allocates to everything in his day.

There is a famous method called the Pomodoro Technique, invented by Francesco Cirillo, which teaches the individual to work with "chunks" of time in a constructive way, rather than in a race. In this method, there are 25-minute intervals in which a piece of work can be accomplished. You split your day into respective chunks of time (the Pomodoro Technique), with small breaks in between each one and the odd larger break at less regular intervals. You then look at what you need to accomplish and allocate various amounts of Pomodoro to get it done.

Checking your emails might take two Pomodoros (50 minutes). Writing a business plan might be three Pomodoros (75 minutes). A meeting might be one Pomodoro (25 minutes). The idea is that the moment the Pomodoro is over, you stop and have your break. You should accomplish what you plan in the given time, not be over ambitious, and the regular break will ensure that your mind stays fresh.

He swears by it, and it makes lots of sense.

He used to eat a single cheeseburger in four bites and would never put another quarter in until the first quarter had been swallowed in its entirety. That takes true patience and iron discipline.

No wonder he is so accomplished at managing his time!

# CHAPTER 69

## *Your Imperfections Are Your Competitive Advantage*

I am sure that you have all heard the phrase that your strengths can be your weaknesses.

You are a quick thinker, but that might make you impulsive. You view yourself as being self-confident, but some might interpret it as arrogance. You always try to be positive, but many view your optimism as being unrealistic. You might view your patience as a virtue, but others might be frustrated by your indecisiveness.

The list goes on and on. There is nearly always a flip side to the coin, but it is interesting that we nearly always look at this phenomenon from this viewpoint. Strengths can indeed be weaknesses, and we guard against succumbing to those weaknesses in certain circumstances. However, it is rare that we view our weaknesses as potential strengths. In certain situations, this is equally true, but most of us fail to take advantage of it. This seems counter-intuitive, but if you think about a few examples, actually, I believe that there is something in it. In your self-dialogue and your dialogue with others, start repackaging your weaknesses as strengths, and soon that is how others will perceive them too.

Imagine the following water cooler conversation with two colleagues talking about you:

"I can't believe how stubborn he was in that meeting. He just stuck to his opinion and wouldn't be moved by any argument. Sometimes you have to be a bit more flexible."

"I agree, but at least he isn't blind to it. I saw him stick to his guns and convince a supplier not to leave us the other day. A less determined person would have taken the easy route and walked out of the meeting."

"I suppose that you can't have it both ways. It is easy to poke holes at the weaknesses and then take the corresponding strengths for granted."

Wouldn't you love to give them more opportunities to see your weaknesses as strengths? If they do, you will be forgiven for the negative aspects of your weaknesses far more often.

This is possible to do from a place of humility and self-awareness. When you are talking about your day, be sure to throw into the conversation how stubborn you were in that meeting, but explain why you behaved that way. You chase what you believe in, and never give up. When people understand the reasons behind the behavior, they will be able to interpret your victories in the same way. Your successful persuasion of the supplier was a result of the same behavior, but this time with a positive outcome.

You can't have one without the other. If you are aware of your weaknesses, try to use them as strengths as often as possible, and you will find that the people around you become that little bit more forgiving.

I'd like to leave you with one last thought to ponder. Our weaknesses are the most natural behaviors that we have. We all work hard to develop our strengths, but our weaknesses are naturally there. They are part of what makes us who we are. We may have been a little stubborn all of our lives, but to turn this into dedication isn't such a big step. On the other hand, there may be other strengths that we aspire to, where we don't have a natural affinity. These are far harder to acquire.

The step from a weakness to strength isn't a big one. Maybe that is where we should be focusing our self-development efforts rather than chasing unnatural targets.

# CHAPTER 70

## *Personal Branding: The Power of You*

In 2001, I co-authored a book published by McGraw-Hill called *M-Commerce Security*. Post publication, I was invited by leading universities and companies nationwide to lecture, participate in discussions, and share my knowledge. I had a great time and felt alive sharing my ideas. I felt I was making a difference. I wish I had continued to remain foolish. As time passed, I became more and more passive, focusing on my career and started consuming canned content like everybody else, reading copious amounts of leading publications online. With time, I realized how exhausted I had become from all the specious content that had consumed my life. Now I just do not know what is real online and what isn't, so I have started to consume more content that reaches me directly from the writer without having to go through a traditional editorial filter. I have also started to write and get back to communicating my thoughts in the form of blogs and articles.

It wasn't too long ago that everyday people built their reputation on respect, wisdom, and fairness, by good, old-fashioned hard work, sweat, and experience. Celebrity is grossly overstated in this new digital world. People with no real talent other than some odd fascination from consumers who retweet their tweets have ended up with large numbers of followers and a false sense of vanity. I call it fake celebrity, and social media has helped amplify this deception.

In the modern world of Internet and smartphones, the need for authentic personal branding has never been greater. Thankfully, this latest trend is more than just another axiom. Personal branding done right can give an individual or small business the power to defeat a large corporation in a modern David vs. Goliath story. Personal branding is essentially about you and your personality, bringing a unique and authentic voice to this world. Large corporations are getting caught up in red tape and are slow to move forward. Replying to a simple tweet has become a major task and questions like, "Does this meet the new social media policy requirement?" have become the norm. Individuals and SMBs that are not restrained by these shackles are changing the digital landscape and leaving the more established companies at bay. Although ad agencies and PR firms are busy trying to shore up the brand equity of their client companies, it is individuals and people-run-SMBs who the masses are relating to in this new online world.

Reports that technology separates rather than unites us are significantly inflated and camouflage the real truth that audiences are buying into people rather than brands. For instance, Virgin Mobile has 198,000 followers on Twitter, while Richard Branson has 6.24 million. This is a perfect example that illustrates how it is the person and personality that resonates with people more than the brand.

In many ways, it feels like we have become our own PR managers who manage our online image to ensure it sends out the right message about us. The resulting image is usually an diluted version of how we would like to be perceived; pretending to be something you are not is the worst mistake one could make.

Thankfully, the days of judging a person's online influence from a number next to their profile is increasingly becoming irrelevant. Technology is helping the online community create digital tribes where people with similar interests also share experiences and learn from each other.

Hundreds of years ago, tribes would migrate to different parts of the world and communities would evolve. It's fascinating to see how we have come full circle as a human race and how technology is enabling the same tribal behavior of our ancestors to break down barriers and build alliances through networks all over the world.

Our worldview has been built around what traditional media has presented to us since our childhood. However, we are now beginning to communicate and work with people all over the world who challenge our thought process and begin to question stereotypes as we evolve through our own personal experience and understanding. We also do not need to passively consume all the re-tweeted and ricocheted commentary on social media from what it deems to be "popular" personalities amplified by social echo-mongers.

There is new hunger for original, authentic content, a thirst for learning from those around us who may not be major celebrities or social media butterflies but whose lives make a difference and help change the world one day at a time. The collective total of such everyday people and their stories is what new media and journalism is about. Be authentic, and don't make the mistake of creating a personal brand that is completely unrealistic or fake. Our interests and values will change as we mature and as experiences shape us in life.

Both businesses and people need to stop being concerned about perceived self-image and celebrate how unique each and every one of us is and the value we bring by simply being ourselves. Content creators who are blogging, podcasting, or even writing articles are all enjoying fantastic success by simply being themselves.

The big question is when are you going to start?

# CHAPTER 71

## *Desperate Thirst for Exclusivity*

The world's worst kept secret is that much of Apple's success can be attributed to a rather unsubtle use of a marketing strategy known as the Exclusivity Technique. However, the internet is supposed to be inclusive, and a new website has appeared on the scene amusingly titled the *Most Exclusive Website*, which pokes fun at our desire to be part of an exclusive club.

The concept is simple, only one person is allowed into the website at a time, and to access it, you need to visit www.mostexclusivewebsite.com and pick up a virtual ticket just as you would at your local DMV for a driver's license. You then wait your turn to enter the mysterious website.

Every 60 seconds a ticket-holder is admitted, and the line moves forward; I am currently #51,062 in this virtual queue, and over 2 million people have frequented this line hoping to be exclusive.

The site's maker Justin Foley said to the Washington Post, "The Internet was designed to be open and accessible; what if I made a website that was the antithesis of one of the defining qualities of the Internet?"

Only one in nine people is supposed to be still around when their number is finally called out. This leaves only a handful people who know exactly what happens when you enter the website, and that's the power of exclusivity.

Internet behavior will ensure many people will leave a tab open so they can tweet, "I visited the site," until the next online fad appears on the scene. Or maybe there lies a serious message behind our weakness for exclusivity.

In the early days, Apple deliberately restricted the availability of their iPhones to create desirability, and a media feeding frenzy ensued, fueling the infectious want-factor for the must-have gadget. This phenomenon equally creates another opposing faction that despises a group of individuals who appear blindly fanatical about a product.

Although encouraging the creation of two opposing groups who either love or hate their products might seem crazy at first, it's important to remember that this conflict ensures Apple is always in the spotlight. Heated discussions continue to dominate conversations, forums, and blog posts across the world.

A perfect example of the exclusivity technique in action is the recent curated orchestration of the Apple Music release; the online community has fiercely debated the pros and cons of the music streaming service.

The illusion of exclusivity has long been exploited by countless luxury brands to attract consumers by making them believe that their products or services will allow access to some peerless, elite world.

Tapping into the aspirations of an audience desperate for being part of "the club" is a proven method of increasing sales. We are constantly told we need to manage our personal brand, and many choose to do this by surrounding themselves with luxury brands that fit their chosen aesthetic.

Brittany Mills, Director of Client Services for B Culture Media in Atlanta says, "A strong brand image is so important for luxury brands because at the end of the day, an affluent customer is not only buying their product, they are buying into the lifestyle that they portray."

When first discovering the concept of the website www.mostexclusivewebsite.com, you will probably shake your head in disbelief, consider moving on, and think there's nothing to see here. But if you dig a little deeper, you will probably find yourself thinking why so many people are relentlessly lining up on this site and chasing the meaningless pursuit of exclusivity.

Maybe the silly website that only allows one person in the world at any given time is actually teaching us all a lesson on the illusion of exclusivity. The use of products and exclusive attitudes as trophies to measure our material and social success ultimately leads to a shallow and unhappy existence.

# CHAPTER 72

## Understanding the Dynamics of Groups at Work

People act quite differently when they are in groups versus when they are alone. When you are in a position to lead a group of people, you begin to see just how different they are and how difficult it can be. From the inside of a group, mitigating disparities, disagreements, expectations, and perceptions can also pose a challenge. This tends to be the case no matter the group.

Be that as it may, learning to enrich the people around us is pivotal to success and happiness. As the adage goes, "You are the company you keep." What the adage fails to convey is that the company keeps you too, and therein lies the opportunity to change it.

In this chapter, I explore three common problems that stonewall group dynamics and present solutions inspired by a collaborative and adaptive approach to relationship building.

### Groups Are Social and That's a Good Thing

I have a few words by way of social psychology.

A saving grace of group dynamics is that the longer a group stays together, the longer the people in it begin to think, act, and live similarly. That's referred to as social cohesion, the stuff of culture.

An established culture allows for identity forming. In other words, you see yourself reflected—either in whole or in part—in the group's members. People derive a great sense of purpose and satisfaction from group identity. The lines can be drawn just about any which way, starting with the more obvious similarities and tapping deep into those that are imperceptible yet lived.

This is a double-edge sword, however. Social cohesion and group identity can cut both ways; it can generate harmony, pleasure, safety, and strength, but it can also generate bias, prejudice, and "us versus them" mentalities, as well as stifle creativity and innovation.

That is why leaders are crucial. Leaders are meant to provide perspective, guide, council, nurture, and grant confidence among group members. Of course, history has shown us that leadership can take many forms—the means and ends vary colorfully.

Sometimes, a leader is blinded by their own interests, biases, and groupthink. That's when coaches and advisors come into play. They should operate on the outside, while keeping the group's best interests in mind.

What is the point of all that work? Being a leader, being in a group, getting advice—it's daunting and cumbersome. Why do it at all?

The answer is easy. Because undeniably, coordinated groups of people can accomplish amazing feats. Whether commendable or not, the magnitude of a group's concerted efforts usually surpasses that of a single person.

That's why every person in a group plays a special role just by virtue of being in it.

Now that we've got the housekeeping out of the way, let's talk about those problems and how to address them.

## Do We Have a Common Goal?

I'll save the preamble and just jump into this one. One of a group's most poisonous problems is **lack of purpose**.

Individuals alone can suffer from lack of purpose, but when you magnify the volume of people, you magnify the problem.

Often a simple conversation about purpose, goals, or objectives can open up into a discussion about preferences, ideals, dreams, and the like. It's a beautiful thing, and when it's handled with care, it can invigorate group members and set everyone on a course toward success.

Being trained on purpose can become an approach in and of itself. When done right, it can inspire people and foster higher levels of shared enthusiasm, decision-making, performance, participation, and morale.

There are **three** fundamental axioms that comprise this group dynamic:

1. *Mutual Accountability.* In a word, ground-rules. Successful groups openly discuss and establish ground-rules. By collectively establishing rules of proper conduct, expectations, penalties, and principles, the group can comfortably check itself and its members when failings arise. Mutual accountability based on the open discussion of ground-rules tends to be more egalitarian and more difficult to argue against. If you agreed to something, then you are accountable for it.

2. *Shared Contribution.* Each person must be committed to the group's betterment. Sometimes that will mean spending extra time, extra effort, and extra work. If the whole group is willing to share the effort and work together toward this aim, individual frustrations can be mollified quickly. When each person feels that everyone is sharing and contributing equally, it inoculates each individual against resentments. Everyone shares the work; everyone shares the glory.

3. *Shared Values.* Every person is unique. Nowhere is this more the case than in the ambit of values. Many conflicts and arguments stem from

value incongruities. They aren't irreconcilable, though. An open recognition of value differences, and an attitude toward finding common ground in a respectful and considerate way can lead people to the same goal, even if they take different paths.

## "Is Our Group Too Big?"

More people, more problems. A group can get too large for its own good. That varies from context to context, but sensitivity to size is ubiquitously important.

When groups get too large, people tend to get lost in them. That undercuts mutual accountability, shared contribution, and makes finding middle ground problematic. That alone can cause rifts between group members, which can go unchecked until they erupt.

Groups would be wise to consider the following tactics and manage group size with an eye toward effectiveness and social cohesion.

***Downsize your groups.*** I think the sweet number is 12. When you are just forming a group, getting to that number is easier. When you have a large group already, aim to sub-divide your clan into 12-person groups that are in communication with one another, yet not necessarily dependent on each other.

***The resource member method.*** The resource member method is simply having a core group that dabbles in all the satellite groups. It serves as the central control, without actually exerting control, but rather facilitates communication, enables discussion, and addresses issues as they arise.

***Intelligent grouping.*** Just having groups of 12 people isn't enough. The way in which people are grouped and sub-divided needs to be purposeful, and purpose-driven. The guiding star of the group must determine who needs to be there and who doesn't such that the group will function efficiently and with a high degree of specialty.

## "Do We Allow a Diversity of Ideas?"

Under the right circumstances, groups are markedly more intelligent and able when it comes to decision-making than single individuals. James Surowiecki's research in *The Wisdom of Crowds* points out that the group is not more able than every single person, yet it is rare that the same person will be right as consistently as the group.

That is the benefit of a healthy diversity of ideas, skills, and experiences. When people take guesses, the aggregate of their guesses reflect reality better than a single individual's could. That's a potent revelation, and a strong indicator of the benefit of cultivating groups with varied perspectives.

A prevalent problem in groups isn't just the suppression of ideas and perspectives, but some social, cognitive pitfalls. People in groups commonly sabotage themselves in the following ways:

***Social Proof.*** People tend to assume that if many people are doing something, there must be a reason. That's why a crowd becomes more influential as it grows.

***Herding.*** People stick with the crowd because it is less risky than doing something radical that could fail enormously, or that could prompt social backlash.

***Information Cascades.*** People with different information, much of it imperfect, make decisions in sequence because they believe that their information accrues to truth. They are making decisions using prior knowledge with the assumption that their predecessors knew something that they don't. This can undermine critical thinking. It's called traditionalism.

Despite these pitfalls, imitating others instead of undertaking complicated calculations before every action is a rational response to our own limits. Used prudently, it is a powerful tool for spreading good ideas fast.

And yet, people must recognize when to stop imitating and act independently when the benefits are high enough. Intelligent imitation depends on an initially wide array of options and information, as well as the willingness of at least some people to put their own judgment ahead of the group's.

## A Group Must Operate as a Group

A group, at its heart, is a collection of people who collaborate or interact in some way. Technology has facilitated collaboration immensely. It has allowed people to share at high-speed, explore alternatives rapidly, and review a gamut of possibilities with greater accuracy.

Putting collaborative technology at a group's disposal can reduce some of the strain of group dynamics through systematization. However, the important thing is to ensure that the group operates as a group. Each person must identify with the group in some way; otherwise they'll never feel a part of it.

A common pain, respect for a central figure, recognition of the expertise of others, passionate leaders, a clearly defined purpose, mutual accountability, transparency—those are the vital ingredients of a healthy group dynamic.

# CHAPTER 73

## Company Culture & the Public Image

I have spent a substantial amount of time considering the threats of specialization to the health of departments within a company. Upon further reflection, I realized that the way we divide departments and the lines of communication that we establish between them have a fundamental connection to public perception.

In general, the existence of departments and the sub-divisions therein stem from a view toward efficacy and productivity. The threat there lies in the latent value-assumptions that those divisions reflect and promote. Since separations of power based on traditional corporate hierarchies are out of touch with today's values, they can disrupt a business's internal culture and create discrepancies between that culture and the business's public image.

### The Threat of Specialization

Historically, companies have improved productivity and quality by designing specialized positions for each necessary step in a production line. The people assigned to those specialized positions are called specialists.

The threat inherent in specialization is that each specialist operates in a vacuum. The specialist can indeed minimize error, enhance quality, and gain intimate knowledge of their step; however, these benefits are also blinders. The narrowness of focus inhibits a purview of the organization as a whole.

To ameliorate this, the company must deliberately promote awareness of the bigger picture among all of its employees.

## The Artist's Eye

Like an artist painting a picture, sometimes we have to take a step back and look at what we've done. The complaint that companies—especially corporate entities—are soul sucking arises in part because of a lack of perspective.

Certainly, the nature and dealings of some companies are questionable. And yet, there are some that are doing great things that few people know about, including the people in the company itself. I do not want to endorse or deride any specific companies here, but I think the point is well taken.

## The Call is Coming from Inside the House

The people who spend hours, days, weeks, and months within a company will unavoidably discuss the company in public.

Today, public takes many forms. The avenues and platforms of public discourse are places where a narrative can take on a life of its own. If the company does not promote an internal narrative that conveys a broad and multi-faceted perspective of the company, then the public narrative will be even narrower.

This internal narrative has a profound connection to the threat of specialization. If specialists feel an overarching sense of purpose, their connection to each other and to the company will grow stronger. More to the point, with this increase in connectedness, the broader perspective will naturally come into focus.

This internal narrative will spill out into public view, shaping discourse and perceptions, and eventually, customer value and experience.

Though, all this must start from within the company.

## As Within, so Without

In business, there are two competing structural approaches: inside-out and outside-in. The inside-out approach places the locus of success within the company, e.g., company resources, company culture, etc. The outside-in approach places the locus of success outside the company, e.g., customer experience, customer value, etc. Each of these approaches manifests itself in different corporate practices and corporate goals.

## Inside or Outside

The outside-in driven CEO may devote most of their time to marketing, enhancing delivery, product quality, and making every facet of the business user-friendly.

The inside-out driven CEO may devote most of their time to harnessing internal resources, reducing corporate expenses, and implementing procedural overhauls.

To me, these approaches are two sides of the same coin. In either case, choosing one over the other can put you in a precarious position because you risk ignoring a crucial human element of your company.

## The Grand Canyon

Specialization alone creates distances among people, departments, and the public. By forsaking one business approach for the other, you either ignore your customers or your employees. This can increase the distance between the people who make your company what it is.

What's worse, your customers can sense this, because today, nothing stays private for long.

## The Same but Different

The distinctions between internal and external, private and public, are blurred, if not eroded. Entities of all sorts struggle to plug up holes through which private information can escape into the public view.

To some extent, this is a good thing. Transparency is valued at all levels of complexity, from interpersonal interactions to international relations. In the context of business, rather than combat this social phenomenon, why not harness it to shape the public narrative about your company?

## Bridge the Gap

When you uphold transparency, cultivate fruitful lines of communication within the company, and promote customer reciprocity, all as company values, it aligns your specialists with your public image, thereby creating a shared internal and public narrative.

## Inside the Company

When it comes to the gaps that emerge between specialists in separate departments or between isolated individuals in the same department, the goal should be to create fertile lines of communication, enriched by pervasive company values, and aimed at reaping nourishment from the insights of employees and customers alike.

## Outside the Company

This can be done inside of the company, and it can be done outside of it too. The juncture of these two lines of communication is a bridge that connects a company to its customer by way of its specialists. By bridging this gap, you invite customers to participate in shaping the company, building loyalty, confidence, and relatability.

## The Company as Human

What I envision here is not some Elysian corporate environment where the bottom-line and productivity are sidelined. In fact, many companies are already instilling the values of shared learning, creative exploration, and customer feedback into their business models.

What I do envision is a corporate environment that thinks functionally and humanly about its resources and its public image. For some time now, the jury has been out on whether companies are human or non-human entities. These steps toward letting our companies be represented by our employees and letting our employees represent our companies will certainly affect the debate.

There are tremendous benefits, both in terms of productivity and in terms of business success, to extolling the human elements in our companies.

## Conclusion

The outside-in and inside-out approaches create a false dichotomy. This dichotomy expands the rifts created by specialization, increasing its threats, and further disconnecting companies from their employees and their customers.

Companies that want to have greater control over their public perception should start from within, promoting company values that align themselves with employee and customer interests, so that their products can enjoy the benefits of good public will.

# CHAPTER 74

## *How to Deal with Conflict at Work*

It seems particularly apropos given our current political and social climate to pay lip service to conflict. We have to deal with it often, despite our best attempts to avoid it. Fortunately, some conflict is minor and innocuous, yet other conflicts are incendiary and damaging.

No matter the scale, the consequence, or the context, understanding how to deal with conflict at any stage is a life skill. I know that some people are even crippled by the thought of conflict. I think that any conflict-related fears arise because we are never taught how to grapple with such moments. It's a shame, and perhaps graver situations could be avoided were we imparted with conflict resolution and avoidance strategies at an early age.

Thankfully, there is no time like the present to pick up a few new tricks. In this chapter, I will share with you my understanding of conflict and some conflict resolution strategies that have worked for me.

### The Two Roots of Conflict

Generally, conflict arises from incompatibilities in goals or perspectives between two or more parties. Conflict can also arise when two or more parties pull from the same pool of resources. For the purposes of this article, this very basic understanding of conflict is enough to get us through. However, if you are curious for a deeper analysis of the roots of conflict, I recommend Howard M. Guttman's book on the subject, *When Goliaths Clash.*

In any human context where people must interact to accomplish goals, conflict is unavoidable. That's perfectly acceptable. Conflict avoidance at all costs is not the antidote, however. The best way to defuse conflict is with an attitude toward peaceable exchange and the mutual satisfaction of all parties involved. Some would call this diplomacy.

In simple terms, there are two main provenances for conflict, be it in personal relationships or business relationships.

***Individual Differences.*** Each person brings a mixed and varied bag of wants, needs, values, beliefs, opinions, assumptions, and interpretations to the table in any given situation. Chances are there will be disparities between two people on at least one of those fronts. This can be a source of conflict, and contingent upon the nature of that disparity, it can be a source of great conflict.

Be that as it may, we don't have to combat someone who is at odds with us on one or more of those points. The key to successful communication in those instances is depersonalization. Remind yourself that although what the person says may relate to you or undercut your beliefs, it isn't about you until they make it about you. This can keep you from getting defensive, which then forces the other person to put their guard up. Stay calm, stay depersonalized, and stay clear headed.

***Stylistic Clashes.*** Style can mean a number of things. In my mind, style refers to the mode of communication or how people speak. That spans the gamut of tone, language, reasoning, attitude, bodily cues, and so on. There are many conflicts that crop up or are exacerbated by stylistic differences.

Although this might appear trivial, packaging is very important to us human beings. The way we communicate largely affects how we are perceived, how our ideas are received, and how likely we are to accomplish our goals. Consider that rhetoric was an art back in ancient Greece and Rome. They too recognized the power of packaging in communication.

That is my best attempt to capture the two main sources of conflict as I see them. Surely there are many more, but those suffice for now. By way of framework, let's explore the substantive features of conflict.

## Two Types of Conflict

Most conflicts can be grouped into one of two types. The benefit of being able to identify what kind of conflict we may find ourselves in is that it gives us some healthy distance and helps us decide how to reconcile it.

1. *Manifest Conflict.* This is the type of conflict most people envision when they hear the word "conflict." It's in your face disagreement between two or more people. This can happen between co-workers, family members, lovers—you name it. This kind of conflict tends to escalate quickly, and people tend to shut down, staying in their corners without giving in. The word that epitomizes where both people err in manifest conflict is competition.

2. *Latent Conflict.* Latent conflict is much more difficult to diagnose. This type of conflict is characterized by an inability to communicate openly about the source of conflict or the emotions that it prods. Perhaps the subject matter is too sensitive, or the power dynamics preclude dialogue, so people tend to find others ways of venting their frustrations. The problem is that those accrue at the subconscious level. Small jabs, sarcastic jokes, sabotage, and lack of cooperation are all steam being let out from a latent conflict that just wants to see the light of day.

Now that we have covered some common sources of conflict and the way in which they play out, we are ready to move on to conflict resolution. Of course, every conflict is unique because the people in it are unique. That is why each conflict plays out slightly differently, but the attitudes and tactics to deescalate and mediate a conflict to the point where resolution can occur tend to be ubiquitous.

## Conflict Resolution

Ideally, conflict resolution aims to pacify the source of disagreement between two people and help each come to a negotiation that satisfies their core concerns.

I am going to cover some general conflict resolution rules, and then get more specific about the three predominant approaches to negotiate conflicts of a financial, personal, political, or emotional nature.

### *General Rules.*

First, describe the conflict. Harken back to first grade when you learned Who, What, Where, and When, but skipped the Why. At this point, it is absolutely crucial to only state the facts, free of interpretation. Each person embroiled in the conflict must do this until everyone has agreed on a version of the situation; or agreed to disagree.

Second, review what the consequences of the conflict are. Think about what is being lost, what is being halted, what is being compromised. This can help put the conflict into a greater context and reduce tensions through pragmatism.

And third, hash out the potentials benefits of resolving the conflict. What can be gained by the people directly and indirectly related? When you do this, you have crafted a comprehensive picture of both the positive and negative impacts of the conflict. A complete picture of the situation can provide some much-needed separation from personal feelings.

There are three common approaches to reaching a consensus after the big picture has been set in place:

1. *The Assertive Approach.* You have a problem and it must be resolved. That is your prerogative from the get-go. Another name for this is a solution-oriented mindset. A face-to-face meeting with the object(s) of conflict is preferable.

   Once you've agreed to meet in person, determine the exact language you want to use at the start of the meeting. This will set the tone for what is to come. The goal is to keep perspective and not get sucked into personal attacks or assumptions. What is the problem? What is at stake? How can we ameliorate the tension?

   Then, when you have made your points, turn the conversation over to the person in a non-threatening and unassuming way. Invite the person to speak and give them the floor openly. Let them know you are receptive. This must be sincere; otherwise, the person's guard will be up.

   Granted, this is a very straightforward approach, and not everyone is keen on it. Despite your best efforts, stylistic and individual differences may impede the intended effects of the assertive approach. If you suspect that is the case, then try a more "beat around the bush" tact: the cooperative approach.

2. *The Cooperative Approach.* You have a problem that must be resolved, but not at this moment. You can temporally accept the disagreement without major consequences.

   You have a conversation with the person and explain to them your position on the matter. Again, follow the general rules stated above, but close with an acceptance of the matter as is. You can perhaps postpone talks for another time. The key here is to express goodwill. You don't want to come off as impertinent and dismissive of the situation. One way to do this is to highlight how much time has been, is being, and could be spent on negotiations when the issue is really not that urgent. This will evoke empathy and realism.

If the approach is not satisfactory to the people involved, and they are too heightened to tolerate the assertive approach, then you are left with one final recourse: the collaborative approach.

3. *The Collaborative Approach.* You have a problem that needs to be addressed immediately but not aggressively. Some finessing is necessary. You need the collaborative approach. This approach is best described as *quid pro quo.* You concede on some points of conflict to gain on others.

   After you have elaborated on the points of conflict and what each side wants to accomplish, one side agrees to grant concessions so long as the other side cedes on other points. It creates a collaborative balance where accord can be reached without losing face. For some people, the competitive side of conflict cannot be avoided, and this approach can work well in those situations.

All that being said, there are sometimes situations that the conflicting people simply cannot resolve together. It happens. It's okay. Emotions run hot and sometimes cloud our better judgment. It may take a third-person with no interest in the conflict to help mediate a resolution.

In a corporate environment, that may be a manager or a fellow co-worker; in a school environment, that may be a counselor; in a home environment, it may be a friend or a family member. Whoever the person, make sure you both agree to their presence and can respect their input.

When you decide to get a mediator, there are a few important tips to bear in mind.

## An Outsider Looking In

I don't want to belabor the point, so I will quickly run down the line of helpful tips for mediators in a conflict. I believe they are self-explanatory.

- *Discuss boundaries and expectations.* Before broaching the conflict, establish rules of conduct, expectations, and a sense of how the conversation will proceed. This helps eliminate ambiguity that can stoke the flames when left unchecked. It also helps keep everyone accountable.
- *Use active listening.* Paraphrase, ask for clarification, make sure that each person's points are being heard and understood. Try to stay outside the content to the conversation to provide an objective perspective.
- *Separate positions from issues.* People tend to get messy in disagreements. Opinions are presented as facts, assumptions are taken as truths, and recounted events are interspersed with interpretation. Tease those apart.
- *Understand and validate.* Listen, paraphrase, and accept. Do not undermine or invalidate anyone's thoughts or feelings.
- *Empathize.* Empathy is key. It ensures each person feels understood. Be careful not to take sides, though.
- *Be.* When you express sensitivity to the feelings of others, they will remain open to your input. Get each person to talk about alternative interpretations, alternative end-results, and other possibilities.
- *"I" statements.* In short, speak for yourself.
- *Be kind.* Find something positive to say about each person. It reduces nerves and disarms.
- *Attack the idea, not the person.*

## Reclaim the Relationship and Move Forward

In the midst of a conflict, we can say things that we don't really mean or wouldn't say upon careful reflection. Sometimes it's because we want to win, because we want to injure, or we just get carried away.

Keeping our emotions in check is very important when trying to resolve a conflict. Often all people involved won't be able to do it effectively. Fortunately, it only takes one person to short fuse the conflictive energy. This is especially the case when the conflict is emotionally charged.

Kerry Patterson, Joseph Grenny, Ron McMillan, and Al Switzler share valuable advice on how to talk about sensitive issues in *Crucial Conversations*. Their kernel of wisdom is that the more emotionally charged the discussion, the less likely we are to keep ourselves in line. That doesn't mean, however, we cannot share our opinions calmly in those moments. There are ways to share while maintaining an air of safety in the space. Safety is essential to conflict resolution because it prompts people to put their guard down, which allow them to listen and open their minds.

There are three ingredients that, when taken in conjunction, reduce emotional tension and foster safety in a conflict-riddle situation:

1. *Confidence.* Have the confidence to say what you need to say and know that you can say it without hurting the other person.
2. *Humility.* Realize you don't have a monopoly on the truth. Others have valuable input, and together you can come to a better understanding of the given situation.
3. *Skill.* Share delicate information willingly. Be vulnerable and don't regret it. People will be grateful for your honesty.

And then there are five tactics that can help you continue a conversation without impinging on safety or exacerbating emotions:

1. *Share your facts.* Share what you know, and put aside assumptions and conjectures.

2. *Tell your story.* Explain your realizations and how you got to what you think you know. Be process oriented.

3. *Ask for others' paths.* Encourage others to explain their realizations and how they got to what they think they know. Urge them to also be process oriented.

4. *Talk tentatively.* Don't use absolute terms. Leave room for error in what you say. Make it clear that it is your perception, and don't disguise it as fact.

5. *Encourage testing.* Make it safe for others to try their theories without fear of being recriminated or brushed off. Don't launch into a monologue. Don't get indignant. Hold your beliefs, but don't bang people over the head with them.

## I Am a Businessman After All

Some of you may be wondering how the heck this could work in a professional environment without devolving into a kumbaya circle. Well, you know what I say?

Professionals should be more willing to talk openly while paying deference to their emotions, because choosing to ignore the role they play in conflicts doesn't mean they aren't playing a role.

Emotions, assumption, experience, and beliefs all influence the way we go about our daily lives, and if you are in society, that means you are affecting others. Learning how to mitigate the impact of those aspects of human psychology on conflict resolution is necessary, be it a business context or not.

More broadly, it is pressing that we learn how to communicate effectively and respectfully with others. Conflict will always reach you, so you should be prepared to deal with it the best way you can muster.

# CHAPTER 75

## *Teamwork Lessons from Monkeys*

Apparently, 98% of our DNA is shared with our distant cousins, the monkey. Given that 2016 was the Year of the Monkey in the Chinese zodiac, and having watched a few documentaries over the festive season (the Harsh family went a little "monkey mad"), I cannot ignore the thoughts that were running through my head as I sat there watching. It was captivating viewing.

You can learn a lot when you observe other people, and you cannot avoid putting yourself in their shoes. When you are observing a group of monkeys, the lessons are still all there, but there is enough detachment to be able to absorb them fully.

What struck me most was how these highly intelligent animals interact with each other and organize their lives. I have been in a few boardrooms in my career where the behavior has been far "wilder" and more irrational.

The success of any group of monkeys depends on the strength of their bonds with each other. It is not just about how they interact with the dominant males or females; they thrive when they take the wellbeing of the entire group into consideration. Monkeys, like humans, might be selfish when it comes to basic needs such as food and reproduction, but they are far better team players than you might think.

Life in a monkey troupe is rarely plain sailing. When tough times arrive, tensions rise, and there are inevitable conflicts. What is fascinating is the innate ability of a monkey for reconciliation. When you live in a tight group, you cannot allow simmering issues to spoil the cohesion of the group. One minute you see two males fighting for the attentions of a female, the next minute you see them grooming each other as if nothing had happened. They fight, but they don't let it spoil the group dynamic. They will go hunting for food together as they always have.

While much is made of the hierarchies in monkey society, there are many species where the senior members will groom the younger members and vice versa. A group needs to be led by the experienced members, but this enforced distance does not need to apply to every sphere of life. I pity the company where the CEO will not have a chat with the latest intern in the pub after work. The strength of a monkey group comes primarily from their inclusive and accepting behaviors—they act as one, and they thrive as one.

Going a step further, the monkey team bond is so strong that many will look after each other's young. The baby and juvenile monkeys are cared for by others when the parents are away. I am not certain that most team members would be so keen to look after each other's projects. This sense of shared responsibility was probably what came across strongest for me. That is not something that you can demand of a team; you simply have to feel an inner yearning to get through it together.

Lastly, when you look into a monkey's eyes, you get the feeling that they are trying to figure you out. They are constantly looking for new sources of inspiration, and their ability to learn from each other is possibly what contributed to our appearance on this earth. When an older monkey is using a stone to crack a nut, you can see all the little ones scrambling for stones of their own. They want to ape (excuse the pun) the behavior of the subject experts—something that is crucial if any team is going to evolve together.

So, next time you are watching a monkey documentary, spare a thought for your colleagues at work. How could you work a little more efficiently together?

# CHAPTER 76

## *Rise of the Collaborative and Shared Economy*

Those who refused to believe in the concept of a collaborative and shared economy are starting to shift uncomfortably in their chairs as modifications to our traditional ways of doing things are evolving at a pace much faster than anyone had ever thought possible.

We seldom stop to comprehend how the Hilton hotel group needed 93 years to build just over 610,000 rooms, whereas Airbnb got there in less than four. As consumers, we purchase items from the likes of Amazon, eBay, and Etsy, but we also know how to sell a few of our own personal items on these same platforms as part of our private ventures.

Tom Goodwin, Vice President of Strategy and Innovation at Havas Media says, "Uber, the world's largest taxi company, owns no vehicles. Facebook, the world's most popular media owner, creates no content. Alibaba, the most valuable retailer, has no inventory. And Airbnb, the world's largest accommodation provider, owns no real estate. Something interesting is happening."

The seeds of our digital future were first planted with the rise of social media, which allowed people from all over the world to connect in a way that we have never thought possible.

Fast forward a few years, and those people who have built their online communities now have the ability to reasonably bypass the shackles of larger corporations that slow things down or force things to move a certain way.

The brave new world allows both businesses and individuals to connect directly to whichever service they require to help complete an important project or even assist them with something in their increasingly busy lifestyle.

These new ways of working in the shared economy are rapidly revolutionizing the way we do business. However, this fundamental change also alters every aspect of our lives at work, home, and how we interact with each other.

Critics of the person-to-person commerce model—where people obtain what they need directly from each other rather than from an organization—will declare this utopian, working together design as nothing but idealistic fantasy, but those that think this way are part of the problem rather than the solution.

The most enlightening aspect of this new era of trust is how old regulations and licensing have been cast aside with wild abandon in favor of just trusting each other, which illustrates how we have progressed both as a society and as a human race.

The growing number of freelancers and solopreneurs is also contributing to the increase in demand for collaborative workspaces where individuals or small teams can pay to share office space or work resources, which further illustrates how the traditional 9-5 grind is changing right before our eyes.

Collaboration is not a silver bullet for every task, and it's important not to throw all your eggs in one basket. We need to understand that it's not always appropriate to use this approach, but equally, there is no substitute when sharing insight, expertise, and development of ideas to ensure that the projects excel.

The rapid rise of the collaborative economy is a wake-up call for established organizations that must learn how their marketplace is changing and adjust their business models accordingly to avoid a disconnect with their customers' changing preferences.

Technology has most definitely become the enabler that we all hoped, and business leaders would be incredibly short sighted to bury their heads in the sand until this latest fad passes by. Widespread adoption from users creating the world that plays by their rules suggests that this movement will only continue to rise in the coming years.

The only remaining question is how will your business adapt to the change?

# CHAPTER 77

## Six Tricks for Amazing Presentations

No matter how proficient you are at giving presentations, every occasion brings fresh opportunities for embarrassing slip ups. The audience may be bigger, the material may be less well-known, or you may simply not be feeling your best. After having given over 1,000 presentations in the last 17 years trying every imaginable trick in the playbook for every type of audience, I now live by one maxim— "Keep it simple." Rather than overload you with the delicate science of influencing, I thought that I would focus on six practical considerations of giving a presentation.

Very rarely do you attend a presentation where each of these six points are spot on:

1. *Talk slowly.* You know what you are going to say next, but you need to give your audience time to process what you are saying right now. A machine-gun approach ensures that your carefully planned speech passes in a blur. If you are nervous, make sure that you take a breath between each sentence. This will help you relax, and it will pace your delivery.

2. *Don't apologize.* Everyone is there to listen to your opinion, very few people are forced to be there against their will, and hardly anyone is expecting that they will agree with everything that you say. Therefore, qualifying every second sentence with "This is just my opinion," or,

"I'm sure that some of you see this differently," will merely serve to make people focus on where they do indeed disagree. Hold your head up high and share your views.

3. *Be enthusiastic.* Enthusiasm and a genuine smile go a long way in getting an audience on your side. Don't be over-confident, simply try to convey the impression that you are glad to be there. If you are monotonous and boring, your audience will switch off immediately. Eye contact helps when you are developing a rapport with your audience—let them see the glint in your eye.

4. *Use filler sentences.* Presentations are rarely one-way affairs. There is often a questions section at the end, and many presenters are happy to allow external questions to shape the presentation as it goes along. It is wise to give yourself a little time to consider a response—phrases like, "That's a good question," or, "Let me think about that one," do exactly that. Jumping in immediately with a response can often distract you if you engage your mouth before your brain.

5. *Don't read your speech.* You need to instill confidence in your audience, and reading your speech on cards is the best way to torpedo your credibility. Your delivery is never as natural as when you are speaking freely, and your body language will also be impeded. Your gestures and facial expressions will be the bulk of the communication "heavy lifting" in a presentation, but if you are standing frozen behind a lectern, they will make no impact whatsoever.

6. *The 10-20-30 rule.* This is a slideshow rule offered by Guy Kawasaki. This rule states that a PowerPoint slide should have no more than 10 slides, last no longer than 20 minutes, and have no text less than 30-point font. Your basic ideas might not light up the world, but it is how you mold the story around them that will ensure the impact of a presentation.

# CHAPTER 78

## *Does Your "Tribe" Have a Shared Interest?*

In his 2008 book *Tribes: We Need You to Lead Us*, author Seth Godin talks about the power of the carefully directed collective. He suggests that a group needs two things to become a tribe: a way to communicate and a shared interest.

The first question has been comprehensively solved in the last six years since the book was first published, but arming a group with a sense of a shared interest is much harder.

People can connect with their leaders and each other, but unless they are connected to an all-encompassing idea, sooner or later their bonds will loosen. Their shared interest in each other is only meaningful if they have something (not just someone) to follow.

Godin discusses the importance of these ideas and suggests that it isn't always the strongest ideas that win through, "In a battle between two ideas, the best one doesn't necessarily win. No, the idea that wins is the one with the most fearless heretic behind it."

Leaders play a huge role in painting the picture of the future for their team, only to then let the team themselves contribute to the painting. Those ideas that are painted with passion and zeal are the ones that will drive the tribe forward. In this way, leaders allow the tribe to connect with one another. If they are all contributing to the same painting, they will have a vested interest in the final outcome.

Godin talks a lot about the concept of "heretic" leaders, those with a fearless belief in their idea who can inspire the same fearless belief in their teams. "Heretics must believe. More than anyone else in an organization, it's the person who's challenging the status quo, the one who is daring to be great, who is truly present and not just punching a clock who must have confidence in their beliefs. Can you imagine Steve Jobs showing up for the paycheck? It's nice to get paid. It's essential to believe."

The ultimate goal is to create a pseudo-religion around your idea, to have people so committed that they will never leave, to have them so involved that even the smallest discrepancy will be picked up and amended with fervor. When people care, they can move mountains.

The key to all this lies with creativity and storytelling. People have been telling stories to foster a sense of belonging for many millennia, and leaders should learn to not only tell the stories to their people, but also let the stories develop a mind of their own within people's heads. Only when the story is a collective story can it truly be called a "shared interest." When it is strictly dictated by the big boss, its hopes of survival live only in the head of the boss.

A shared interest takes a while to evolve. It works best when there is a small core of believers who can communicate clearer and quicker, and the vision will soon solidify. Then is the time to "spread the word."

Ask yourself this question: does your "tribe" have a shared interest? Do you even see each other as a tribe?

# CHAPTER 79

## *Seven Ways to Reduce Stress at Work*

There are certain people who walk around the office telling everyone how stressed out they are and how they are at their wit's end. They aren't the ones that you should worry about.

The genuinely stressed are trying to hide it—from themselves and everyone else. They have bags under their eyes from lack of sleep, their mind is dulled by the plethora of broken records, their confidence is shot by (perceived) rejection after rejection. They are scared of whatever is coming around the corner next, and a small part of them truly doesn't know how they will cope.

Stress is a disease that affects millions of people every year. No one is immune, not everyone can fight it, and in certain situations you simply have to accept that you are stressed and do your best to work through it. I have had a good few situations like this in my professional life and here are seven suggestions for how to deal with it:

1. *Breathe.* When stress overpowers you, the easiest first step is to release its hold on your body. When you breathe deeply, it sends a message to your brain to calm down and relax. Your brain gets more oxygen, your heart rate slows, your blood pressure lowers, and the urge to fight or flight diminishes.

2. *Sleep.* When you are anxious, your brain is in overdrive, your sympathetic nervous system doesn't shut down correctly (as normal), and it is harder to fall asleep. A vicious cycle ensues as the resultant daytime exhaustion makes it harder to cope with the daily stressors. In order to get a good night's sleep, you really need to deal with the stress directly, and relaxation techniques in the evening can help.

3. *Escape.* Stepping away from (or avoiding) stressful situations doesn't make the stressor go away, but it does give you some temporary space to deal with your response. You do need to take positive action to resolve the stress, and escaping for a while gives you the chance to think things through in a calm and logical manner.

4. *Act.* It is ever so easy to close your eyes and hope for things to get better. Feelings of helplessness are never far away in this scenario, and unless you do something positive about your stress, it will likely only get worse. Doing anything but giving in to the stress will seem like a positive step.

5. *Understand.* It is only truly possible to understand stress in retrospect or through the eyes of others; when you are in the situation, it is almost impossible to think rationally. Understanding how you respond to stress and what triggers these responses is crucial in managing any future risks.

6. *Prioritize.* Many stresses arise because situations seem "too complicated." By simplifying the choices that you have to make and prioritizing your actions (by doing the difficult stuff first), you can deflate any stressful situation into more manageable portions. Prioritizing helps you feel more in control of the stress, and that is never a bad thing.

7. *Realize.* We all get stressed sometimes—realizing it is nothing out of the ordinary makes it all seem that little less scary. If you stop thinking that you are a super hero who can deal with whatever comes

your way, then you will realize that sometimes failure is acceptable. Stresses will come and go, but you will survive and prosper, despite it seeming like the end of the world at the time.

# CHAPTER 80

## Work & Exercise

Companies have an obligation and self-interest to look after their employees.

People are spending ever-longer hours slaving away at their desks, forced into a sedentary lifestyle that is reportedly more dangerous to their health than smoking. Companies realized the dangers of passive smoking years ago—it is about time that they addressed the true elephant in the room:

### *Office life is inherently bad for your health.*

Many companies choose to turn a blind eye to the fact that they are growing while their employees are destroying their health. They might be of the opinion that it is down to the individuals to keep themselves healthy in their spare time, but actually, with long commutes and long days, not everyone is able to make that choice. People with families will value time with their loved ones over time in the gym. Younger employees will value time with their social circle, and older employees may simply not have the energy after a long and draining day sitting still.

Yes, sitting still is incredibly tiring. It saps your energy, deflates your morale, weakens your body and dulls your mind.

The benefits of exercise are so well known that I personally believe far more companies should be offering exercise opportunities as part of the working day. I wouldn't go as far as to say it should be compulsory, but it should be made an integral part of every company's culture. There is nothing more important than giving people a choice to have a healthier office life.

There is a lot of science behind this.

Fit employees are likely to take less time off for illness. One survey conducted by the Integrated Benefits Institute that represents major US employers and business coalitions showed that absenteeism due to illness costs employers $576 billion in lost revenue per year.

Regular physical activity can improve your muscle strength and boost your endurance. Exercise and physical activity deliver oxygen and nutrients to your tissues and help your cardiovascular system work more efficiently.

Working up a sweat can help manage physical and mental stress. Exercise also increases concentrations of norepinephrine, a chemical that can moderate the brain's response to stress and release higher levels of endorphins, which make us feel on top of the world.

Being fit improves your concentration and sharpens your memory. Exercise boosts the chemicals in the brain that support and prevent degeneration of the hippocampus, an important part of the brain for memory and learning. Working out even helps create new brain cells (neurogenesis) and smooths out those neural pathways for better decision-making.

Exercising helps with productivity and regulates the circadian rhythms of our bodies, helping us to sleep better at night and have more energy in the day. Some experts believe that midday is the perfect time for a workout. Lunchtime step class in the office anyone?

Studies have even suggested that a person's creativity is given a boost in the subsequent couple of hours after a workout. I am sure that we have all had that feeling of both physical "exhaustion" and mental sharpness upon exiting the shower at the gym. Get your laptop out immediately and tackle that tricky problem.

From my point of view, one of the biggest benefits of organizing exercise classes at work is the camaraderie and culture that it creates. There are very few opportunities for people to bond within the office setting, but if half the team sweats it out twice a week in a spinning class just before the end of the official working day, you can be sure that they will feel that little bit closer to each other.

*Mens Sana In Corpore Sano* – a healthy mind in a healthy body

# SECTION 3 – CAREER DEVELOPMENT

# CHAPTER 81

## *Is Disruptive Learning Crucial to Transformational Career Progress?*

How long have you been "making do" with your current skillset?

You have hit every target and progressed in your career, but the path has been more incremental rather than transformational. You feel that you are dealing with everything that life throws your way, but are your sights really being set so high? Everything seems so comfortable, but that is because the neural pathways in your brain are so well worn. When did you last step off the neural beaten track?

For most of us, the last time we learned something significant was back in college. Incremental learning doesn't count—that will happen every time you step out of your front door. I am talking about the sort of learning when you stand in front of a task and have 1,000 hours of work ahead of you before you master it.

However, in the disruptive times that we live in, and with an economic slowdown looming on the horizon, taking that giant leap to learn something entirely new could make the difference between just surviving or potentially thriving. If you want to make a step change, there has to be fundamental learning to back it up.

To start with, you have to understand the value that this learning will add to your life. It is all well and good wanting to learn how to code, but if you work in marketing, this is unlikely to provide an immediate benefit.

You could, however, take a course in video production and scriptwriting. This might not be immediately relevant to your role at the moment, but when the chips are down and the redundancies threatening, those extra skills could prove crucial in a slimmer marketing department.

Just because you are not using a skill doesn't mean that it won't add to your future worth.

So, how can you tell what you might want to learn?

Not every skill needs to be work-related, there are many new skills that will add pleasure in your leisure time, but if we are talking about the future of your employment, this search for new skills has to start with some serious reading. Look at where your industry and function is likely to be in 10-15 years. Read some blogs by futurists and check out presentations by consultancies and academic institutions. You don't have to gaze too far into the crystal ball to be able to understand where the skill gaps will be.

There are an increasing number of ways to learn these skills in a flexible manner that will not have a great impact on your current activity; innovations in EdTech are making material more digestible and learning more personalized. Once you have found a method of learning that fits, there is nothing stopping you.

There are probably two reasons why you haven't learned something for a while: there hasn't been a requirement and you think that it is too demanding. Neither of these things are true, and in reality, there is nothing stopping you adding to your skillset.

If you haven't learned something radically new by this time next year, you are being left behind.

# CHAPTER 82

## *Is Your Career Stuck in the Wrong Gear?*

Imagine Tim Reynolds (not his real name), a hard-charging and absolutely brilliant young man. He's an insightful strategist who can create a plan or presentation in one-third the time of any of his colleagues. Present him with a complex problem, and Tim will have a workable solution before most people can even grasp the challenge at hand.

Did I mention that Tim just got fired?

The only speed Tim understood was full speed ahead.

He couldn't slow down to explain a solution to people in other disciplines who lacked his knowledge and experience. He alienated every team on which he worked. Tim couldn't even hide his disgust with executives who did not immediately embrace his ideas.

The moral of the story is you can't succeed today with just one speed.

In industry after industry, data and insight is growing at a staggering pace. No one person can absorb it all, not even Tim. You need to be able to work with other people, because other people possess talents you lack and knowledge you need.

This means being able to switch gears from

- "I'll take charge and carry the ball," to

- "Yes, I can sit quietly for two hours and listen very carefully to what others have to say," to
- "We have to find common interests and shared strategy that we all can embrace," to
- "We have waited long enough for consensus; let's just go with our original plan."

There is no single approach to business that always works. That's why I look for people who not only are resilient and driven, but also have the flexibility to switch gears when the situation demands that.

"One-note" people are ineffective and boring. If all you can do is pontificate about project management, you will become the person others avoid at social gatherings.

But if you can be tough and driven in the morning and compassionate and open an hour later, then you have true potential.

It disturbs me when I encounter experts who present a single framework for navigating our insanely complex world. Badly-run companies embrace such gurus for six months before they bounce to another idea. Well-run organizations know that there is no secret sauce, no magic formula, no one-size-fits all solution.

You need multiple talents and the ability to shift gears from what worked yesterday to what will work today. Even more importantly, you need the judgment to be able to discern which skill and which strategy is most likely to work right now. This is no easy task, and I don't wish to minimize it. That's why people who know how—and when—to switch gears are so valuable.

As you manage your career, be careful not to get stuck in a rut. Once you demonstrate a special skill, clients and colleagues will ask you to use that skill repeatedly. While it's good to be valuable, if all you do is perform the same function again and again, you run the risk of getting stuck in one gear. Stretch your wings. Try new approaches. Seek out new assignments.

Flexibility will always serve you well.

# CHAPTER 83

## *Does Doubt Help or Hinder Your Career?*

That little voice inside you—you know it all too well. Sometimes it is barely audible, quietly harkening back to tougher times. At other moments, it is so overwhelming that you cannot concentrate on anything else. It can save you from making a mistake, but it can also stop you from fulfilling your dreams.

The voice of doubt.

When you are making trivial decisions like whether you need to take an umbrella on your walk as the dark clouds gather, doubt can serve as a useful reminder. Remember that last time you didn't take one? You got soaked. It could happen again, you know. Acting on these little voices can be useful, but in most such trivial situations, it won't be life-changing if you don't heed the doubtful voices.

When it comes to other matters, however, not heeding them can be a high-stakes decision. How we deal with those doubting voices can make or break us. When it comes to making crucial life choices, there are few areas more prone to doubt, and more complicated, than our careers. To me, a successful career should be a progression, an accumulation of learning and experience to then be passed on to the next generation of leaders. Does doubt have a role to play in this developmental journey? Does it help our career growth or hinder it?

As with most things, the answer is not clear-cut.

The worst kinds of doubts are those that cause you to freeze and avoid making a decision. We've all been in that situation in our careers. We know deep down what we need to do, but the potential consequences of the action are worrisome, so we end up doing nothing. This sort of doubt destroys futures and ensures the continuation of a far-from-ideal present.

But not all doubts are destructive. Some are productive. Some can help shape our thinking.

A career is rarely a linear progression from small victory to small victory. There will be times when targets are not met and goals are not achieved. Each time that this happens, the natural reaction is to look inwards, sowing the seeds of doubt for the next time a certain activity comes along.

These more manageable doubts are useful to us.

If we are worried about public speaking and doubt our ability to present without stuttering over our words, more often than not, we do something about it. We will read a book, take a course or maybe chat with a colleague about how they handle it. The doubts force us to take action in order to deal with difficult situations. If we had no doubts and thought, "Ah, it will be fine next time. No worries," then the likelihood of repeated failure would be higher.

If we don't let them build into foreboding monsters, small doubts in our career can often galvanize us to improve and be better than we were.

# CHAPTER 84

## *Is Your Boss Taking You for Granted?*

This happens a lot.

### There are multiple reasons why your boss could be taking you for granted.

Your boss might be used to your stellar performance and doesn't praise you as much as they used to. They might not understand what you do and exactly what you have to go through to make it happen. They might be intimidated by your abilities, view them as a potential threat, and consequently seek to inhibit your career growth. Maybe they think that they know best and ignore the value that you can bring to various situations.

### There are always ways in which you can redress the balance.

Employees are taken for granted when their relationships are not strong. They can do their bit to make them closer. It is partly their fault if they do not speak up and defend their position. Their boss may not be aware of the situation, or they may simply need a reminder of the employee's value. If a manager steals your glory, their agenda is clear; next time ensure that your efforts are more visible with the wider team. If your boss doesn't value your work, ask them for feedback and act on it. Don't sit there and let their negative opinions intensify. The employee should make every effort to inform their boss of their input. It is the employer's job to help the employee optimize their performance, but they have to be aware of the details in the first place.

In the above couple of paragraphs, you may think that I have given the topic a rather cursory treatment. Surely there is more to the phenomenon than these rather brief lines. Well, yes, of course there is, but in my view the next few lines are more important, and, in particular, the next four words:

## Why Should You Care?

Bear with me. For many of us, our childhoods were filled with "rewards" for good behavior—you felt worthy and secure when people praised you. This tends to dry up when you enter the real world, so it is so important to learn to value yourself and feel secure in your own ability.

What does praise from a boss give you apart from stroking your ego? Why should you spend your energy on seeking this recognition when it can be perfectly well spent elsewhere? In most organizations, the results of your activity will be visible enough for you to be in line for promotions and important projects. Why get all upset about not getting the praise that you think you deserve?

Maybe you just need to learn to be content with yourself a bit more. Try to take a step back and realize that your good deeds need to feel good to you. If you do things in order to be put on that "pedestal" by someone else for five minutes, maybe you need to rethink your priorities. Why do you need praise in order to feel loved?

If you feel this way, you are not alone. Millions of us live our lives doing things that we think others expect of us in order to please them. It is somehow part of the human condition—we live to please.

Sometimes, I wish that we could learn to please ourselves that little bit more. Then we wouldn't care so much what others think of us. If you live a good life and try your best to make a difference, the praise will come, but don't live in anticipation of that pat on the back.

If you are confident in who you are and what you mean to others, that pat on the back doesn't really matter.

# CHAPTER 85

## *How Therapeutic Hobbies Can Power Your Career*

Therapy often conjures up the image of a psychologist's couch—the last resort of personal sanity. I would wager that not all of us would feel it necessary to visit a psychologist, but in fact, giving our minds some tender loving care is crucial for everyone, no matter how self-confident.

Our brains are incredibly strong organs, but they are still open to abuse. Too much pressure and stress can shut them down entirely, turning a captain of industry into a whimpering kitten overnight. We all need to find our own pressure valves to help let off steam and gain a sense of perspective.

When times are tough at work, hobbies can help you retain your sanity.

I personally enjoy playing and watching tennis, and I love singing (I even sang solo at the Carnegie Hall a couple times). I find that when I focus on perfecting my skills in an activity that I enjoy, my brain gets a productivity boost as well as a well-earned rest from the daily grind at the office. An hour spent improving my tennis serve might have very little to do with the latest publishing deal that I am finalizing, but the knock-on effects of the feel-good factor will very much be felt at that negotiating table. If a deal falls through, and your self-confidence takes a knock (it happens to the best of us), excelling at your hobby can give you that crucial boost.

Hobbies can also be excellent for expanding your network.

Finding common ground with others outside the office environment is often the basis for the strongest relationships with colleagues or clients. People might play golf, watch football together, or go fishing—sharing a common pastime breaks the ice and allows you to get to know each other on another level. When someone sees how you deal with the disappointment of losing a fish, they will subconsciously be "rooting" for you when they are agreeing terms on that next deal.

Most importantly, hobbies give you a chance to think.

Amongst the thousands of thoughts tripping around your brain is the one "breakthrough" thought that will take you to the next level. If you are living life at full speed, that thought is likely to be swamped, and you will act on the "nearest" sensible thought in the front of your mind at any given moment. If given space to sort itself out, your brain naturally pushes the great ideas further forward. The less active your brain is at any given moment, the more likely it is for you to realize the power of the unthinkable.

How you spend your time is always a conscious decision. Going for a run or even just a walk seems "wasteful" if you have a huge to-do list, but it might just help you to get in the right frame of mind.

# CHAPTER 86

## *Are You Likely to Lose Your Job?*

Stock markets are trembling (some may say crashing), investment decisions and projects are being delayed, and certain industry sectors are freezing recruitment and even starting full-on redundancies.

Are those worrying times around the corner again? Did they ever go away? If you look at the stock markets, then theoretically, yes, we have had a decent run for a few years. The numbers of jobless are low, but we all know how easily they can be fudged.

No, for every ordinary office worker, the trauma of the 2008 recession (that didn't really see a satisfying bottom) lives long in the memory—the boxes, the en-masse collective culling, the shattered dreams and crying kids. It was messy, but increasingly more of us are worried that it may happen again sometime soon.

I am not going to explore how likely the "part two" scenario is to happen. For the sake of this chapter, let's assume that there is a reasonable chance of something similar to 2008 (if not worse). If that were the case, what would be dominating your thoughts? I would say that the one thought at the front of many minds would be this one:

"Will I lose my job?"

It is in the hard times that we stop taking our jobs and employers for granted. We worry less about pool tables and more about the increasing empty tables that surround us. "Did you hear who left yesterday? Yeah, I thought he would be here until the end. Obviously, no one is safe."

Now, I run a successful digital media business, and I do not wish to alarm any of my employees. The doomsday scenario is still some way off. However, if it were to come closer, what would be some of the things that every employee should consider in terms of their job security?

Firstly, consider the industry that you work in. How did it perform in the last downturn? Are there certain niches that could be more resilient? Is it realistic to move to a more recession-proof industry, while retaining your specialization? Are there any extra skills that you would need to acquire should such a move be required?

Then, it is well worth considering your function. There will be a high demand for procurement professionals in a recession, but maybe less so for recruitment professionals. Sometimes it is hard to retrain, but even a subtle shift of role could pay dividends. Are there growing sectors that you can take advantage of? A specialist in sales could become proficient in "social selling" without too much difficulty, for example.

Thirdly, the more difficult questions come. How well are you doing at your job? Are you valued? Are you invaluable? Look at yourself from the perspective of your colleagues, your boss and their boss. What would they say if you were gone?

These are difficult questions, but if you have even the slightest worry that you job may be at risk, you can start to address them. Make sure that people understand the value that you add before it is too late.

Don't stick your head in the sand. Be prepared for all eventualities. One day, you might be glad that you heeded this advice.

# CHAPTER 87

## *Market Yourself: A Job Won't Find You Anymore*

For something that only happens once every few years, it is hardly surprising that people are a little nervous and rusty when it comes to looking for a new role.

They will often have been comfortable, working away for their previous employer, and even if the move is a planned one, the first day of "job hunting" can seem a little daunting.

I believe that there is a huge skills gap in terms of people having the knowledge of how to go about managing their job search and making the most of the opportunities out there. There are always thousands of opportunities, in all sorts of weird and wonderful areas, but unless you seize them with both hands, they will float right by you.

In my view, the main sea change in recent years has been the prevalence of social media in the job search. For those who are well-networked on LinkedIn, Twitter, and Facebook, a whole arena of opportunity opens up for them. They are immediately able to access second-degree connection decision-makers, and they will have built up a following that is more than happy to help them make the right move. The choice to invest in your networks when it isn't "needed" is one that will pay off for many people.

On the other hand, the "passive" individuals rely on third party recruiters and running the gauntlet of the keyword checking ATS systems to get their chance to shine. Why leave your future career prospects to chance?

Another aspect of candidate marketing is the level of innovation required to stand out from the crowd. Video CVs are becoming common place, candidates are blogging their way through the experience, and social proof (i.e. lots of likes) is becoming a pressing reason why someone should get in interview. If they can use social media to get 5,000 likes and 100,000 views, imagine what they could do for our company when they set about a difficult task?

The simple fact is that jobs don't find candidates anymore.

Recruiters still play an important part in the process, but they will also spend their time with the clued-up rather than the clueless. If your CV is poorly formatted or has grammatical errors, feel free to assume that the recruiter will not spend a great deal of effort on your application. If you cannot get the simple things right, how will you perform in the white heat of an interview?

I am not a job-hunting expert, but I see plenty of potential candidates come my way for work. It only takes a few seconds to see those who are switched on to the new realities of the job search and those who are being left in the dark ages.

No one wants to hire someone who lives in the dark ages.

# CHAPTER 88

## *Are You Too Important to Be Ill?*

Let's be honest, we all think we are a little more indispensable than is actually the case.

How will people cope when we are on holiday? We fret when our phone runs out of juice, and we are not contactable for a few hours. We make sure that we are in all the important meetings on the off-chance that someone needs our precious pearls of wisdom.

Well, deep down, we all know the answers. Business ticks along just fine when we are sunning ourselves on the beach; our team may well even be more productive without us breathing down their necks. If people can't contact us by phone, they will likely make the same decision that they would have made anyway—they know our views, they will make the right call. Lastly, it is a sure thing that our presence in 90% of meetings is superfluous.

Why, therefore, do we insist on going into work when we have a highly contagious illness such as flu? We soldier into the office, coughing and spluttering, half-expecting our annual appraisal to consider the amount of days spent at our desks when we really should have been tucked up in bed.

We play the unfortunate hero part to a tee, and it makes us feel that much better about ourselves. In reality, however, we are the opposite of a hero—a clueless and dangerous villain.

We covered our mouth when we sneezed on the way to work, didn't we? We all know that sneezes can travel at the speed of light. That may be, but the germs will have stayed on our hands for a few minutes until we touched the overhead rail in the train or the door handle of the office (flu germs can remain infectious on hard surfaces for 24 hours). We may sneeze into our hands before we get to the office, but unless 5-10 minutes has passed, it is unwise to shake anyone's hand. Germs do become less infectious very quickly if they are on our skin tissue, but there is still a period where they can be transferred.

Somehow, we have forgotten what it is to be ill, do everything possible to make ourselves better, and then get on with our lives, refreshed and renewed.

No, instead we struggle on, prolong the period of our illness, and risk further complications. It is true that some workplaces have a "no illness" policy, and they will be that little bit healthier and more productive for it. If only our society as a whole had the same sort of mindset.

I was at a classical concert a couple of weeks back. Not only did the man behind me spoil the wonderful music when he coughed, I also felt the full force on the back of my neck. I can still picture the germs floating around my head even now. I was lucky not to get ill, but you never know.

So, next time you feel ill (the early days are the most infectious ones when it is flu or a cold), do everyone a favor—get well! If this means a few days of rest and recuperation at home, then so be it. You can work remotely, and no one will catch your germs over Skype.

# CHAPTER 89

## *Put Away the Recruitment Top Trumps*

You might remember "Top Trumps" or a similar sort of card game. Each player picks a card, which contains various characteristics of a given subject. These characteristics are then measured. It may be the height of a building, the top speed of a car, or the fear factor of a monster. Each card has multiple characteristics, and the idea of the game is that someone chooses a characteristic and the player with the highest figure wins the "hand." They then go on to choose the next characteristic, etc.

It is a fun game where the cards with the biggest numbers are the "Top Trumps."

To give a fun example, an ogre has a maximum score of 100 for "strength" but only 2 for "magic power." A wizard with a "magic power" of 99 would easily beat him on that metric, but with a score of 80, would lose on "strength." Well, you get the idea.

So, what does this have to do with sound recruitment decisions? Well, everything, actually.

Recruitment technology and Big Data advances are threatening to diminish the human element in recruitment. Ranking candidates on the keywords on their CV has been around for quite a while, but if the net is spread wider and people are "ranked" on all their online content (it could happen at some point), then those with the highest "scores" will automatically be pushed to the front of the queue.

I understand the methodology of scoring people for performance, but that mainly works when you are intimately involved in the process. Giving someone a "score" just because they have written certain things on their CV or because they have worked in certain roles or at certain companies doesn't give anything like the full picture.

You can't score a charming young lady with a stellar attitude. You can't score an older gent with a resume as long as your arm, but who still has passion burning in his eyes. You can't score a mother who is returning to work after a four-year absence.

You can score them, of course, but the result wouldn't be a truthful reflection of their potential.

Potential. That is what great recruitment is all about in my view.

No one job is the same, and no one will have worked at an identical company to yours. They won't have worked for the same personalities or had to contend with the unique challenges that your organization poses. You have to look them in the eyes, consider their attitude, and make a judgment call of "would they fit in here?"

Many of the best recruitment decisions that I have made in my career have seemed illogical on paper. In the world of Big Data and Top Trumps, they simply wouldn't have stacked up. In my world where recruitment (and management) is more of an art than a science, it makes total sense.

So, just because something can be measured, doesn't mean that it should be.

Big Data and recruitment technology will inevitably facilitate some great hires, but they are not the only option! Look beyond the numbers. There are hidden stars out there; you just need to look with your heart, not your head.

# CHAPTER 90

## Meet Opportunities Before They Arrive

### Carpe diem - Seize the Day

*Carpe diem* is a Latin aphorism meaning "seize the day" and taken from book 1 of the Roman poet Horace's work *Odes* (23 BC). Let me start this blog with an English translation of a piece of text from *Odes 1.11: Tu ne quaesieris, scire nefas, quem mihi, quem tibi.*

> *Ask not ('tis forbidden knowledge), what our destined term of years,*
>
> *Mine and yours; nor scan the tables of your Babylonish seers.*
>
> *Better far to bear the future, my Leuconoe, like the past,*
>
> *Whether Jove has many winters yet to give, or this our last;*
>
> *This, that makes the Tyrrhene billows spend their strength against the shore.*
>
> *Strain your wine and prove your wisdom; life is short; should hope be more?*
>
> *In the moment of our talking, envious time has ebb'd away.*
>
> *Seize the present; trust tomorrow e'en as little as you may.*

Unlike what's stated above, popular culture has constantly been telling us "the best things come to those who wait."

In one sense, there is no truer phrase. Some of the best things in your life right now will have taken years to come to fruition. Patience is the finest virtue, as very little happens at the click of a finger.

However, for me, this phrase implies a certain passivity that does not ring so true with our competitive modern life. You can wait months or years for an opportunity, only for someone with a bit more hustle to steal if from under your nose. You react indignantly—that opportunity was yours. You had been waiting longer for it; therefore, you have a right to the first bite of the cherry.

This is a manifestation of the victim culture that I sometimes think we live in. It is far easier to blame someone else for not playing by your perceived rules than realize that you need to do more to take these chances.

Waiting isn't enough. The moment your opportunity appears on the horizon, you have to run toward it. No, maybe running isn't enough, you need to get on the next train and meet it halfway.

So many people will be waiting passively, like you, hoping for an opportunity to come in their direction. When it is on the horizon, it can take all sorts of twists and turns before it may or may not get to you. The passive you knows that it might never arrive, that is why you prefer inactivity. The active you learns to anticipate the twists and turns, and makes a beeline for it without a second thought.

You can waste a lot of time like this; there will be a lot of opportunities on the horizon that simply won't be "right" for you when you get closer to them. There are hundreds of reasons why your pursuit might stop, but the most important thing is to proactively put yourself in the position to make a decision before the rest of your peers do, whoever they might be.

It is better to try and fail in the pursuit of four out of five things and succeed at one of them, rather than the alternative of not having any of these opportunities at all.

I can relate this to my blogging journey over the past year. So many of my friends are still unsure about the value of content. They wonder why I spend so much effort on conveying my thoughts on LinkedIn. For me, it is simple; it is a wonderful opportunity to share my thoughts with whoever would like to listen, and while everyone else is umming and arring, I have decided to redouble my efforts. As well as my lighter blogs, I am also writing digital and tech blogs. These fit nicely with my day job, and I hope they might further the discussion in this fascinating area of our new economy.

For me, *carpe diem* became personal when I lost my young father to a 10-year battle with Progressive Supra Nuclear Palsy and cancer a short while back. He had just retired from his professional life, and over the past decade had written 800+ pages of management insights from his field of work—one finger, one key press at a time. Besides causing difficulties with reasoning, problem-solving, comprehension, and decision-making, among many other severe neurological impediments, the progressive diseases also took his ability to speak almost entirely, his motor functions, as well as his ability to write by hand.

I was faced with the challenge of trying to decipher 800 pages of unintelligible text and charts in scores of Word files, wanting desperately to publish his works posthumously as books, but eventually giving up on the effort since the text had become so incomprehensible. It then dawned upon me the importance of *carpe diem* or seizing the day, which my father kept drilling into me all his life, something that never really quite clicked until that moment. Dad wanted to write his thoughts all his life but never got around to doing so until it was too late.

The moment the opportunity presented itself for me to write, I embraced it with both arms.

*Carpe Diem - Seize the Day*

# CHAPTER 91

## A Career Lesson from Bird Seed

No matter what part of the earth we live in, winter can be bearable and actually quite enjoyable. We wrap up warm, muck around in the snow with our kids, and maybe even hit the ski slopes every now and again.

For birds, life gets considerably harder. There are no extra layers to put on, and they need to expend extra energy to keep warm. Juicy worms are no longer wriggling in the grass every dewy morning, and the berries have long since disappeared from the trees. Pickings are slim, and their territories are looking pretty barren all of a sudden.

Then their savior walks out of the house. The birds tweet in anticipation—they know what is coming. Their focus shifts to the bird feeder hanging precariously off the apple tree. The human carefully takes it down, pours it full of seeds, closes the top and, with a satisfied smile, hangs it up again.

The nimble robins, finches, and sparrows are first in there, stealing the first fresh seeds before the heavy mob arrives. They, in turn, are forced out of the action by the bigger starlings, and then the crows come along. They all take a few quick pecks and move out of the way. They too know what is coming. The heavy wing beats herald their arrival. The local pigeons are here.

They land clumsily on the flimsy feeder and send cascades of seed scattering to the ground. The apex seed guzzlers in the garden, a pigeon's appetite is rarely sated. There is only space for a couple of them at a time at the feeder, and with other pigeons waiting on nearby rooftops, there is no look in at the feeder for anyone else.

The less intelligent birds wait on the branches waiting for their turn at the feeder. It almost never comes. The savvy ones, however, don't even bother with those first hurried gulps of seed. They know that the ground is the place to be. The pigeons cause the feeder to rock to such an extent that much of the seed is spilt over a wide area on the ground. The smaller and more nimble birds are the winners here. They run rings around the clumsy pigeons (who didn't get a place at the top table), and they eat more than their fill.

You see, there are often multiple places to get a piece of the action. As a business, there might be a primary source of income for your market, but it will often be crowded and inaccessible. It is far more interesting to exploit the niche opportunities that the "big boys" are largely ignoring, or are too cumbersome to take advantage of.

In the era of the "gig economy" and the rise of the solopreneur, the ground will provide all the seed you need—as long as you are nimble enough.

# CHAPTER 92

## *Why Solopreneurs Will Rule the World*

A solopreneur is defined in the Urban Dictionary as "an entrepreneur who works alone, solo, running their business single-handedly." A solopreneur believes in putting in an honest day's work; they don't care about pitch decks or profitable exits. They have a talent, and their sole focus for the foreseeable future is perfecting their craft. They have no ambitions to build a business and are perfectly happy with their laptop, tablet, and phone. They have a diverse mix of clients and are flexible in terms of how and where they work.

They are the future of the fast-growing "Gig Economy," and they are the solid and dependable bedrock of the entrepreneurial landslide that is carving its path through our global economy.

Solopreneurs are a sub-species of entrepreneur, but they differ in some key ways from their investment-chasing cousins. Entrepreneurs are currently getting all the press with sky-high valuations and unicorn rhetoric, but soon it will be the sheer numbers of the solopreneurs that will steal the show.

Here are a few of the key differences, from my point of view:

- Entrepreneurs seek investment in specific business ideas, look to gain investment for those ideas, rapidly scale their company, and then take profits at some point down the line. Big is beautiful, but big is often associated with huge amounts of burnt capital and little to show for it.

- Solopreneurs do not seek external backing. They invest in their specific talent and seek to build a long-term business with themselves as the "brand." They aim to develop niche and truly value-added relationships with a small number of clients, which means that they are highly reliable partners. They rarely have ambitions to take on a team, and they often create a sustainable income stream.

Given the two descriptions above, you could call the life of a solopreneur a little dull when you consider the billions floating around in the start-up scene. However, when you are a father of two kids, do you really want your lives to rely on the next round of funding? No? Well, you are not alone. Many solopreneurs are making an excellent income, and when the hard times come, they will be able to reduce their fees, reduce their outgoings, and "tough it out."

Corporate giants used to be the key drivers of the global economy, but now, increasingly, the fate of these solopreneurs is going to determine our future.

You see, many of these very same corporate giants are coming around to the idea of working with solopreneurs. When someone has a very specific talent, but you only need them for a few hours a week, why would you take on a full-time employee when you can pay a market-leading individual for their time? Yes, they might work with 20 other clients, but that doesn't matter as long as the work gets done to the highest possible standard.

This is the model of the future workplace in so many service-based industries, and the "little man" will be the winner. The solopreneur should receive far more recognition than they currently receive. Their steady rise will underpin the growth of the world economy for decades to come.

You probably know a solopreneur. Make sure you give them a pat on the back the next time you see them. They definitely deserve it.

# CHAPTER 93

## Is Grammar Important for Career Progress Anymore?

Times have certainly changed. The Oxford Dictionaries Word of the Year for 2015 is not a word. It's the "face with tears of joy" emoji. A pictograph. The runners-up include "ad blocker," "Brexit," "Dark Web," "lumbersexual," "on fleek," "refugee," "sharing economy," and "they (singular)."

We all send and receive emails more than we speak on the phone. We all write presentations and proposals. Some of us even write research papers or marketing material. We all certainly write our own resumes. In the end, we hope that our readers are comprehending exactly what it is that we had wanted to tell them.

Have you ever received an email where you wish you had the opportunity to speak with the sender on the phone or in-person, so that you didn't have to decipher the conundrum of an email you just received? I know I have. In fact, I get such an email at least once every day.

Lately, I seem to be reading business communication with grammar, style, typographical errors, and punctuation that is so far off the cuff that I wonder if people think that basic grammar and punctuation have indeed become optional in the new digital age. I'd like to argue the opposite by asserting that grammar has become even more vital in today's digital age, simply because the devices at our disposal have allowed us to write at a frequency and volume that we never did before. Most importantly, nobody wants to be misunderstood.

I don't profess to have a perfect understanding of the English language, but I would hope that my understanding is on a par with the majority of native English speakers on the planet.

For me, the building blocks of language are words, while the glue of language is the grammar. If the glue is loosely applied, you can still infer much of the sentence's meaning even if the workmanship isn't perfect. If there is no glue at all, the walls collapse, and the meaning is lost very quickly.

In an age of instant messaging and mobile communications, many of us seem to have forgotten about that glue altogether. Just because a message takes five seconds to read and only slightly more to write doesn't mean that it has to be incomprehensible. This kind of writing is transferred to our children's speech patterns. I am no expert in the abbreviations used in text messages, but I am sure that the language of school kids is unduly influenced.

Who cares if that word needs a capital letter or if that sentence requires a comma? Well, not many people, by the look of it. I am sure that many blog readers would say that even blogs themselves don't typically comply with the so-called "rules." Blogs tend to be conversational pieces. The author is speaking to the reader as they would over a glass of wine in a bar. Are you hearing me? I don't speak like Shakespeare, so why should I write like he would have written?

Technology is speeding up our lives; we value efficient communication. However, in our haste, the grammatical correctness of the message suffers. But since the recipient will probably still understand the message, does the poor grammar ultimately matter?

The main argument that I would put forward is that we are setting a bad example for the younger generation. They don't spend enough time reading well-written books and far too much time on text and instant messaging, where butchered English is *de rigeur*. I am certain that I don't understand or use every grammatical rule correctly, and neither do most people.

We could all brush up on our grammar from time to time. Here are a few areas that are particular offenders:

- Its and it's
- Who and whom
- Your and you're
- Their, they're, & there
- Fewer and less
- Farther and further
- Affect and effect

- Bring and take
- May and might

I don't mean to preach or seem too sanctimonious, because everyone has attained their own level of education in their native language. In my view, however, there is a basic standard that every person working in a business environment should be able to achieve. You should be aware of your shortcomings, and if you are mixing up there/they're/their or making some other obvious mistakes, people may make other assumptions about you.

# CHAPTER 94

## *Seven Bad Habits That Get People Fired*

We are all creatures of habit, set in our ways to varying degrees. Thus, when we understand that we need to change a certain aspect of our behavior, it requires a weighty reason to ensure we follow through. When the neural pathways in our brains are set on autopilot, it takes a conscious effort to change the record.

Many of us have settled into a comfortable existence in our personal lives—we are the way we are, and our friends and loved ones accept many of our shortcomings. However, there may be certain situations at work (especially if we have just moved companies), where our habits may need some reassessment.

Annoying habits should be tolerated to a certain extent. Our differences make us stronger, and no one wants to work in an office full of clones, but there are certain habits that should be nipped in the bud. An accumulation of these habits over a period of time could have serious ramifications for job security. As always, there are too many to mention in a short chapter, but here are my top seven habits that get people fired:

1. *They don't tell you how it is.* There are many shades of grey to what constitutes a lie, but the moment someone sugarcoats a response, exaggerates an opportunity, or conceals their true opinion, a guessing game

begins. If you cannot rely on someone to give their honest opinion, you may as well not ask them in the first place.

2. *They leave things until the last minute.* People like to feel busy, and for some there is no greater buzz than getting their work completed just before a deadline. This motivation may work for them, but there are often knock-on effects on others, who are less happy to live on the edge all the time. There are enough things to worry a manager at work—the timely completion of projects should not be one of them. Disorganization is a destroyer of relationships.

3. *They play the blame game.* The blame game is the disease of the modern office. From email black holes to stony silences in meetings, there are many ways to hold your hands up and say, "It wasn't my responsibility." Pointing the finger and focusing the blame on someone else may work once in a while, but if this is a constant tactic, questions will be asked as to the team ethic of the individual concerned.

4. *They can't stop checking social media.* When everyone is stressed out trying to meet their deadlines, there is nothing worse than seeing your neighbor browsing their Facebook or Twitter feeds. Social media is indeed becoming an integral part of certain roles, but there are always those who take liberties. The people around will assume that they are taking on a greater burden, and this resentment can build very easily.

5. *They don't take care of themselves.* Image is still so important is many businesses. People come to work as individuals, but they work as part of a collective. If they do not fit in with this collective in terms of their dress and personal hygiene, the exit door will beckon sooner rather than later. Greasy hair, unkempt fingernails, or grubby shoes are visible and may send the wrong messages to external clients or customers.

6. *They don't contribute.* "It's not my job" is a phrase that ties in with the blame game behavior, but in many organizations, merely doing the basics is also not enough. Contributing to your company and your

colleagues means going the extra mile, putting in the overtime, and suggesting creative solutions to tricky problems. Sitting back and just "doing your job" is letting your team down.

7. *They love the sound of their own voice.* I purposefully left this one until last. So much vital working time is lost when people dominate meetings (and email exchanges) by vociferously voicing their opinions, whether they are relevant to the topic of conversation or not. They are not content until their voice has been heard and are often so focused on their views that they miss the point of the conversation entirely. Two ears, one mouth—use them in that ratio.

# CHAPTER 95

## *Why Everything Is an Investment in Your Career*

Most actions in our lives have consequences. Their effects may be immediately visible, or we may have to wait years for their ripples to touch our lives again. Much is made of the "butterfly effect" of unintended and distant consequences, but if we act with purpose and meaning, our actions have every chance of giving our lives a push in the right direction.

Every action that we take is an investment in our future.

We do, however, need to be aware that there are bad investments as well as good investments. The bad ones come and bite us on the backside when we least expect it. Unless we analyze the origin of these events, the flawed decisions that lead to them will repeat themselves time and again.

Think about what you have done today at work.

Maybe you supported one of your colleagues in a meeting when they seemed to be isolated. People may not have agreed with your viewpoint, but they will have noticed your willingness to stand up for interests other than your own. People will turn to you in times of trouble in the future.

Maybe you helped a junior colleague get to grips with a common problem. Sharing knowledge with others without expecting anything in return is one of the best ways to strengthen relationships. You never know how that will benefit you in the future, but you can be sure that it will.

Maybe you sent off a curt email to someone who was politely chasing an update on a project. It is never so easy to ascertain emotions over email, and they may have read it as being overly defensive. The moment you start to build walls in your relationships, it becomes ever harder to dismantle them. Anything other than open and honest communication will lead to future misunderstandings.

These are just three examples of potential interactions. You probably have hundreds of such moments every day with all sorts of colleagues and customers. Unless you are 100% present and aware of the ramifications of your actions, the laws of chaos dictate that your future will be taken out of your hands extremely quickly. Very few events happen in a vacuum. For every thing that happens to you today, you will have had a contribution at some point in the past.

Some people talk about fate in our lives. I firmly side with those who say that we make our own luck, and for me, this means the accumulation of all the little investments that cumulatively add up to something that seemingly happens out of the blue.

Nothing happens out of the blue—it is not only the return on your investment, but also the investments in you by others.

If you invest in other people, they will certainly invest in you, and the potential of your life is the sum of all the investments that people have made—your parents, your first boss, your friends and even your kids. Investment is a two-way street; the more you put into it, the more you will get out of it.

# CHAPTER 96

## *The Myth of Multitasking*

Technology has delivered on its promise to be an enabler that is reshaping our world and continuously improving or simplifying almost everything we do. However, it is also responsible for perpetuating the myth that we are all now master multi-taskers. The question is, do any of us actually possess real multitasking powers?

We now find it completely natural to watch television while checking important emails and commenting on social media. Sure, we make old-school jokes that men are incapable of multitasking, and maybe this is most apparent when trying to hold a conversation with someone face down in their smartphone. But can anyone actually multitask?

Although multitasking might sound quite impressive, many will tell you that it's impossible, and we have just become more effective at task switching. It doesn't matter if you were born into this mobile world; the real challenge is the ability to focus with clarity on one given task at a time.

Self-confessed multi-taskers who claim to be super-efficient are often clumsy, stressed, and easily distracted with much slower response times and fractured concentration spans than those who focus on one task at a time.

Rather than increasing our efficiency or productivity, we often achieve quite the opposite results while being in a constant state of stress. Our overall performance usually suffers, such as accidents caused by foolish drivers who believe they can send a text message and give the road ahead their full attention at the same time.

We have all shaken our heads in disbelief at the rude individual who sits checking their phone during important meetings blissfully unaware of what is being discussed around them. If you commit to nothing, you'll be distracted by everything, so maybe it's time to focus on doing one thing at a time in order to produce a more efficient, higher standard of work.

Rather than running around like headless chickens dipping in and out of various tasks, maybe it's time we embraced the more productive technique of cluster-tasking where you simply group related tasks together to prevent getting sidetracked. For example, it has become too easy to allow emails to steal our time and attention every few minutes when we could simply set aside specific times during the day dedicated to emailing and focus on completing more important tasks instead.

Humans officially have a shorter attention span than a goldfish, so it is time to stop kidding ourselves. Multitasking is a myth of epic proportion that destroys performance, leaving us easily distracted and scrolling down an endless feed that ultimately just lowers our overall enjoyment and happiness.

To truly enhance our performance and help build our attention span again, we need to get back to basics and simply concentrate on doing one thing at a time. Close the door, switch off your music streaming service, turn your phone to silent and place it face down in front of you. Step away from the increasing notifications to focus on the task at hand and reap the rewards offered by clarity.

We have become too envious of those self-proclaimed multitaskers and their ability to spin plates, but the reality is that upon closer inspection, they are actually busy doing nothing, working the whole day through.

The concentration of doing that one thing involves working smarter but not harder and will dramatically increase your productivity. It's time to stop pretending that we are proud members of a super-efficient, multi-tasking workforce and face up to the fact that this digital utopia is one big urban myth.

# CHAPTER 97

## *Is "Likability" Truly Essential?*

The link between a happy team and a productive culture has been well documented. Collaboration is easier, staff retention is higher, and people come to work with smiles on their faces. In the tough times that we live in, this is vital for the success of any company. We are often told that one of the key factors in a cohesive team is the likability of its members.

However, a brief glimpse around us shows that not everyone is so likable.

To some people, it comes naturally; they are social butterflies, flitting in and out of the office circles with ease, spreading positivity with every emoticon in their emails and often going out of their way to help others. Others are drawn to them and feed off their relentless optimism.

Others try their best to be a team player, going out of their way to help others. They make an effort (sometimes against their nature) to support others and create a pleasant working atmosphere. They are harmonious and unobtrusive colleagues and probably form the majority of any typical office.

Then there are the less likable individuals. They might have certain personality traits that make them hard to cooperate with. They might take a more self-centered approach to work, rarely going out of their way to help others if it is not part of their job description. They might simply not "fit in" with everyone else; they are there to do their jobs, not become a clone of everyone else with a permanent grin on their faces.

However, it can sometimes happen that these disliked individuals can be the most productive. They come to work, concentrate on their job, and can be some of the most valued people in terms of adding to the financial bottom line. This is where a distinction must be made; there is undoubtedly a cultural bottom line where the "feel-good factor" resides, but the true bottom line should not be forgotten. At the end of the day, this is what ultimately dictates the fortunes of any company.

In the search for cultural fit and conformity, recruiting and HR departments are in danger of forgetting this second factor. Hiring for culture and attitude is great, but hiring for results and effectiveness should not be forgotten. Ok, someone is a little surly by nature, but if they are the most qualified candidate and have an impeccable record of delivery, should they really be discarded?

This is a fine line. If too many people feel that it is okay to act in their own best interests rather than follow the company's cultural norms, there will be anarchy. However, if companies unfailingly put personality ahead of performance, they will lose out on some star contributors who simply aren't so likable.

I believe that it goes back to the diversity argument. The more diverse the team, the better the chances of success. If a team is filled with lovely, likable people, the hard truths may not be said and failures may not be acknowledged. You need a mix of personalities to complement each other. The "miserable sorts" are often unafraid to call a spade a spade—you don't make much money with your heads in the clouds.

So, from a business point of view, likability is still desirable, but being less likable doesn't always equate to being entirely undesirable.

# CHAPTER 98

## *Surviving Office Politics*

There are certain rules in this life that are unwritten and certain skills that cannot be learned from a book or training course. The mix of personalities involved in certain situations ensures a unique set of subtleties and nuances, and there is seemingly no right way to behave.

I am talking, of course, about negotiating the maze of office politics, but this is a maze where the passageways are constantly shifting—nothing is as it seems. Reputations can be destroyed with a well-directed comment, projects derailed without the right people on board, and survival of the fittest (or most politically savvy) can reign supreme.

There are a few crucial questions to ask yourself that could dictate the trajectory of your career: Can you afford not to play? How can you be sure to avoid collateral damage? How do you minimize the potential risks?

Let's make something clear—you can't truly be involved in office life without playing at least a small part in the office politics. If you want to progress in your career, you have to be involved, so by definition you have no choice but to work out your own way of navigating the currents.

While I acknowledge that everyone is different and everyone has their own approach to solving certain issues, here are a few suggestions to think about:

***Be inclusive.*** Cultivating relationships with everyone in the business is crucial, no matter what the level. You never know which sort of allies you might need in the future, and it is important that you don't get involved in the "them and us" games that can go on. The broader your social circle in the office, the less likely you will be drawn into the gossip circles of cliques.

***Wait before you judge.*** People will always be quick to influence you with their thoughts about other people. They will use their relationship with you to sway your opinion in a certain direction, but it is vital that you are seen to be even-handed. If you always judge people and situations on their factual merits, others will be less likely to persuade you to join their judgmental crusade.

***Be open and honest.*** The moment you start listening to secrets and confiding your secrets with others is the moment you start to concoct a spider web of deceit that can become almost impossible to unravel. Tell other people what you think of them and give them your honest opinion of their ideas. There is nothing worse than saying "great idea" to their face and then "that's rubbish" behind their backs.

***Put yourself second.*** The "big idea" in office politics is that there has to be this "big cheese" influencer who can snap their fingers and make things happen. People play the game to further their own agendas – this automatically makes others suspicious and creates a competitive atmosphere. If you put the business agenda first, people will be far more likely to listen to you, as your opinion will be unbiased. Influence is far easier to gain when you are not at the center of the conversation.

***Don't get personal.*** When others are making personal attacks, it is hard not to jump on the bandwagon. The mob mentality takes over, and you feel "better" about putting someone down because you are part of a crowd. There is no difference. The victim will remember your part, even though your voice is one of many, and that will be another relationship that you have to mend down the line. If you don't get personal with others, they will be less likely to get personal with you.

In a room of highly intelligent people, some of whom may be your direct rivals, you have to be on your toes to flourish. “Winning” in office politics is, however, not the answer. Do all you can to survive or bypass the politics, by all means, but you have to be able to spend your energy on other things.

# CHAPTER 99

## *Why We Need Competition at Work*

Sometimes the little voice in our heads isn't enough.

Life can get a little comfortable sometimes. You have a good job, which affords you all the creature comforts at home. You have reached a level that is challenging but not too far away from your comfort zone. You go to work with a whistle and leave the office with a relieved sigh. Nothing and no one can touch you—finally you can relax a little.

The moment that you feel you have "arrived" is the moment that you are in danger of mentally switching off. You feel that you have deserved to sit back and enjoy the fruits of your labor, but it never quite works out that way. Other people will make sure of that.

Some describe work as a treadmill, others might describe it as a rat race, personally, I like the analogy of a tennis match. You can return the ball to your opponent, but you never quite know what sort of ball they are going to return back to you. The moment that you stop to admire your assumed winner is the moment they come up with a miraculous drop shot to win the set.

Most of our work is involved with other people. They embody this precise *je ne sais quoi,* and you never quite know what is coming next. You are in control of your actions, but you cannot hope to control other people. You never know when a newcomer may come in to smash all your sales records and become a rival for the Sales Director job. You never know when someone might be promoted and prove to be a more competent Project Manager. You never know when your best friend at work might get consecutive promotions and start moving in different corporate circles.

If you stand still, all of this could easily happen.

Of course, you have another choice. You can choose never to assume that your return is a winner. You can choose to train harder and practice more than ever before. You will take on opponents who would have wiped the floor with you last year, and you will win a few more games from them than usual. Being able to compete when you couldn't compete before is an amazing feeling—it gives you heart and a determination to carry on.

Seeing a colleague achieve something that you previously thought impossible should spur you on. If they can do it, why can't you? Most of us do not have the willpower to push our personal "bar" beyond the limits of our imagination, but when we see someone else do something amazing, it can inspire us to greater heights.

Some of the greatest achievements of man have only been achieved because of intense competition—all because people have stood on each other's shoulders and raised expectations that little bit higher.

It happens at work every day. Ignore your competitors at your peril; they will make you great.

# CHAPTER 100

## *What Is Your Storytelling Quotient?*

Creativity has never been so valued in the workplace. What was once confined to the dark recesses of someone's personal life is fast becoming the differentiator in a competitive world where ideas are king.

Everyone has had periods in their lives where they have been bitten by the creative bug, only for their passion to be dampened by the reality that their efforts have a limited audience. While creativity is enjoyable and beneficial on a personal level, many of us yearn for it to have a wider purpose. When that purpose has been lacking, the priorities of our busy lives have taken over and that creative drive ebbs and flows like the tides.

Ironically, it is technology that has enabled the rise of the corporate storytellers. Mobile phones are their medium, social media is their loudspeaker, and instant messaging, their oxygen. It has never been easier to engage an audience of thousands, but herein lies the challenge: they are not exclusively your audience.

People are being bombarded by information like never before. In order for your employees or customers to retain your messages, they have to be memorable; they have to "stick." This is where storytellers come into focus.

Tell someone a fact, and it will likely be consigned to the wasteland known as "Sorry, what was that again?" Invoke an emotional response by telling them a story around that fact, and it will be far more likely to be retained in their memory. When you involve them in the story by appealing to their emotions, you are taking the first step to influencing them.

Of course, you have to tailor your stories to the audience. You should understand what is important to them and make them feel as if it is their story rather than your story. Companies and individuals with a high SQ first seek to understand to whom they are speaking before even thinking about their story.

When you let a meaningful story out into the world, it takes on a life of its own in the heads of those who hear it. They will all interpret it in subtly different ways, and it melds in their imaginations with all the other dialogues that make up "their world." If (that is the important word) it is meaningful to them, they will accept it. If it doesn't resonate, it will be dismissed, crashing like a wave against the harbor wall, never to leave its mark.

Storytelling is not only the territory of the marketing department. Finance tell stories to give their figures some context. Operations need to listen to stories of employees in order to make things run smoothly. Sales need to tune into the stories of their customers rather than force feed them their "own" stories. HR are increasingly molding the company culture through storytelling, letting their employer brand develop organically through a constant internal dialogue.

So, coming back to the question of the title, do you have a high SQ?

Do you take every opportunity to fire the imaginations and stimulate the creativity of the people you work with? Do you foster a dialogue with your colleagues, or does information flow only in one direction? Do you make time for your team to tell their own stories and make sure that everyone's thoughts are heard? Can you talk about something totally unrelated to work, only for people to find parallels and lessons within your words?

Storytelling takes time, it doesn't have an obvious ROI, and it defies measurement. Despite this, it is the most important movement in modern business. Its magic takes place in the hearts and minds of its audience, influencing them once but touching them forever.

# CHAPTER 101

## How to Cold Call a Hiring Manager

"Hello. We've never spoken or been in contact, but I'd like to request five minutes of your time to discuss how I might add value to your team. I understand that you are busy, but I believe that it would be worth your while."

What response do you think this hopeful applicant might receive? The probability is that it won't be fantastic. The hiring manager doesn't know them at all, and is highly likely to put a black mark against their application there and then, no matter how good they might be. This simply is not done – you should never cold call a hiring manager. Ever. Apologies for the misleading title, but not every glaringly obvious bad idea is glaringly obvious to everyone. Yes, it might work out in rare circumstances, but only after you have burned countless bridges with previous failed attempts. Don't even consider it.

So, apologies for the clickbait. Maybe the title should read:

### How to Call a Hiring Manager

See what I did there? Ah, so if the call isn't cold, then there might be a bit more hope? Yes, very much so, but you have to put in the groundwork to ensure that the manager will be happy to take that call first.

But first, a question. Isn't it a good idea to follow the usual channels of sending your resume to the HR email inbox? Surely, they have everything under control and won't miss your undoubted value to the company. Well, yes and no. Many companies do have extremely thorough hiring processes, but, given the volume of applications, the opportunities for human and software errors are still considerable. Maybe you don't have the right selection of keywords on your resume, and the system doesn't suggest you for your ideal role. Maybe the HR Manager doesn't have the subject matter expertise to realize how your unique experience might be a perfect fit for the specific role.

Building relationships with the hiring managers before the hiring process is nearly always a good idea. But how do you do this without jeopardizing your chances? The answer is to start before you are even looking for a job. You need to get on their radar when you haven't got an ulterior motive.

That isn't as hard as it sounds, and initially you don't even need to be in direct contact with them anyway. Participating in online groups and discussions where they are active is one idea. You might want to write a blog about your industry, or alternatively, you could become an active (and valued added) commentator on other industry blogs.

The next step is to reach out in a small way. Online this might mean "liking" or "sharing" their updates every now and again. As long as you ensure that this isn't obsessive, it will simply remind them that you are around. They will appreciate the support, and many of them will be curious to check out your profile.

Once you are sure that they have a certain level of awareness of you (maybe they have reciprocated some of your likes), you can start to share things directly with them. Maybe you could send them a message with a link to an industry event and ask if they were aware of it. Again, gently let them know that you were generally informing your network,

so as not to seem like a stalker!

Lastly, I would advise dropping them a message first before you call so that it doesn't catch them at a bad time. You only get one chance to have this conversation, so do it on their terms. You'll be surprised at how many people are prepared to give someone they know a helping hand.

All this entails a lot of investment and patience from your point of view, but when it comes time for that "make it or break it" phone call, they will know your name, they will picture your face, and they will be far more likely to welcome a chat. They may not have something for you, but if you have the right level of relationship, they may well be happy to refer you to a friend.

Calling a hiring manager could lead to wonderful opportunities. Make sure that you give that call the best chance of success.

# CHAPTER 102

## *Ten Signs That You Should Leave Your Job*

These moments come more often than we would like. Sometimes it is possible to nip them in the bud and make a few changes, but at other times you simply need to face the inevitable music. It may be time to start looking for a new job when:

***You dread going to work.*** It›s normal to be tired in the morning, but you shouldn›t feel thought-consuming anxiety when it›s time to get up. The sunrise is hidden behind foreboding dark clouds, and you shuffle into the office like a convict dragging a ball and chain.

***You are not yourself.*** Who are you anyway? If you don't recognize yourself in the way you react to certain people and in certain situations, you have let yourself be influenced by the situation. When you have lost your mojo, often only a change of scene will help it to return.

***You have an abusive boss.*** This is one of the big ones. Whether your boss is a bully, a manipulator, or a coward, you deserve better. Sitting there and suffering in silence is tantamount to giving permission; there is always an alternative. People don't leave jobs, they leave bosses.

***Your health is suffering.*** Stress is a silent assassin and can creep up on those who are not self-aware. If there are no explanations for those headaches, stomach aches, and fatigue, it›s time to consider a psychological explanation. The link between mental instability and physical illness has been well documented. Don't let your job cause a long-term health problem.

***You are playing dumb.*** Constantly having to play down your intelligence can be a prime cause of frustration. If you have more experience than the boss, it will either lead to conflict or stagnation. You need to find a place to work where your talents are used to their full potential.

***Your company is struggling financially.*** There is nothing worse than the sword of Damocles hanging over you every time you look at your company's stock price. The best people left long ago, what is stopping you from escaping the inevitable? If the writing is on the wall, why are you still standing there reading it?

***You enter a spiral of negativity.*** The voices in your head won't stop, and you find comfort in complaining with others. This alienates you yet further from the productive types in the office, and the exit door opens that little bit wider. If you surround yourself with negative people, the specter of depression looms large on the horizon.

***There is no work/life balance.*** You have left work, but your head is still there. You are in the restaurant, but you can't shake those worries about the presentation the next day. People stop inviting you to events, as they know the answer anyway. You'll be working… The more time that you spend in the office, the less work you actually get done.

***There are zero job prospects.*** You know more than the boss, but you aren't going anywhere. Most people enjoy a sense of accomplishment at work. Reaching the limits of your job removes that incentive, and you feel stuck in limbo. If you are ok with being on a treadmill, then carry on. If the thought of perpetual motion without progress scares you, it's time to get off.

***No one tells you anything.*** You feel like an outsider, you aren't invited to work social occasions anymore, and people stop sharing gossip with you. It is as if you have fallen off the edge of the Earth and simply aren't considered worthy of people's time. You might share an office space, but that doesn't automatically make you part of the team.

# CHAPTER 103

## *Managing Change in Your Career*

What do you do when something unexpected happens? Was it really that unexpected, or did you just shut your eyes and hope for it to go away? Had you gotten so used to your current situation that contemplating a new reality seemed impossible?

Questions like this pop into our heads when disruption enters our lives. This may take the form of a stock market crash. It may be the loss of a job or the breakdown of a relationship. In these situations (and many others), there is one thing that you can be sure of: change is constant and should be expected.

You have two options: evolution or extinction.

This life-long struggle is nicely captured in the famous book *Who Moved My Cheese* by Spencer Johnson, M.D. I would like to share the basic story with you and relate it to our modern world where, rightly or wrongly, disruption is celebrated.

The four main characters in the book live in the middle of a maze. Their daily activity consists of putting on their running shoes and setting off into the maze in search of cheese (fulfillment).

There are two mice named Sniff and Scurry. They are simple animals, led by instinct, Sniff pointing out the direction of the cheese and Scurry racing ahead to find it. The other two are little men the same size as the mice named Hem, a worrier, and Haw, a dreamer. They are more organized in their search for the cheese, using maps and rational thinking rather than instinct.

Using their various methods, all four of them find "Cheese Station C" and return every day to eat their fill. Hem and Haw become lazy, throw their running shoes away, and start to take the cheese for granted. Meanwhile, the mice notice that the stockpile of cheese is going down and get ready to run back into the maze as soon as it finishes.

The inevitable happens; the men mourn the unfair loss of the cheese, but the practical mice run off and soon find another Cheese Station with a huge mountain of cheese. Hem and Haw debate what they should do. Haw instinctively imagines looking for new cheese and can almost taste it, but Hem discourages him and destroys his dream. To begin with, both men felt a sense of entitlement to cheese, but Haw finally sees the light. He laughed and realized that it is folly to "keep doing the same thing expecting something to change."

Haw plucked up the courage to leave Hem, ran off into the maze and finally found the new source of cheese. However, this time, he didn't take it for granted. He measured the cheese every day and knew that one day, it too would run out…

Haw then wrote seven rules on the wall of the new cheese station to remind himself of reality in a world of moving cheese:

*Change happens. They keep moving the cheese.*

*Anticipate change. Get ready for the cheese to move.*

*Monitor change. Smell the cheese often, so you know when it's getting old.*

*Adapt to change quickly. The quicker you let go of the old cheese, the sooner you can enjoy new cheese.*

*Enjoy change. Savor the adventure and enjoy the taste of new cheese.*

*Be ready to quickly change and enjoy it again. They keep moving the cheese.*

*Change and win! Move with the cheese.*

For me, the biggest learning from the book is not to fear change. When you move beyond fear, you feel free, and at that point you can make the decisions required to move your life forward. Let go of the old situation, accept the "new normal," and you will find the next lot of cheese soon enough.

# CHAPTER 104

## *Why Do Your New Recruits Keep Leaving?*

The recruitment process doesn't end when someone walks through the door on their first day. In the current market where a top candidate may have multiple head-turning offers, it is vital that a comprehensive onboarding process seals their emotional decision to join.

If recruitment is seen as a production line that ends on that first day, the percentage of "returns" will be high. You can't simply put someone down on their chair with minimal support and expect them to flourish in what are often the hardest few months of their time there. Too many companies pay lip-service to the first day induction—a few semi-useful presentations, lunch with a load of other new starters, many of whom they will probably never see again, and then spending the last few hours sorting out their stationary, etc.

I am obviously exaggerating, but I do believe that companies could do an awful lot more to ensure that the relationships built up during the recruitment process transfer into the first month's work. The success of a recruit sits with the recruitment team, and in my view, the responsibility for their successful integration should lie with them as well.

The best companies give the candidates an HR contact to approach with any issues that might crop up. Most new employees want to hit the ground running as quickly as possible and don't generally want to bother their bosses or colleagues with too many concerns in the early days. The possibility of having a contact from outside their team with whom to discuss the various issues is key to their integration. They shouldn't spend days worrying about the subtleties of processing their expenses, for example; these are easy questions, and they should get easy answers.

However, I would question that the recruiters themselves could potentially take on the more relationship-orientated parts of this activity in conjunction with HR. They get to know the candidates, understand what makes them tick, and then they can be the constant factor to integrate them into the further workings of the company.

Companies lose hundreds of thousands of dollars in lost recruitment fees every year. If just a little more time and thought were spent in this specific area, maybe even SMEs would reap the benefits.

Another aspect of the new starter process is that the existing employees have little incentive to giving them the best possible start. Many will be welcoming, some will be hugely helpful, but ultimately everyone has their own agendas and will be wary of getting too close to the unknown quantity of the new person too soon. If there were a small part of their company bonus linked to the success and longevity of new recruits throughout the company, the initial 3-6 month period would be more productive, less stressful and result in far closer relationships.

It all comes down to process and expectations.

If new recruits are expected to integrate themselves, there will inevitably be mixed results. If a company ensures that existing employees are actively engaged in this integration (long after that intense first day), then wonder how much better their retention numbers might be.

New recruits leave for all sorts of reasons. Many of those reasons can be addressed if the recruitment process carries on for at least the first three months. Should companies see this as a bit more of a priority? In my view, yes.

# SECTION 4 – SALES

# CHAPTER 105

## The Art of Closing: Top Sales Negotiation Strategies

Sales negotiation has not decreased in importance, although the glamor may have faded. Think of the term salesperson. It's unequivocally pejorative. And yet, the practical knowledge of sales negotiation is more important than ever. The market is growing globally, and goods and services are cropping up every day.

This has caused department heads to absorb traditionally sales specific tactics into their business models. In other words, no matter what sector you operate in, buying and selling will make up a natural part of its dynamics. That's why stepping into a negotiation, whether big or small, armed with the skills that have kept sales departments at the front lines of business—in spite of social backlash—is indispensable.

The fundamentals of sales negotiation have not changed much, despite cultural and social oscillation. People are people, and we've been dealing with money and goods for quite some time now. To understand the art of sales negotiation is to grasp the interplay of psychology, economics, decision-making, and market trends.

Throughout my time as a businessman, I have learned invaluable lessons about sales negotiation. These lessons have helped me grow my businesses and other people's businesses. Now, I will share some of them with you.

## Step into the Buyer's Mind

Buyers are always intent on improving their bottom lines. That won't stop anytime in the foreseeable future. There are three primary ways that buyers go about doing this, and it's often at your expense as a seller.

The first is to sell competitively. That usually results in price-point matching or beating a competitor's price. This can happen in a number of ways, but more often than not it is through innovation. It's risky and expensive, however.

The second is cutbacks. In a simple and unsympathetic sense, that implies the reduction of operating expenses.

The third is better negotiation. This is by far the easiest path to improve profits. Buyers want to negotiate lower prices with their suppliers because it directly affects their bottom line. This is the alternative that directly applies to you as a seller.

## The Art of Negotiation

This section of the chapter will read much like a step-by-step interspersed with tested advice. I will start with the three types of gambits: beginning, middle, and end. They denote the three phases of a typical negotiation.

## Gambit: Beginning

Broadly, gambits are the lifeblood of negotiation. When you first initiate a sales negotiation, you establish the bedrock of your buyer/seller relationship. Early preparation and the demands you make, including how you propose them, will set the tone for subsequent transactions, even within that same conversation.

***Preparation.*** To establish a solid foundation, your initial offering must reflect an accurate and studied assessment of the buyer, the market, the buyer's organization, and any other relevant and crucial conditions. This preparation is vital.

***Wiggle Room.*** There are a few rules of conduct that apply universally for beginning gambits, aside from preparation. Henry Kissinger once wrote, "Effectiveness at the conference table depends upon overstating one's demand."

In other words, anticipate haggling and compromise. Start high. This gives you room to negotiate without the compounding fear that your bottom line might suffer because you started where you'd like to be in terms of profit.

This strategy is called, Maximum Plausible Position. It's a fine balance that requires you to identify what the highest amount you can ask for is without forsaking reasonability. In laymen's terms, create wiggle room.

***Initial Proposal.*** The best starting point for price negotiation is to have your buyer state their position before you do. Once you have that expectation, you have immense power.

***Saying Yes.*** An affirmation to an initial offer from a client or counteroffer instantly—painfully—raises two regrets. One is, "I could have done better." This one is self-explanatory. The second, "Something must be wrong," is a bit more complex. In that instance, our intuition about the buyer will be undermined because whatever our mental picture was of the buyer, it seems to be misaligned with reality. This is a seller's existential crisis, if you will.

This experience can be very frustrating because getting past an initial offer or counteroffer is a central step in good sales negotiation.

## Tips & Tricks

In the beginning gambit, a few strategies can help you gain an advantage and advance your position. Here are three such strategies.

***Body Language.*** Always pay attention to body language. It can belie your buyer's words. The flinch is a telling bodily cue. It singles surprise, simulates pain, and tells your interlocutor that they've reached a maximum point.

***Reluctance.*** Whether you are dealing with a reluctant buyer or playing one, remember that the strategy here is to disarm the interlocutor. This is an iteration of good cop/bad cop. Chances are they are trying to get you to divulge your maximum plausibility point. Don't succumb.

***Detachment.*** Detachment is absolutely essential when tensions rise and anger flares. Don't lose your cool, and remember that this is not personal. You don't know what the buyer has at stake in this negotiation, so bring it back to the issue at hand. One method for re-centering yourself is to keep a running tab of where you've gotten in the negotiation.

## Gambits: Middle

Middle gambits are based in your initial conversation and the bedrock you've established—whatever that may be. This phase depends on you successfully responding to the pressures that arise in the conversation. There are some that can help move you in the direction you want while others derail you and force you to salvage lost ground.

***Higher Authority.*** "I'll have to speak to my boss about this." It signals all sorts of things. What it does best, however, is displace responsibility from you to the shoulders of some nebulous "boss" figure that we can all relate to. It's precarious because it can signal—among other things—that you aren't the decision-maker.

On the other hand, if someone deploys this tactic against you, be prepared with counterarguments, such as: ingratiate their ego; secure a commitment to you; ask for a commitment that you can refer to at a later date.

***Concessions.*** Reciprocity is the norm in the world at large. When babies are just about newborns, studies have shown that they possess primitive intuitions about fairness and punishment. Adults are no different. When you make a concession, or vice versa, there must be give-and-take. It places greater value of your concession and indicates that you aren't being pushed around, but rather making a carefully considered decision about value exchange. Never expect or trust that the other side will compensate you for your concessions later. Negotiations are in the moment. They are here in the present, in the now.

***Non-confrontation.*** Some people tend to argue over anything. They are reactionary and tend to suck you into their whirlwind of anger. Don't let them. Don't argue with someone who attacks what you say. In a negotiation, there must be a level of trust, however leery. Arguing back perpetuates a vicious cycle. The more you respond or retaliate, the more they'll argue their point so you won't be able to get them past whatever is impelling them to argue in the first place. Regain composure, lend perspective, and move on.

***Split the difference.*** It's quite simple, yet effective. When you are at odds with someone on a price, ask them to split the difference. It's fair, balanced, and easy to say. The boons are plentiful. What will happen here sometimes is that your buyer will try to get more out of you to compensate for their concession. Generally, that means taking their problem and making it yours. There is no quick fix for this. Each problem is unique. What you could do is propose alternative solutions that don't involve spent time or energy on your part.

## Gambits: Ending

In short, the ending gambit prepares you to solidify the buyer's commitment to a negotiation.

***Good Guy/Bad Guy.*** Believe it or not, negotiators use this ploy more often than I'd like to admit. It's time-old and surprisingly effective. It takes at least two negotiators to pull this off. You can already imagine what it looks like. When you see it, call it out. People are usually embarrassed and move-on.

***Nibbling.*** Small wins amount to big gains. I say it often, and I can never overstate it. Some people call it upselling. Whatever you term it, the point is that after you've established a commitment, you can create an additional buying opportunity that is only available to the person once they've made that commitment. This is treacherous, however, so be vigilant.

***Halt.*** Stop yourself when you conceded too much or too often. It can create the expectation that you always give in, especially at the end. This is easy when you have secured a deal. The fear of losing it can lead you down the road to perdition. Halt, and turn around.

## On Concessions

Concessions are where negotiation gets sticky. In a sense, it is the spirit of negotiation. Be warned that buyers will always try to grind away at your offers. It happens. Don't be alarmed.

***Habit.*** I mentioned this above, and I'll say it again. Don't create the expectations of concession. Also, be careful how much you conceded because it establishes latent benchmarks. For example, if you make a $500 concession the first time, your buyer may expect you to do the same the second time.

***Accrual.*** It's called sunk-cost effect. Basically, when you've lost a lot already, you are willing to lose more, but in smaller increments. It's surprisingly efficacious.

For example, let's say you concede $500 in the middle of negotiations. Chances are that you will concede $100 more easily later on because you don't want to lose the business. Plus, you've already conceded $500, so what's another $100? The antidote is to bear in mind the total rather than the discrete amounts.

***Big Reveal.*** Buyers will try to force your hand through dismissal or apathy. They'll say things like, "I don't negotiate," or, "This is a waste of my time." Don't let yourself be intimidated. Chances are they are just trying to shake you up so you reveal your price-points, make concessions, and feel uncertain.

***Modesty.*** The guiding principle with concessions is the opposite of the Maximum Plausibility Point. Rather than starting high, start low, very low. If your buyer rejects a small concession, you can comfortably raise it without fear of losing too much. Remember *Habit*, also mentioned above. You don't want to create an expectation. So, keep track of your concessions. If you make a concession here, then increase the amount elsewhere. This raises the stakes and dissuades your buyer from asking for further concessions.

***Peak-End Rule.*** When you make a small, last minute concession it can make the buyer feel good about their wins, at little cost to you. The ideal negotiation is when both parties walk away feeling that they got what they wanted, or best when they feel that they outdid the other person. You can concoct this emotion.

Peak-End Rule refers to the psychology heuristic in which people retrospectively perceive a situation in relation to the last perceived emotion. In this hypothetical, if the emotion is good, then the person will recall the whole situation positively. A last-minute concession can accomplish this.

## Power & Personalities

What is a conversation about sales negotiation if we don't discuss power dynamics and personality types? Incomplete, that's what. I saved this section for last because it is speculative at heart. People are complex and often elude our best efforts to generalize accurately. That doesn't mean, however, that the entire effort is fraught.

In my experience, there are a few power dynamics and personality types that I've identified time and again.

***Titular Power.*** This is power derived from a title. Titles, whether people care to admit it or not, confer influence. Just as you would not treat the President of the United States the same as your mother, you would not treat the CEO of a company like you would their sales rep. If you have the title, leverage it. On the same token, do not fear someone else's title.

***Compensation Power.*** This is power derived from promises. To gain ground and shake out concessions, buyers will promise future rewards. They'll say they have a big job coming up, or that they can guarantee you an in to some business. Don't fall for it.

***Deferent Power.*** This is power derived from adherence to set standards and values. If you establish that certain values are important to you and that you cannot flout them, it builds trust and respect. Your buyer might be frustrated but they'll acknowledge your character, and that can secure long-term relationships.

***Personability Power.*** This is power derived from personality. There is no easy way to subsume this or delimit it. The goal is to get your buyer to like and trust you. Finding common ground is a good place to start. Ultimately, this is a matter of intuition and would take several books and trial-and-error to master.

***Knowledge Power.*** This is power derived from insider information. I am not referring to illegality here. I am referring to expertise. If you can demonstrate expertise, or knowledge, on a topic, the buyer will be less likely to contradict you and more likely to acquiesce to your demands.

If you are on the receiving end, however, and someone is wielding expertise against you, make reference to another expert with a similar or opposing view to diffuse the situation. In any case, the goal isn't to contradict. The goal is to subvert the power that knowledge grants.

***Sharing Power.*** This is power derived from sharing information. This is a tactic more than a power relationship. It easily fits underneath any one of the abovementioned categories. When you share information, you share power, and that creates the urge to reciprocate. It bridges the gap between you and your buyer.

Well, that just about covers the power dynamics that I've identified in my time in sales.

Here are the personality types I've encountered.

***Practical.*** Practical buyers tend to be domineering. They veer on hostility and imply that things will not bode well for you if they don't get what they want. These people are bottom line oriented and tend to know what they want stepping into the conversation. Don't waste your time with small talk. Zero in on the negotiation point and do not show hesitancy. Don't overload the buyer with information or show over-enthusiasm. You'll come off as farcical. Be quick, factual, and steadfast.

***Extrovert.*** Extroverted buyers tend to be friendly, open, and decisive. Their strategy tends toward the affective. They will influence you with charisma. They are usually not savvy enough to unveil your ploys and tactics, but they won't shy away from saying, "No," nor will they shy away from saying what's on their mind. Talk about their interests and about their excitement. If they feel you are enthusiastic and excited, they are far more likely to go along with what you are putting down.

***Amiable Personality.*** Amiable buyers tend to avoid things that make them uncomfortable. Trust is central to an amiable buyer. If they cannot trust you, they will not do business with you, no matter how competitive your offer. They are innately skeptical. You can easily sway an amiable buyer by building on emotional cues and taking care not to offend them. Tread lightly and check in constantly. Ask about doubts, hesitancies, and the like.

***Analytic Personality.*** Analytical buyers tend to need and provide lots of information. They appreciate accuracy and concision. They are flawless organizers and require it for all their negotiations. They tend to eschew relationship building. To sway such a person, lead with the facts, with benefits and losses, and support your conclusions with reliable information.

## Last Remarks

This covers most of what I have gleaned of the art of negotiation from my years as a businessman. I don't see the art of negotiation as a smoke-and-mirrors practice. Not even a little. I see it as a delicate balancing act—a practice in receptivity, active listening, and purposeful communication.

If you take away anything away from this chapter, let it be these four points:

1. Do not limit yourself to one negotiation point. Negotiations are multi-layered.

2. Realize that not all negotiations are personal. It's healthy to acknowledge that you and your buyer have diametrically opposed goals, but that does not mean you can't reach an acceptable compromise.

3. Greed is disdainful and impractical every time.

4. Reciprocity and equity are central tenets of the art of negotiation. Give and take.

# CHAPTER 106

## *Discover Your Inner Salesman*

From the moment a baby smiles at their mother because they want her to smile back, they are entering a transactional world.

Like it or not, most of our actions provoke some sort of reaction, and our behavior partly dictates the behavior of those we interact with. Consciously influencing the behavior of others is a complex business, and definitely something that takes a lifetime to understand fully.

Do you think the mother would be so cheery if the baby were crying all the time? If the mom ignored the child, the crying might soon stop. If the mom showed the child the attention that it was craving, the crying might continue. The behavior in that particular relationship would become self-reinforcing, and would probably continue until the child enters pre-school. The derision of the other children would soon curb the attention-seeking crying, but the child would find other attention-seeking behavior. It might seek to be the loudest, the cleverest, or the most popular.

The baby that craved and received attention on tap could be seen to become an extrovert in life. They understand that their actions always carry some sort of reaction, and over time these actions might become ever more exaggerated. These types are the natural salesmen of our world, they exude confidence and seem to thrive on attention. As long as their ego has not been stroked too many times, these extroverts will not find it hard "making friends and influencing people."

However, what about the babies who maybe cried and were left to their own devices? Many of them will grow up to lead balanced lives, but for those with a more insular bent, a slightly more introverted life beckons. Now, being introverted is no bad thing. Many introverts are hugely contented with their lot in life; they don't need external reinforcement of "who they are," and many have a healthy internal dialogue around what they value in life.

It is when they need to influence others that introverts sometimes struggle. They may not have had the attention-seeking upbringing, but that doesn't mean that there isn't an inner-salesman inside each of them. If their parents had given them that attention when they cried, they might have been hardwired to seek it out later in life. I believe that "nurture" plays a significant role in the development of our personalities, but that doesn't mean that we don't have the inner potential to act in a different way.

So, for every introvert going into a sales meeting or an interview, I would like you to think about this:

You can choose your behavior in any given situation. Just because you are used to downplaying your role and being modest doesn't mean you can't "talk yourself up" when it is really needed. If your voice is not heard and your actions not noticed in the race to be promoted, there is every possibility that you will be overlooked. If you can't examine and explain your past experiences in detail at an interview, how will your potential employers gain an insight into your ability? If you can't sell yourself and your company at a sales pitch, will the potential clients think that you don't want their business as much as the others?

You do want to be promoted, you do want that job, and you do want that business. There is nothing stopping you from switching on that inner salesmen, and when you have done it a few times, you will know that he/she is always there to be called upon.

You may not want to live your life like that, and you certainly don't have to, but sometimes that inner salesman can make a big difference to where it takes you.

# CHAPTER 107

## *Redesigning the Broken Sales Function in America*

Sales departments across the US are in a serious state of dysfunction. Sales management is well aware of this, but rather than targeting the root cause, they are busy with incremental—and peripheral— improvement initiatives: sales training, automation technology, or lead generation tactics (e.g., outsourced digital marketing, social media activities, influencer marketing, etc.). Because these initiatives don't address the dysfunction directly, they amount to beating around the proverbial bush and pouring money down proverbial drains.

### Why Are Sales Departments Dysfunctional?

Sales as a business activity is as important as it was even 50 years ago. The issue is that other business activities are improving while sales departments cling to the same structure, the same management approach, and the same practices that have been in place for ages now.

The predominant approach to sales is individualist at heart. Usually, sales is the sole responsibility of an independent, sometimes outsourced, individual. This individual is incentivized rather than paid, and is valued on the basis of what they return, not what they do.

This creates an insidious culture of outcome- rather than process-oriented success. The salesperson gets entrenched in contacting prospective buyers, generating new pitches and spreading themselves thin just to meet a quota. That time spent devising methods is time that could be better spent actually selling products.

The issue is a lack of adaptability in sales, not a lack of relevance. This is not to say that an out-with-the-old-and-in-with-the-new approach is always the answer, but in this case, some updating is long overdue.

What I am getting at is that sales should no longer be considered the responsibility of a sole individual. It should be the responsibility of a team of specialists, who each perform crucial tasks oriented toward big picture objectives.

In this new sales approach, perhaps contrary to intuition, the incentives to perform will not diminish and the bottom line will surely not suffer. The complete opposite should happen.

## Let's Get a Little Meta for a Second

This is the first part of a two-part chapter meant to provide a new approach to sales. This first part sketches out the general framework of that approach, while the second gives a detailed example of how it would play out in real-life.

The approach as it is laid out here is theoretical yet practicable. It may not apply as described to every single business with a sales department. Nonetheless, the business philosophy that motivates this redesign certainly can.

## Looking to the Past: The Division of Labor

Under the new approach, sales would be the result of various interconnected mechanisms, rather than the output of a single individual.

Salespeople would become components in a larger machine, supported by key teams of specialists—divided according to a predetermined workflow—and management would be solely responsible for infrastructure and day-to-day operations.

As surprising as it may sound, this is not the nature of most contemporary sales departments.

## Adam Smith's Division of Labor Theory

In his magnum opus *An Inquiry into the Nature and Causes of the Wealth of Nations,* Adam Smith predicted that the division of labor would drive a massive increase in productivity. Essentially, the division of labor theory dictates that separating production into distinct and interconnected steps managed by select individuals (specialists) would save time, resources, and money.

## Adam Smith's Pin Factory

Adam Smith conceptualized the division of labor theory into the classic thought experiment known as the Pin Factory.

As the experiment goes, a pin factory with 10 workers divided the pin making into 18 distinct steps. Then, each of the workers was assigned a step to specialize in. In so doing, the factory could produce thousands of pins per day by channeling the energy of each worker into easy steps that together produced a pin.

## The Division of Labor in Today's Companies

If we were to peer into the windows of a contemporary company, we would probably discover the division of labor in just about every production environment.

From quantitative-heavy engineering factories to psychology-heavy human resources departments, the division of labor is everywhere. Oddly, the only business environment that seems to have ignored the lessons of the division of labor theory is sales.

This oddity is at the root of the dysfunction experienced by many sales departments.

## Four Basic Lessons from Manufacturing

Manufacturing departments have truly embraced the lessons of the division of labor theory. This business sector is a salient example because it has experienced significant improvements over the past few years—in part due to advances in technology and in part due to its practices.

By looking at the typical functioning of contemporary manufacturing departments, we can glean a few basic lessons that will help us put the new approach to sales into practice.

1. *Scheduling Is Specialized.* Manufacturing departments typically have some form of centralized scheduling. Most work is broken down into two basic components: critical activities and scheduling.

   Broadly described, critical activities are those that significantly alter physical or informational matter. Scheduling refers to how tasks are sequenced and timed. When these two components coalesce, you have synchronization. As your workforce gets bigger, however, scheduling rapidly grows more problematic.

There are ways to avoid this: divide the labor. Assign specialized teams or groups to specific critical activities and other specialized teams or groups to scheduling.

So, before we divide labor in sales, we must relieve salespeople of all scheduling activities and assign those activities to teams who will just focus on scheduling.

2. *Workflow Is Standardized.* Manufacturing departments typically have standardized workflows and procedures. The efficiency of those workflows usually depends on specialists responsible for scheduling and on separate specialists who perform critical activities. In the context of sales, workflow and procedures are aimed at sales objectives.

   The problem in sales is that those workflows are often the sole responsibility of a single salesperson. The salesperson is expected to independently develop, coordinate, and carryout each part of their insular workflow. They must do all this to meet benchmarks that determine rewards.

   The continual time, energy, and resources necessary to sustain each of those responsibilities runs contrary to efficient standardization. Eventually the inefficiency wears the salesperson down, detracting from their ability to actually sell the product or service.

   Standardization along manufacturing lines, i.e., who does what and when, can enhance efficiency and allow for easy identification of procedural shortcomings.

3. *Human Resources Are Specialized.* Manufacturing departments typically have a specialized workforce with each worker solely dedicated to very specific tasks that aggregate to larger objectives. The benefit of specialization is that it increases productivity through practice and habit. It also eliminates the need to switch between substantially different activities, thereby drastically reducing stress levels

That is why specialization is tightly linked to standardization. A standardized workflow or procedure is made more viable when your human resources are specialized. To standardize a workflow that is supported by specialized human resources, the division of labor must happen along three axes: (1) Location, (2) Work Type, and (3) Cadence.

These divisions of labor (*which we will explore in the second part of this article series*) should be made based on the nature of the activity, on whether it is profitably an outdoor or an indoor activity, and on whether it has a short or long lead-time.

To successfully implement these divisions, sales departments must assess their resources, their target market, and their unique corporate goals.

4. *Management Is Unifying.* Manufacturing departments typically have a strong management network. Management is fundamental because scheduling, standardization, and specialization impose particular problems. Yes, those divisions do increase productivity; however, they also force workers into virtual isolation from one another and from their shared objectives.

   Proper management can make up where the scheduling specialists leave off, helping keep everyone on track, and resolving problems as they occur without taking anyone off task. In this sense, sales department managers must make decisions respecting design, workflow, resourcing, and the overall infrastructure of the work environment.

## Conclusion

The lessons of manufacturing serve as guidelines for the new approach to sales. If we think about sales as a collaborative group activity, where process rather than commission and incentives keep people focused and motivated, we can undermine much of the dysfunction and individualism that pervades sales departments today.

In the second part of this chapter, I delve deeper into the topics of scheduling, standardization, specialization, and management, describing divisions of labor along those lines. I also explain how the newly divided labor force can work together—under proper management—to increase productivity and reduce stress on workers.

## Out with the Old and in with the Older

The approach to sales that I propose here is not novel, per se. It is based on Adam Smith's Division of Labor theory, published in 1776. The concept is simple yet revolutionary.

When you take a workflow or procedure and separate it into distinct steps, then assign people to each of those steps whose sole responsibility is to perform them (specialists), you increase productivity and reduce the probability of error.

Manufacturing departments, along with other work environments, adopted this theory and are structured by it. By looking to manufacturing, we can abstract some basic lessons that will inform how we can change sales departments for the better.

## A Day in the New Sales Department

Every business is unique yet similar. Workflows and procedures vary from business to business and yet, businesses in the same industry tend to be similar in some crucial regard: the structure, distribution of labor, and procedures exhibited in one are often exhibited in the other. Thus is the nature of market forces.

Up to this point, the conversation has been predominantly theoretical. However, this trend ensures that the divisions of labor, the structure of sales, and the interrelations that I will discuss below are generally applicable.

That being said, let's jump into what a day in the new sales department would look like.

## Divided We Stand

Divisions of labor that result in specialization should be made according to three variables: (1) Work Type, (2) Location, and (3) Cadence. In brief, these variables account for the nature of the work, where it will be performed (either inside the company or outside), and the lead-time, respectively.

Under this approach, at least five new specializations will emerge to help standardize workflow and safeguard the integrity of the department.

## Who Are the Specialists?

Two central figures in any sales department would be the scheduler and the salesperson. When you divide their labor according to the three variables mentioned above, their positions end up quite different from what would be traditionally expected.

### Specialist 1. The Scheduler

The scheduler would be expected to push work to the salesperson. This would entail managing calendars, interfacing with production, coordinating client deliveries, and instructing the salesperson on when and where to pursue sales objectives.

Due to the intermediary role of the scheduler, they must remain inside the company. This preserves the lines of communication, eases the dissemination of important information from executives, and helps the scheduler quickly access company information that would influence planning.

### Specialist 2. The Salesperson

The salesperson would be expected to pursue sales objectives, nothing more. Any planning, customer service, workflow or procedural design, and interfacing with the production or technical side of the product would not be within the scope of the salesperson's job duties.

This added time and energy to focus only on selling and increasing expertise to better sell would accomplish two things. It would relieve the salesperson of historic stresses and free them up to leverage and refine the very attributes that make someone a good salesperson.

The salesperson would be in constant communication with the scheduler, who would inform them about calendar dates, changes to client profiles, changes to products, and other considerations that would directly influence the salesperson's ability to sell and their relationship to the client.

### Specialist 3. The Campaign Coordinator

The campaign coordinator would be expected to maintain a healthy queue of sales opportunities in the scheduler's stockpile. This would ensure that the scheduler always has sales objectives to schedule for the salesperson.

The campaign coordinator would need to conduct research—much like procurement research—on potential buyers and sellers in the company's target market. Although they would not be expected to make contact with the potential buyers, they would be expected to provide comprehensive viability reports backed by their research.

The campaign coordinator would need to update the scheduler about leads, on-going research, and changes in the market that would affect target opportunities or the company's decision-making.

### Specialist 4. The Project Leader

The project leader is a contingent position. The project leader would be expected to work hand-in-hand with the salesperson on products that are technical in nature; further, the project leader would be expected to follow the solution all the way along the production process up to delivery. In other words, if you were selling a technical solution, the project leader would be the main point of contact between the client and company.

If your company provides engineering or technical solutions, then you are probably painfully aware of why a project leader is necessary. Salespeople (who aren't technical or engineering experts) often complicate the delivery of the solutions they sell because of their lack of expertise. In those cases, the salesperson's selling capacity is impaired and catalyzes a host of problems for the company. The presence of a project leader can mitigate those problems.

### Specialist 5. The Customer Service Team

The customer service team takes full responsibility of the entire customer service caseload so that schedulers, salespeople, campaign coordinators, and project leaders can extricate themselves entirely from that task.

Some of the customer services tasks can include lead generation of standard proposals, processing repeat transactions, and after-sales support (i.e., issue resolution). These activities are significant and make-up a large portion of a company's success.

Customer service is a critical activity that promotes the health of any business, especially in today's economy and consumer culture.

## Everything Happens for a Reason

With a company profile in hand, the divisions of labor, their interrelations, and the structure of the sales department can all be properly established. Once that is done, workflow standardization should follow simply.

After some trial-and-error, a standardized workflow should confer predictability, resilience, and confidence. In a best-case scenario, it might seem as if every output is the result of necessity, rather than careful planning and some luck.

## Workflow Standardization

When standardizing a workflow, do not aim to map-out the existing complexity, instead reverse-engineer a more efficient workflow given the existing complexity. Parsing out what needs to be done and who will do it takes care of this to a great extent.

It requires a macro-analysis of the production line, company objectives, and current constraints, such that reality will not be forced into impractical divisions of labor. *Beware!* If the divisions do not parallel the reality of the production line, the workflow will never be truly efficient.

## A Standardized Sales Team

Once the division of labor is completed, responsibilities assigned, and guidelines created, we should have a potential, standardized workflow.

In project management terms, we now have a project plan (our standard workflow originating and pursuing sales opportunities), a project manager (our scheduler), and various resource pools that contain single resources (our salesperson, our campaign coordinator, and our project leader). The last key ingredient is the specialist who will oversee the whole mechanism.

## Get Me Your Manager

Management is indispensable to a successfully standardized workflow—the reason being that specialization has its own problems, namely specialization.

When a person is specialized, their labor narrowed, they operate in perceived isolation from other people in the production line. In an effort to sustain their energy and harness expertise through habit and practice, the bigger picture is lost.

Management is necessary to keep an eye on the bigger picture. The sales manager must be aware of all the goings-on inside the sales department to help keep everyone on track, making changes to design wherever necessary without compromising the efficiency or the integrity of the standardized workflow.

Management's directives will flow primarily from executives, memos, and the like. All that information reflects the company's overarching objectives, and someone must be responsible for them.

## Change Beats Perfection

Standardization is an active process rather than a passive one. When you standardize a workflow, it isn't enough to layout the timbers and imagine how they might operate. A standardized workflow must be put to the test in real-world conditions, so that shortcomings, holes, and oversights reveal themselves quickly.

All the elements of a standardized workflow are subject to change; in fact, they should change. The reason sales is in the current predicament is that it hasn't changed for almost 50 years. Other departments are adapting to contemporary social, cultural, economic, and market circumstances, and sales should be no different.

I would take change and adaptation over perfection any day.

## In Sum

In businesses with sales departments, the tendency has been to let them operate in a vacuum and to treat salespeople much like glorified telemarketers. This has created a culture of individualism and outcome-oriented success that undermines the very existence of sales.

This new approach based on Adam Smith's Division of Labor theory and the lessons of manufacturing is my attempt to disrupt that cycle with an alternative. I will restate that this approach might not apply precisely as described here to every business.

As always, we must be careful not to embrace new ways of thinking without carefully evaluating our own experience first. Be that as it may, the general belief that motivates this approach and its theoretical backdrop are applicable no matter the nature of a business.

# CHAPTER 108

## *Is It Time We Retired Sales Commissions?*

Social pundits tell us that sales commissions at work are old school, unscientific, and ineffective. It's usually the end of the year when each business thinks about bonus allocation and commission payments. This is also the time when many sales executives think about new ways to structure sales compensation and incentive packages so that the sales teams are able to deliver on the lofty targets that the company might have set forth for itself in the year ahead.

There are many indisputable facts in life one cannot argue with, such as the supremely elegant Newton's first law, which states that an object either remains at rest or continues to move at a constant velocity unless acted upon by an external force. Can't argue with that. It's common sense.

Similarly, we do not question where the sun rises and sets any more.

The third incontestable fact is that "salespeople are best encouraged only by commission." I mean, they have to be since this is how we have been structuring sales since the medieval days. Notice I used the word "medieval," because that's exactly what it is. The reason we pay sales reps a commission is because the concept is entrenched more in belief and folklore than in raw logic. I mean this annual drill is so paved with canon and convention that it's not even an actual choice any more. While meeting clients from all kinds of industries, I learned that some of them have started questioning this ancient tradition of motivation by commission, and are uncovering that commission can, in some circumstances, be even detrimental to the business and to the rep. Doing away with them altogether can open the doors to higher earnings and happier employees.

This may all appear a bit like going against basic human instincts, but there has been abundant scientific research conducted over the decades that supports these claims. In fact, Professor of Psychology Adam Grant from my alma mater Wharton, as well as leading innovators in the field from the University of Rochester Edward Deci and Richard Ryan, have written extensively on the subject of human motivation in different life situations and enunciated a more delicate approach to the topic altogether compared to offering a conditional bounty.

Professor Grant's research focuses on generosity, motivation, and meaningful work, championing new ideas, personality traits like introversion-extraversion, and leadership, collaboration, culture, and organizational change. His pioneering research has introduced evidence-based techniques that increase performance, reduce burnout among sales professionals, and enhance overall sales productivity.

These academics have discovered that the efficacy of incentives fluctuates with the job. Specifically, they have determined that conditional bounty (i.e. "If you deliver $x of sales or accomplish such a task, then you will get $y in commission.") is effective when the duties being undertaken are mundane or almost mechanical. These researchers even have a word for it—algorithmic. According to them, if you were folding flyers, packing 500 lunch boxes with the same produce, or turning a screw clockwise all day in a factory, then such a carrot in the form of a cash incentive will likely get us quite motivated to get the task completed on time and accurately.

However, for tasks that are heuristic in nature, involving a high degree of creativity, complexity or out-of-the-box thinking (such as sales or product development to name a couple), the conditional commission has proven to be substantially less effectual. Not only sales, but also many other white-collar jobs where one might be creating a new product, trying to solve a problem with the help of others, or any such work where a wider viewpoint is crucial, the research proves that conditional if-then commissions are just not that effective.

Back when Shakespeare was writing *The Merchant of Venice*, sales was probably not terribly complicated. I think it might have even been pretty one-dimensional; the salesman shows up with a script, hopefully commits it to memory, opens his "wares" for the world, responds to questions or concerns with scripted answers he has memorized, then rinses and repeats the job the following day all over again until sales start to trickle in—the law of averages, the principle that supposes most future events will likely balance any past deviation from a presumed average, working its best in support of the salesman.

As in the above case, back in the day, sales might have been primarily transactional, mundane, and repetitive in nature. That's certainly not the case anymore. Anything routine now automatically gets automated what with all the tech improvements we have had over the decades. What happens with automation is that the collected data is accessible not only by the salesman, but also by the prospective customer, making things interesting. In such cases, it is the salesperson's heuristic talents that bear the most value. In this context, such skills might involve the interpretation of the data as opposed to just providing it, the resolution of complications while identifying new ones, and most importantly, offering knowledge, solutions, insights, and a vision, instead of merely peddling a product.

For many industries, the standard sales plan is a 60% base salary with 40% commission. I would urge CEOs and sales leaders to explore a new, simpler plan – that of giving your salespeople 90% of their comp as a flat base salary, with the other 10% associated with company achievements (i.e. growth in top line revenue, EBITDA, net profits, and EPS). Based on my conversations with several company leaders from a variety of industries over the years that have deployed such a system, they claim some remarkably positive changes, such as an increase in total sales while keeping a flat cost of sales, higher sales rep retention, and lower attrition. Among the list of such companies are Microchip, a $6.5 billion public company; Thoughtworks, a software company based in Chicago; Hunt Big Sales, a consulting firm based in Indianapolis; New York Label & Box Works, a 135 year-old company; the Islandia, a N.Y. based company which produces $20+ million a year of manufacturing specialty packaging, and Red Gate Software in Cambridge, England.

Even Pharmaceutical giant GlaxoSmithKline joined the no incentive society, removing commission from the comp packages of its pharmaceutical sales reps in over 150 countries worldwide. I find this quite revolutionary, because GSK salespeople are not paid bonuses based on the volume of prescriptions they convince their doctors to write, but instead, their bonuses are based on product understanding, business wisdom, and complete comprehension of the needs of patients and physicians. How refreshing, indeed. I am sure this effort eliminated the pressure GSK salespeople may have felt to coax doctors into writing prescriptions that often led to some unfitting marketing practices anyway.

To show their commitment to this unique compensation structure, a GSK Spokeswoman said this on behalf of GSK's new head of North America Pharmaceutical Operations Jack Bailey:

*Glaxo has led the industry by changing the way we reward our sales representatives. Our approach is based on the core principle that we will not link the compensation of our individual sales representatives with the number of prescriptions generated. Throughout the program, we've looked for ways to simplify the process, but the fundamentals remain the same. This approach has now been rolled out in 150 countries where we operate.*

I am not saying every company should retire sales commission. Every job, company, and industry is unique. All I am asking is for us to challenge the convention and appreciate that we are living and working in a highly sophisticated and technologically advanced period in our society where the sales function is complex, creative work, and the sales people selling your products or services consequently deserve a form of motivation that ventures beyond that of a hanging bag of cash.

# CHAPTER 109

## *Good Sales People Are Not Pond Scum*

You know that slimy green stuff that sucks the life out of a pond ecosystem—well, that is called algae. Colloquially, it might be also called pond scum. Algae are microscopic, simple plant-like organisms, and, in large quantities, they can suck the life out of an ecosystem, only to eventually die, sink to the bottom and poison the water yet further.

I'm not sure that anyone sees "pond scum" as a good thing. Water should be blue and clear, not green and murky. Ponds can survive perfectly well without it, but you can't get rid of it for long.

Many people view all sales people as a similar type of scum, choking the ecosystems wherever they are, whether it is overly aggressive self-promotion on social media or narcissistic tendencies at networking events. "But that's enough about me. What about you?"

The "good" sales person (and most of us are in sales one way or another) is not looking to suck the oxygen from your life with enthusiastic pitches and machine-gun-like delivery. They stand and listen to your problems, and maybe, just maybe, the sales person has a solution for your particular problem. However, they'll never know unless they listen. They are confident, but not arrogant. They are tenacious, but they stop before they become overbearing. They have personality and an innate charisma, rather than droning on and sending you to sleep. Their aim is to make your life easier, not fill it with noise and hot air.

Many people say that toxic salespeople lie, cheat, and pressure people into making decisions that they otherwise may not have made. They cover the pond with a thick film of green scum, and no living creature can escape. Those poor little pond skaters have no chance. Most "bad" sales people resort to these tactics because they simply don't have the first clue about what their customer's needs are. They don't care. They have a historical ratio of success with their current bullying tactics, and they will move from potential victim to potential victim until they get a bite.

On the other hand, good sales people take their time with their prospects; even if it initially seems that there is not a fit, they will still work through the issues until the end. If they can't help, they will suggest someone who may be better placed. They are consultative, they ask the right questions based on the intelligence that they have gathered, and they add value. That doesn't sound like pond scum behavior to me.

It is so much more entertaining regaling people with tales of nightmare meetings and horrific presentations. Maybe that is where this "pond scum" myth arises. In actual fact, the vast majority of sales people are quickly trying their best to discover value for their customers. They provide the vital oxygen for life to continue rather than suck the ecosystem dry.

It is the toxic minority who are the root cause of the stereotype.

# SECTION 5 – MARKETING

# CHAPTER 110

## *How to Disrupt a Market*

Disruption is the order of the day. There are so many articles about digital transformation and disruption that it's dizzying. I am guilty of having written prolifically on the topic. So, I decided to consolidate.

Disruption is an inexhaustible topic. Every day disruptions occur, and the business landscape changes. It's paradoxical because almost as soon as I'm done writing, my analysis will be outdated. Such is the nature of disruption in the twenty-first century. Nonetheless, there are some enduring trends.

In this chapter, I attempt to capture the two central aspects of disruption today. What it is and the common ways that businesses have created it.

### What Is Disruption?

Simply put, a technology or product is disruptive when it creates an entirely new market, consumer base, or user and destroys (or displaces) the market for the technology or product it destroyed or displaced.

That's enough theory for one day.

## Identify Solutions and Kill Them

The key to disruption is problem solving with this formula in mind. Identify the biggest opportunity in the value chain to shift money away from its present course. Then, identify a problem and solve it using digital technology. The larger the problem, the more far-reaching the solution and—in most cases—the greater the revenue.

Problems are just business opportunities waiting for the right problem solver to tap into them. Insight and drive are all the skills you need. Everything else can be hired. By carefully studying your environment and analyzing your daily frustrations, you'll find that opportunities for transformation start to jump out at you.

Once you've compiled and refined all your observations into one comprehensive and tangible idea, you'll probably experience a bout of fear. It's understandable. This is a natural reaction. You see the behemoth before you and think, "How can I take this on?" That reaction is the best indicator of whether your idea is good or not. A big idea should face challenges and opposition; not just from others but from you, the originator.

You should do all you can to kill your idea.

When you try to kill your idea, you'll find all the ways it can fail. Then, you'll know how to fix it and make it stronger. Your idea will start out big, but it'll eventually become a zombie: battered, bruised, and immortal.

One surefire way to accomplish this is through collaboration. If you have a truly original and potent idea, others will sense that. Of course, be selective with the people you take on-board; but do so, because there is no way you can conceive of all the possible ways your idea will perish, alone.

There are also many possible ways a single idea can disrupt. A zombie idea can take down an entire industry. At this point we have many, many examples of successful zombie ideas.

## The Many Ways to Disrupt

There are four common ways to disrupt an industry. They are research and development, design, sales and marketing, and distribution.

1. *Research and Development.* For the problem solver looking to disrupt, inspiration abounds. Research and development is at its peak right now. There are scientists working 24/7 who make discoveries that could fundamentally alter an industry landscape, yet give little thought to business applicability. There is tremendous financial opportunity there.

   In recent years, dozens of small companies have sprung up and started making millions in the open-source space. Adafruit uses open-source technology to enable over 350,000 of its customers to build cellphone jammers. Bug Labs open-sourced Lego-like interlocking computers. In 2010, *Wired* magazine's Editor-in-Chief Chris Anderson launched an open-source company focused on creating military drones and quickly generated over $1 million in sales.

   The beauty is that we all have equal access to this research. Billions of dollars' worth of research knowledge lie dormant at American universities waiting for the right problem solver to come along and create a business.

2. *Design.* Remember, a problem solver doesn't *need* to invent something new. They can simply take something old and rework it.

   Michael Kors, Kate Spade, and Tory Burch didn't invent the handbag. Nike and Converse didn't invent the running shoe. Innovators who disrupt through research and development must find ways to introduce nuance to the marketplace. Design disruption, on the other hand, emphasizes the art of piggybacking.

   With design disruption, it's often the small, incremental improvements in design and manufacturing that generate billion-dollar results. For example, Nestlé Waters North America—maker of Arrowhead, Poland Springs, and Deer Park bottled water—re-engineered its bottles to use 50% less resin. Nestlé Waters North America manufactures roughly 20 billion bottles per year. With this change, it not only saved millions of dollars, but also reduced its carbon footprint by 55%.

Another example of design disruption comes from brand strategy. You can leverage the relationship customers have with an existing brand to catapult a new one. This is referred to as brand extensions. When it's done well, you get products such as Reese's Peanut Butter and Chocolate Dessert Bar Mix or Arm & Hammer Advanced White Toothpaste. These new products are familiar to customers because of the trust and reputation of the brand affiliation.

Yet another example of design disruption comes from web development. User-experience is absolutely vital to success, and one of the first customer touchpoints is the website. By redesigning your website with user-experience principles and a digital journey in mind, you can topple an industry.

One of the first value chains shattered by smart web development was travel. The advent of Expedia, Priceline, Orbitz, and Travelocity wiped out the independent travel agency. Two serial transformers, Reddit co-founder Steve Huffman and BookTour co-founder Adam Goldstein, founded Hipmunk in 2010, an online booking agency. The user experience was clean and graphic. Travelers could clearly see each possible flight as a color-coded bar, and the information could be customized with one click. This was a game changer.

The impact of design disruption hinges on the power of design. Design determines how users feel about a product. Poor design presents a world of opportunity for transformers looking to make their mark without having to invent or introduce a new product to the world.

As with all disruption, design disruption comes from identifying problems where others failed to see one.

3. *Sales and Marketing.* Sales and marketing transformation may be the easiest of all transformations. You can rely on your customers to tell you where there is room for improvement. You don't need gimmicks or flash, just a well-thought-out customer journey informed by the customer.

   For example, people hate waiting in lines to check out at retail stores, so Apple Stores reimagined the consumer experience, designing their brick-and-mortar locations without cash registers or checkout lines.

   That reminds me of another piece in the sales-marketing link that has only recently received attention, customer service. Customer service should be thought of as marketing, because it influences how customers feel about your company. Great customer service can have vast repercussions. It creates brand loyalty and enduring product differentiation.

   The key value captured by great customer service is a reduction in customer acquisition costs. If a business has to market and advertise to get each and every sale, its costs are substantial. On the other hand, if each customer tells five friends, then the business grows virally.

   The challenge of the digital age is that retailers seldom see their customers in context. The antidote is that retailers have access to data that informs *when* and *if* those customers come back. Use customer feedback and data collected to devise ways to disrupt the sales-marketing value chain within your business and compared to other businesses in your industry.

4. *Distribution.* Distribution disruption is essentially redefining the customer. Prior to the Internet boom, research and development, design, and production were the main modalities of disruption. Distribution, it turns out, holds the most value in the digital age.

We saw the greatest number of store closings in U.S. history in 2012. Sears Holdings, once the champion of retailing, closed out nearly 200 Kmart locations and over 100 Sears stores. GameStop and Radio Shack, both traditional fixtures at nearly every major mall in America, each closed out nearly 500 stores. Add to that the hundreds of closings for Office Depot, Barnes & Noble, and Office Max, and the pattern is unmistakable.

One way companies have transformed distribution is through online product access. Amazon, eBay, and iTunes capitalized on online distribution while offering consumers maximum selection availability. Jeff Bezos identified Amazon's competitive advantage as providing the most complete selection of inventory. "There are two kinds of companies: those that work to try to charge more and those that work to charge less," Jeff Bezos of Amazon declares. "We will be in the second."

Amazon was able to offer more than brick-and-mortar locations ever could. Customers have an ostensibly unlimited selection at their fingertips. By investing heavily in state-of-the-art automated distribution centers and by partnering with other suppliers that would drop-ship directly to the customer, Amazon disrupted and dominated.

It took Amazon nearly $1 billion of capital and six years to make its first profit. By that point, the mighty retailer was grossing over $1 billion in sales and had created new users (cyber-shoppers) by the millions.

Distribution transformation isn't just about shipping and handling, it's also about individual products.

Apple's iTunes transformed distribution by adopting an agency business model, wherein the retailer takes a predetermined commission on every sale. When EMI originally negotiated the first iTunes deal with Steve Jobs, Jobs was adamant that all songs retail for 99 cents, regardless of a song's variable costs. So, while many consumers benefited from the flat pricing, behind the scenes there were many songs that EMI sold to Apple for substantially more than a dollar.

For one, classical pieces of music that could be up to 70 minutes in length used to command the price of an entire album with a wholesale price of $6 and yet retailed on iTunes for just 99 cents. Nevertheless, the company has extracted the greatest possible value out of its combined bricks-and-mortar and ecommerce strategy.

Although there are many iterations of the abovementioned four ways to disrupt, I chose the common ones. The takeaway is that the sources of disruption can come in all shapes and sizes; the impacts, however, are always massive.

## Supply Chain Disruption Is Still a Thing

The next topic is heavily political, but I won't politicize it. I want to talk about supply chain disruption. This election cycle has evoked traumas from our national past, many of which stem from the adverse consequences of offshoring.

The truth is that the lack of manufacturing jobs in the United States has left many people destitute. It's inarguable that most of the items we purchase, wear, and consume are manufactured in factories abroad. It isn't that factories stopped making things; it's just that in America, we stopped making factories. Even if the raw materials for our goods were harvested in America (cotton, iron, wood), production too migrated to countries with cheaper labor.

We are the world's Costco.

In a free-market economy, there will always exist a demand for cheap labor. Outsourcing to third-world countries is a means to that end. But it isn't a viable long-term solution. Problem solvers need not tackle the systemic problem of labor supply and demand head-on, because the means of production are changing and creating new avenues for value.

A single disruption in the production of physical goods is bringing jobs back to America and other developed economies. Namely, on-demand manufacturing facilitated by 3-D printing technology. The 3-D printer is shattering the existing value chain for physical goods in much the same way the Internet destroyed the value chains for intellectual digital goods such as music, movies and books. With 3-D printing technology, camera parts and pharmaceuticals can be downloaded and printed as quickly and easily as a song. Any physical item can be produced anywhere, at any time. Never has so much manufacturing capacity been available to so many people.

The McKinsey Global Institute estimates that 3-D printing will affect 320 million manufacturing jobs globally. The opportunities for transformation abound in countless fields. Just think. Everyone has the power to compete on a global scale without having to raise millions of dollars for equipment and tooling.

Look to the future means of production to disrupt your supply chain and capture emergent value.

## History Doesn't Reminisce Fondly on the Status Quo

History forgets those who maintained the status quo. The glory comes from being a problem solver. Every man and woman would like to leave their mark on this world. Whatever your mark, it doesn't have to start big to have a big impact. Remember the power of incremental changes.

There is a Latin proverb apropos of our conversation about disruption, *Guta Cavat Petra,* the drop cleaves stone. Persistence over time can break the mightiest of industries.

# CHAPTER 111

## Why Do Consumers Purchase? Understanding the Customer's Mindset

As of right now, a number of structural changes have become institutionalized in the business world that have forced companies in every sector to reevaluate the way they view the customer. As Robert H. Bloom points out in *The New Experts*, "the seller's new role is customer engagement." That means that those who can provide customers with substantial interaction and involvement will have the most success. That is, in some measure, because consumers constitutionally distrust corporations.

### The New Relationship Dynamic

These independent and inter-informed buyers support each other in the pursuit of good companies and the persecution of bad or terrible ones. And they don't respond well to aggression or arrogance. They prefer sellers who are uninvolved and passive. And, they aren't interested in lifelong friendships. The new consumer demands clarity, transparency, expertise, and service when it benefits them most—and that the seller will anticipate their needs.

These benefits can take many forms.

Consumers are not merely drawn in by financial benefits. They want meaningful and conscientious solutions that directly relate to their wants, needs, aspirations, apprehensions, concerns, and fears.

The fundamental question to address is one of trust. Do I like and trust this seller more than I like and trust other sellers?

## The Rules of Engagement

With this corporate undoing, there are new rules and trends that have emerged which can help sellers navigate the uncharted waters to the benefit of consumers.

The first step is to reframe all transactional interactions, and remember that attention-giving is indeed a transaction.

1. Engagement is not the consumer's job.
2. Engagement doesn't happen. It must be made to happen. It is the yield of practiced discipline, strategies, and training.
3. Other business issues, customer involvement, or distractions must not hinder engagement. Anything squarely outside of engagement must be dealt with independently, or risk compromising the interaction between customer and company.
4. Engagement is backed up by a written promise.
5. Engagement from a senior executive is of the highest value in trust building.

The point of all this engagement is to build trust to assuage the distrust and uncertainty endemic to considering whether to purchase a product or service. Once you have succeeded, your work has only just begun.

You must maintain and cultivate the logic behind decision-making, or risk making the customers feel deceived and dissatisfied.

## Holding onto Trust

You've managed to develop a trust relationship with your customer. That means they've paid for your product or service and have used it or plan to. Whatever the case, your customer is relying on the product or service in some way. This is the best time to reinforce the customer preference you tapped into during the initial transaction.

To reinforce the customer preference, there are three objectives you should aim toward:

1. Ensure that your customer is benefiting from your product or service, check-in about performance expectations and verify whether they are being met, and confirm whether any promises you made during the engagement phase are being met too.
2. Communicate with the customer on a regular basis to ensure that your brand stays at the forefront of their mind and to demonstrate your personal commitment and involvement in their life.
3. Lay the groundwork for your customer to be a repeat customer and advocate.

Failure to follow through on these objectives at this critical juncture in the customer journey will cost you potential to generate revenue that accrues from repeat purchases and referrals.

## Unlearn Habits of Deceit

I know "deceit" is a dirty word, but that's what the old marketing and business paradigm condoned, if not demanded. Nowadays, that paradigm has eroded, and consumers have grown allergic to the residue.

In their book *Tuned In,* Craig Stull, Phil Myers and David Meerman Scott say, "Successful companies focus on buyers and the best ways to reach them, and they develop compelling content and programs accordingly."

This has a number of entailments. For one, marketing is no longer about pitching, but rather about providing concrete and honest information that addresses real concerns and questions. You don't know what those concerns and questions might be? Ask your customer. All of your company material—including material that isn't customer-facing—should be created from the customer's perspective.

To make matters simple, here are five bad habits to unlearn that linger from the old paradigm:

1. Unlearn the practice of interrupting people with messages. Instead, publish online content they want to consume.
2. Unlearn vacuous and trivial phrases that convey nothing substantive about your product or service.
3. Unlearn spin. Now. Unlearn it. It's inauthentic and non-transparent.
4. Unlearn forcing consumers into actions. Your terminology will reflect this master-slave mentality.
5. Unlearn that you have to buy access. If you create content that people want, they will flock to it.

If you haven't delved into any one of these practices, it means that in addition to unlearning many things, there's a lot you have to learn about the Internet and Internet culture. Take notes.

## Be User-Experience Centered

The above points apply to the physical experience that consumers have in your store as well as the digital one. Many brands have adopted experiential models to provide added value and craft a memorable in-store experience. Doing so reinforces your digital strategies and harnesses innumerable conduits inaccessible to you online.

A memorable and valuable physical experience starts with the five senses.

1. Crayola uses color in its store to draw attention and evoke emotions in space. **Sight**
2. Abercrombie & Fitch carefully selects its music to match the tastes and preferences of the target market. With sound, it created a soundscape that customers are delighted to return to. **Sound**
3. Bath & Body Works relies almost exclusively on fragrance to keep customers coming back. **Smell**
4. Apple's stores are designed to encourage physical interaction. They want people to walk away with a tactile experience. **Touch**
5. Costco is famous for its manifold samples. Some analysts have premised its success on just that. **Taste**

These are shopper experience strategies that work. They define the store, make each memorable, and provide value that furthers user experience and the product.

## Relinquish the Notion of Control

You don't control consumers. You don't control the market. You don't control buyer decisions. You can exercise varying degrees of influence that spring from a number of factors and intersections, however. In this sense, the word "control" appears hyperbolic, and words like "guide," and "influence," seem more apropos.

Guidance and influence can fall into one of three macro-categories:

1. *Framing effects.* Framing the presentation of a product deliberately and strategically.

2. *Choice context.* Creating a context of differently priced items to spur comparative assessments.

3. *Task effects.* The manner in which consumers are asked to evaluate the offer.

However, there is a vast stumbling block to the effectiveness of these tactics. We are now sunk in an information ecosystem of unprecedented proportions that produces noise, deafening and distracting noise. You must fully acknowledge the ecosystem that you are operating within to defuse its unwanted effects.

The best place to start is by asking yourself, "What would happen if everything went exactly right?" This is the heart of the Ultimate Customer Experience (UCE)®, according to Scott McKain in *Create Distinction.*

When you deploy this stratagem, the questions must start from the first interaction you envision between the company and the customer. Then consider details like how many times would the phone ring before it was answered? What percentage of your calls should be fielded by a live person instead of via digital technology? What sensations would be experienced by customers when they walk into your store? What would the temperature be? What would customers hear? What would the store smell like?

The single most important factor here is to keep drilling down to the smallest aspects of your interactions with customers and prospects. Constantly push for what would have to happen for that contact to be exactly right.

You must examine your interaction with your customers and prospects with extraordinary precision in order to get it exactly right. That's the point of all this.

In order to build trust, you must be customer-centered, think from their perspective, think about their values and preferences, and what your product or service adds to their life.

Only then, you will position yourself to build relationships that are mutually beneficial and reliable.

# CHAPTER 112

## How to Keep Your Customers Loyal to You

This is a buyer's market. The company culture has shifted toward appeasing buyers and their newfound influence. The Internet has empowered them to demand more from companies, including transparency, competitive prices, and the opportunity to capitalize using digital technology. There are more options available to buyers in every market segment. The choices have never been so varied and accessible.

This has put serious demands on customer loyalty. The average consumer is far more scrupulous than they once were. Companies have responded to this by expanding their ability to provide. They have multiple locations, facilities equipped to enable 24/7 purchases, and websites that deliver truckloads of valuable information about products and services.

At this point the trend has revealed some clear wins and losses from which we can extrapolate strategy.

### Win Them Over

***Make contact (now or never).*** The first moments of contact are crucial. It's your one opportunity to grab hold of attention. Your website is likely the first site of interaction between you and a potential customer. Make sure that your site is geared toward providing information, culls the unnecessary, has a clear user trajectory, and is easy to navigate.

***Thinking about it (make or break).*** Keep transactions short and fast. A lengthy transaction process is deadly and downright cumbersome. The more seamless a process, the more likely a consumer is to trust it. Transparency is one way to evoke trust. The other is clear and simple language that speaks to the customer. You want to start a conversation on equal footing, jargon, ambiguity, hyperbole—all these things foment distrust. Distrust will break you.

***I do (stay or go).*** Your consumer is using your product or services. How are you nourishing their experience toward maintaining a relationship? Product or service performance is essential, but so too is user experience. The user experience is based in the preference that drew your customer to the site in the first place. Why are they there? What does it say about them and their needs?

If all this goes well, the person should not only become a repeat customer, but should evangelize on your behalf. They will recommend your product or service whenever reasonable.

***Maintain (here or there).*** Maintain top of mind awareness. Check in with your customers. Show them gratitude. Remember that they are the lifeblood of your business. Without them, you will not succeed. Channel that importance to them. Rebates and discounts are financial. They don't trigger the warmth of human relationships. To maintain loyalty, you must relate to people on a human level.

The more interaction the better. Requesting feedback, being open to discussion, treating people with respect, and honoring their complaints is a way to cultivate loyalty.

***Who's inside? (for you or against you).*** Your employees and partners can be catalysts for brand loyalty. If your employees can't stand behind your brand, then how will others? Employee engagement is a powerful vehicle for success that operates on two dimensions: favorability and defensibility. They will pump out comments and feedback that favors you, while coming to your aid when someone decries your brand. Brand evangelists will do the same.

You can make this easier for them. When you define the brand experience, remind employees about expectations, communicate openly, hold everyone accountable for their actions, and draw connections between that, their behavior, and financial results of the company, not just the bottom line. It's a holistic picture that involves the employees.

## Don't Put the Customer First: Be Customer-centered

There is a stark difference between putting the customer first and being customer-centered. The customer-first approach means you place the customer first in every interaction, yet create the company experience independent of the customer. The customer-centered approach means you tailor the experience to the customer. With the latter, you kill two birds with one stone and generate an organic, human brand.

***Explore customer desires.*** Think about desired outcomes. They are what customers want as a result of doing business with your company and its products or services.

***Uncover experience obstacles.*** An obstacle is what gets in the way of an ideal customer experience. Obstacles can be ways employees falter during or after a customer interaction. An obstacle may also be something that is out of your control.

***Craft the experience mindset.*** The experience mindset is a description of how you want employees to think with respect to customers. It is not a marketing tagline.

***Draft job-specific behaviors.*** Job-specific behaviors are the job norms, so to speak. They are the non-negotiable "must do to keep your job" behaviors.

***Uncover above and beyond opportunities.*** These opportunities are situational behaviors that employees can do to deliver a great experience.

***Prioritize processes.*** Inevitably, you will uncover a series of processes that are either needed or already in place but not followed consistently enough. If a behavior is dependent on a process, then the process must be addressed.

## Engage--Don't Broadcast

Broadcasting is momentary and instantaneous; engagement has longevity. You don't want people to just receive your messages; you want them to want to interact, to engage. That's where your value proposition comes in.

Your value proposition is a statement that tells the person what to do, what to expect in return, and gives them a reason why to do it. It's a sentence that packs a punch.

You may want to contact a copywriter or a brand language consultant to craft one for you. And just one won't do. You should have an arsenal of svelte and nuclear value propositions.

Remember, give value, generate substantial content, be customer-centered, and give your employees reasons to love the brand they work for.

# CHAPTER 113

## Five Steps to Change the Perception of Your Brand

Brand perception is never set in stone. With every new generation of consumers and changes in the markets, a customer's view of a well-reputed brand has the potential to change—for better or for worse.

This process is sometimes a passive and gradual change, but it could also just as easily be a more abrupt transformation—driven by external events that are beyond one's control. However, whether the changes in your brand perception are forced upon you or *driven* by you, there will always be an element of uncertainty. After all, you can't control the thoughts of your customers.

For me, brand perception became top-of-mind when I took over the reins of a new digital publishing company. I underwent a rather elaborate process of figuring out what the brand really stood for, both for the readers of the websites I was representing, as well as for the hundreds of advertisers that were making products to reach these readers. We conducted internal and external surveys in which I asked questions such as:

- How do consumers and advertisers view our brand?
- What is our website's reputation with regard to other websites?
- What would advertisers gain from our website's offerings?
- What is our internal perception of who we are as a brand?

- How did we fare against other leading publishers within our category in terms of brand power?

Using these survey results, I then underwent a five-step process in order to determine our existing brand equity and a strategy to further boost its perception. Here are the steps I took, and how you can leverage them to evaluate your own brand, and make changes accordingly:

1. *Examine the reality.* To change a perception, you must first understand what people think, and not what you *think* they think. Asking for open-ended feedback without leading questions is the only way to determine how you are seen. Social media provides ample opportunity to listen to your customer, and if you listen enough, you'll gather a better understanding. In my scenario, we learned from the reader surveys that the brand's perception was that of a tired, lagging brand not entirely in tune with the times. This was the reality for us, and we had to change it.

2. *Understand your customers.* Gathering feedback is only the first step—now it is vital to understand why they have these thoughts. Does your marketing only hit a certain demographic, leaving vast swaths of your customer base in the dark? Are there geographic or cultural differences? It is vital that you create opportunities for conversation and act upon that feedback. In my situation, we discovered that our customers considered the logos to be old-fashioned and reminiscent of a dying era. We also realized that the brand was skewed toward a slightly older demographic. Our customers wanted more mobile content, when our focus at the time was on desktop content. All of this information needed to be taken into consideration before developing an actionable plan to give our customers what they were looking for.

3. *Get your people on board.* It is one thing to understand what your customers think, but it is another matter entirely to explain to your team why they might need to do things a little differently. Many of them will be one or two steps removed from the customers, and it is vital to explain why changes are required. Your brand perception starts with

your people, and once you have decided what it is you need to change (an important step!), the changes will only take place if they adopt them as their own. In my case, I had to sit with each of the key stakeholders within the editorial, ops, ad sales, and marketing departments to show them the survey results and get their buy-in on a process for pointing the ship in the direction of a new era.

4. *Make a big splash.* Small, incremental changes will not have a significant impact on the way your brand is perceived. If you are going to change something, do it for the right reasons, and make sure that you shout it from the rooftops. It is incredibly powerful to tell your customer, "We have listened to you, and we are going to do things a little differently now." Boldly stating what your brand stands for is the best way of resetting your customer relationship. It requires you to live up to your promises. In my case, our logo was completely revamped into a simplified one to give it a fresh feel. We also completely redid our desktop, apps and mobile sites to make them more visually appealing, and launched downloadable digital magazines that were edgy, fast, and built on the latest tech.

5. *Look to the future.* Enjoying your current success is fine while it lasts, but in the age of disruption, there are bound to be challenges that will turn your business model upside down. Being proactive regarding the demands of your future customer base is the best way to manage the relationship. Letting your customers know that you are looking forward and growing with them is the best way to ensure their long-term loyalty. At my workplace, we continued to evolve and communicate with our customers by embracing the latest that digital had to offer. Nowadays, advertisers and readers completely trust our content, both of which are extremely important in digital publishing. In the end, I feel we were able to translate our customers' feedback into tangible improvements that have redefined the brand.

Changing the perception of your brand is a heavy undertaking, but it could make all the difference in whether or not it stands the test of time years into the future. Staying relevant and meeting the needs of your customers will make you untouchable.

# CHAPTER 114

## *Money Can't Buy Love, or Even a Like*

Marketing is not what it used to be, not even a little bit. Long gone are the days of gimmicks, clever phrasing, and seduction. The well of false enchantment has run dry. Consumers stare down attempts at persuasion and flashy advertising because they expect authenticity from corporations and individuals alike. This shift in consumer expectations comes on the back of the digital revolution and unilateral skepticism toward companies and their products. As consumer psychology changes, marketing enters a new era, when human needs, values, and connections define success and failure.

To meet this call to action, marketers must change their perspective toward consumers. They cannot see them as conquest or gullible money-bags. They must see consumers as community members, tribes-people, human beings who crave trust, predictability, transparency, and respect. This is the pathos of the Relationship Era.

In this era, your corporate value must resonate at every level infrastructure and emanate outward through your employees, customers, suppliers, stakeholders, neighbors, and your relationship toward the Earth. Merely projecting an image is akin to falsity; you must genuinely and steadfastly practice what you preach.

## Better Late than Never

This ascendant paradigm in marketing is completely natural—almost expected. When you look at the history of marketing, it becomes patently clear why this new era came about. There are four global ubertrends that contributed to the fundamental shifts ongoing in marketing.

The first is the unsustainability of mass media and advertising both economically and socially. The cost of advertising continues to increase as technology allows marketers to reach highly targeted groups of people; and yet, customers are conspicuously opposed to advertisements. They are perceived as an encumbrance and in some cases, invasive.

The second is that the Internet dissipated the curtain of shadows that once hid corporate activity. No longer are corporations impregnable fortifications. What remains of them is transparent, and it must be if companies are to win the confidence of their customer-bases.

The third is the rise of social media channels as news outlets where people share current events as they happen as opposed to retrospectively. Daily events are live conversations.

The fourth is the overturn of the morality of consumerism. The public cares not only about the cost and quality of its products and services, but also about the values and conduct of the providers. Trust, reliability, and ethics often supersede quality and affordability.

These four ubertrends represent an unseen disruption in industry at large. They have profoundly altered the status quo, the strategies, and the very sociology of marketing. The question before us is this: What can we do to adapt while preserving our bottom line?

## The Middle Way

The apparent choices before brands and marketing agencies are threefold: pour money into all sorts of media channels at the expense of their budgets and ad agencies, jump into social media and hope for the best, or be purpose-driven and suffuse media channels with a distinctive and human set of core values. In a sense, it is the convergence of all three choices that can win the day.

To understand why a convergence is preferable, we must delve into the origin story of marketing.

## Marketing—an Origin Story

Marketing began in what you can call the Product Era. It's defining characteristic was an emphasis on the intrinsic—to put it charitably—properties of a good or service. In copy dating back as early as 1659, we see advertisements like this: *PANACEA, or the Universal Medicine: Being a Discovery of the Wonderfull Vertues Of Tobacco Taking in a Pipe.*" The copy is simple, blunt, and hyperbolic.

Curiously, by the mid-nineteenth century, marketing schemes had remained just about the same. It wasn't until 1965 that the Consumer Era began.

## The Consumer Era

The Consumer Era was characterized by a change in focus from the product to the consumer. The goal became to penetrate the minds and hearts of consumers, rather than just extol the "vertues" of a good or service. A quintessential example of this is Nike's slogan "Just Do It."

During the Consumer Era, the reigning marketing methodology was a four-step, universally applicable approach.

1. Use research to determine what the public wants.

2. Offer the good or service.

3. Devise advertising campaigns to entice, entertain, impress, or flatter the public.

4. Carefully choose the media where your campaign will be featured.

The Relationship Era is the result of consumer reactions to this approach, in addition to fluctuations in the basic externalities that compose the marketing environment.

## Shift in the Marketing Environment

Marketing as an environment has always been ruled by three externalities: consumer psychology, the market itself, and the economics of marketing. To date, these three externalities have fluctuated in measurable ways.

***Cost.*** In the past, there were gargantuan barriers to entry for marketers. Only the most lucrative agencies and brands could afford to advertise on popular media channels. Now, media is myriad and comparatively inexpensive. Anyone with a social media account can launch highly targeted ad campaigns locally, nationally, and internationally.

***Ecology.*** In the past, advertisers would saturate the market with campaign ads, constantly burning money for the promise of greater returns. Now, there are far too many channels and too much content being produced every day. Saturating the market is simply unsustainable.

***Practice.*** In the past, businesses were slaves to consumer preferences, the competition's activities, and capital markets. Now businesses must look inward to ascertain their core values and earnestly live them out in order to survive in the market. It is no longer acceptable to create the impression of reliability, trust, and quality. It is necessary to foster genuine relationships built on equality, reciprocity, respect, and attention to feedback.

These profound shifts constitute an entirely new marketing environment, heretofore known as the Relationship Era.

## The Relationship Era

This is what the Relationship Era looks like.

Type, "I love Apple," into your search bar. You will get something like 387,000,000 hits in about 0.42 seconds.

Type, "I love Starbucks," into your search bar. You will get something like 35,900,000 hits in about 0.53 seconds.

Some companies spend billions of dollars every year to get the attention of their customers and don't boast nearly this many hits, likes, or love. That's because money can't buy love in the Relationship Era. It can't even buy you likes.

Citibank, Dow Chemical, and Exxon spend roughly $2 billion dollars every year on marketing. Type, "I love Citibank," into your search bar. You will get something like 12,900,000 in about 0.30 seconds. The others do not fare any better.

These results reveal that money spent doesn't correlate with love received. That doesn't mean that you don't have to give to get, however. You just have to give the right kind of stuff; the reality of the market will take care of the rest.

What is the reality of today's market?

***People Talk.*** There are billions of people online, and millions of them are talking about brands, their experiences, posting reviews, and reading consumer feedback. When your customers like your brand, they will express affection for it. People will care about you.

***Providence.*** Those relationships and what people say about you online does, in fact, dictate your success. You might not want to accept it, but that doesn't make it untrue.

***Transparency.*** This is both an edict and an admonishment. Be transparent and continue to be. What happens in the boardroom is no longer a secret, and any discussions had can, and probably will, find their way into a public forum.

The Relationship Era. It is unique in that success or failure depends not so much on what you say, but rather on who you are. To thrive in it just takes some flexibility and willingness to upend the status quo.

## Not Business as Usual

The Relationship Era has many requirements. It demands much more from corporations and marketers. Doing business successfully in this milieu will depend on moral conduct, positive customer relations, and continual cooperation with stakeholders. The imperative at every level is to build trust, and not through subterfuge, but as an aim in and of itself.

The relationships that companies tended to build with customers were detached and self-interested. They were meant to lubricate negotiations. Many people built long-lasting relationships on these grounds, but they were superficial and opportunistic connections. This would make corruption and duplicitousness easier.

When you build relationships on trust and equity, it is harder to abuse someone for money. Relationships of fidelity are not purely transactional, and yet, they result in greater shared value and reduced expenditures on promotion.

When you establish connections that are genuinely and mutually satisfying, you cultivate sustainability and resilience. In economic terms, these relationships yield high financial premiums. You increase share prices, improve ROI, and concurrently safeguard the bottom line. Best of all, you transcend economics and create the opportunity for admiration and respect, which permeates every interaction.

## Relationships Are Built on Social Media

Always being connected is a boon and a curse. Consumers have perpetual access to social media and to the information that flows through it. This can carry you to glory or down into the pits of forget. The power consumers wield has changed their psychology greatly.

Consumers realize that they have this power, and they brandish it in their favor. They live the "social" part of social media on a daily basis. They take no relationship for granted, whether it is human or corporate. You should give equal priority to this facet of social media.

That means viewing consumers as constellations of interlinked relationships. They are connected to their families, their friends, their co-workers, and their lovers. They are roads to bridges that exist online in perpetuity. As a marketer, if you think effectively about advertising, you can enter those circles fluidly.

The way to accomplish this, first and foremost, is to understand how social media works, especially Facebook. You must think of social media less as channels and more as roads to human lives. What are these roads paved with? They are paved with human observations, ideas, concerns, hopes, dreams, fears, opportunities, failures, and all the things that make us complex and exciting.

To put it bluntly, until you establish genuine relationships with your consumers, no one will care what you say on these channels. You can spend millions of dollars on social and never see a return on investment.

What's great about this from a financial standpoint is that money spent on relationship building pays in spades. When you cultivate these relationships from the heart, your consumers stand behind you like they would a friend. The more they let you into their lives, the more they share your content, your thoughts, and your brand with their intimate circles. You don't necessarily pay for that with money, just with time and affect.

## Trust. What Does It Mean?

I have already made it abundantly clear that trust is the basis of marketing and business success in the Relationship Era. For a company, trust means humanizing the institution. People trust companies for much the same reason they trust people: Predictability, reliability, support, honesty, loyalty, respect, shared values, and empathy.

To get into the nitty gritty of trust, MEplusYOU parsed out the concept of trust into three, living components:

***Credibility.*** The presumption of reliability and dependence must take primacy. The brand should connote credibility so that its claims and promises can be assumed to be as good as given.

***Care.*** This is about engaging your customers where their lives matter. It's about constructing your business around their needs and addressing them happily.

***Congruency.*** Consumers are consistently reading into the actions of corporations. They try to divine true motivations, beliefs, values, and purposes. Your actions must align with your motivations in tangible and perceptible ways. Take risks to promote your values.

## The Brand Is All-Encompassing

The brand is what people see and experience. Your starting point with the brand must be the Why behind your business activity. Why do you do what you do? Once you have identified that, let it inspire every part of your business. If that Why is less about corporate success and money-mongering than it is about relationships, then your customers will feel better about jumping on the band wagon.

The Why should determine everything about the company—your hiring practices, your corporate structure, your product design. Your Why must be reflected in all that you do. Only then will the brand become synonymous with your Why, and only then will customers grow to trust it.

Here's an example from Secret.

Secret has been around since 1956. It was advertised as the first deodorant for women. Throughout its long and successful history, it spearheaded its most famous slogan, "Strong enough for a man, but made for a woman." With this, Secret played satirically on the stereotypes of patriarchy, letting women know that with Secret you could be active without the awful and inhuman effect of sweating.

Looking to pivot its brand identity, Matt Hollenkamp, Secret associate brand manager, picked up a compelling story. Olympic medalist Diana Nyad, at 60 years-old, was training to swim 103 miles of open sea between Havana, Cuba and Miami, Florida. Secret identified an opportunity to associate with Diana's fearlessness, and to promote its newest product, Secret Clinical Strength Waterproof Deodorant specially designed for swimming.

After some negotiation, the team agreed to a sponsorship. All Diana's team had to do was develop a Facebook presence and visual identities for garments and gear, decals for the accompanying fleet of boats and kayaks, and some other branded signage. All within one week.

The agency shot three promotional videos with Diana. Then, a day before the swim, she postponed. Subsequently there were additional postponements because of hurricane season. She was forced to put off her historic effort until the following year. Counterintuitively, this was a great occurrence for Secret. They shot another video with Diana, launched a unique website and received hordes of well-wishers who wanted to follow her preparations for the historic swim.

When the time came, Diana set off to the South Atlantic on what proved to be a doomed journey. She started the swim with a fleet of kayakers with shark repellant electronic technology and other protections, but none against box jellyfish. A swarm repeatedly stung Diana. It compromised her breathing. This eventually forced her out of the water.

She tried again and swam 49 miles in 40 hours before jellyfish stings put her at risk of anaphylactic shock. Her third and final attempt had a similar fate.

This story exemplifies the power of relationship-based marketing.

Even before Diana dove into the water, Secret sales had skyrockets. Despite never finishing the race, she won the respect of millions who had followed her intently on the Secret-sponsored Facebook page and website.

The brand succeeded not because of its products but because of its support of and association with someone whose struggle was inspiring to its customers. They wanted to be a part of her journey and of Secret.

## Relationships Are About Membership

This story and others like it show us that brands nowadays are about membership and less so about products or services. In a sense, the goods and services become secondary.

There are a few questions that marketers should ask themselves when such membership opportunities come about.

- Does the campaign hinge on the experience of the person(s) at the center of the initiative?
- Does the campaign gratuitously exploit the emotions of the audience?
- Is the association between the brand and the initiative transparently genuine and equitably transactional?
- Does the campaign adhere to the stated or implicit Why of the brand?

To put this in perspective, consider that Coca-Cola's Facebook page has roughly 45 million fans. The approximate cost of reaching that many people in TV advertising is about $1 million dollars. With this mass of followers, Coca-Cola has 24/7 access to droves of followers for free.

The best part is that the people who liked the page wanted to be members, and every positive interaction reifies their decision of membership.

Membership in the Relationship Era goes far beyond an approval to join, however. That's because it operates at a primitive level where the intuition of reciprocity impels human decision-making. What do I mean?

## Sharing Is a Form of Currency

I'm sure we have all heard about increasing consumer engagement. The problem is that we may not quite grasp why this is positive at all. Yes, the bottom line is to increase revenue, so you may wonder how getting a few followers and having them engage with content will help boost revenue.

The answer is quite elementary.

Sharing is a human need. Evolutionary psychologists tell us it is hardwired into our genes. Theoretically, without this primitive need, complex human societies might not have developed.

According to psychology professor Samuel D. Gosling of the University of Texas, sharing is not just about action. It is also about display. When we display sharing, we tell people about ourselves, about our character, about our preferences. When we do this we both maintain and create social bonds. This has discernible evolutionary advantages. It also has marketing advantages.

From a marketing perspective, the display of sharing is a form of currency. When your audience engages through shares, likes, and comments, they are informing others that the content is worthwhile. There is something good here. It is so good that I interact with it. That alone builds credibility.

If you as a brand respond on those sites and engage, then you engender care.

Contingent upon what the substance of those interactions are, you can generate congruency.

With those three things in one environment, you have built trust.

The point about substance is key. The content you put out and the content that others put up tells others something about your brand.

## The Content Revolution Is About Relationships Too

The content revolution denotes the rise in the demand for high quality content. Some will describe that as providing value. No matter the nomenclature, the heart of the content revolution is strong relationship building.

When you provide high quality content, you give people more reasons to share. When you give people more reasons to share, you build stronger relationships to those people and to the people that they share with. Over time you are associated with content that matters because more people engage with it. This is great because the content matters only as much as the people who engage with it.

It's quite simple.

Slightly more complicated are the layers of engagement. There is definitely a hierarchy there. For instance, a like is not as impressive as a comment; a comment is not as impressive as a share; a share is not as impressive as a video reaction; a video reaction could be as good as a written post about the content; and so on.

As you rush along with this content revolution, make sure that what you share on your social media channels reflects your company values, beliefs, and identity. And make sure that what you share is worthwhile.

The goal should be to increase strong, relationship-building engagement and to make sure that the content people engage represents your brand identity.

## How to Decide What Kind of Content to Share

The recipe for deciding what content a brand should share is simple enough. Just think about how you build relationships with individual people.

***Listen.*** Is the content a reaction to customer feedback? Brands can monitor what is being said about them. Your customers will tell you what is worthwhile about the brand. Listen to them and act accordingly. Be transparent about this.

***Define.*** Is the content aligned with your brand identity? With your Why in mind, delineate your brand's personality traits. Much like a person has a character, your brand does too. The brand needs a social voice, a perspective, a set of values. Define those early on and stay the course.

***Converse.*** Is the content responding to customers directly or indirectly? Interact directly with your customers on social media and elsewhere. When you do so, do not act like a detached voice from up above; be a person with opinions. Tell people what you think as a company, and do not be afraid. The customers you actually want to reach will support you.

***Promote.*** Does the content promote your values? Promote your values across other media sources. Stand behind worthwhile causes. Do not be afraid to lead the charge. The brand can wield a substantial following, and when you use it to promote your Why inside and outside the company, your customers will feel an affinity.

***Inspire.*** Does the content inspire people to action? When you break-down all walls between the brand and the customer, you inspire loyalty and action. Do not be afraid to reach out to specific people with opportunities for engagement. This can take any number of forms. Your stakeholders especially should be willing to engage and promote. You have to find ways to inspire them into action.

***Collaborate.*** Does the content motivate others to join in? This is the ideal of the Relationship Era. When you succeed in building those relationships, you both become promoters. Your customers will feel connected to the brand. When that happens, reach out and give thanks. Do not let your promoters feel that they are screaming into a void. Send them tokens of appreciation; give them a platform. When someone gives, you should too. That is collaboration.

## A Call to Action for the Relationship Era

I have tried my best to describe the mechanism, spirit, and psychology of the Relationship Era. For some brands and marketers, this will be an intuitive process. For others, it will be difficult to depart from the transactional model of marketing.

The middle way requires tremendous effort, listening, and thinking deeply about identity, but it will cost less and gain you much more.

To summarize what I have written thus far, I will leave these parting thoughts.

- The more you sell, the more you scare.
- Embrace relationship building not as a strategy but as obligatory.
- Know what you stand for and champion it.
- Listen to your customers.
- Spread content that is valuable and resonates with your customers' feedback.
- You can't fake authenticity. Don't try it. Be sincere.

# CHAPTER 115

## *How to Really Influence Customers*

The way customers make decisions today is quite different than the way they made decisions 10-15 years ago. In the past, the factors that influenced consumer behavior were more superficial and more limited: brand name, advertising, and brand messaging were crucial and limited to shelves and catalogs. Now, consumers demand strong content, consumer reviews, and clear-cut technical information about products and services. Consumers have reached a point where products can be assessed not only based on their individual merits, but also in isolation from other products in the market.

The advent of expert assessment, vast quantities of easily accessed information about a product and its components, reviewer feedback, and company transparency all put power in the hands of the consumer. Unlike before, consumers are now able to predict the likely experience they would have with a product or service using that information. The total unconditional value of a thing is right at their fingertips.

### Total Unconditional Value

The "total unconditional value" of a thing refers to supposed subjective quality of a product or service, whether experienced or not. The increased access to this volatile yet vital information marks big changes for the marketing industry. What I see is that as consumers rely more and more on the total unconditional value of things, they are becoming less susceptible to context and framing manipulations, to traditional marketing strategies, and are more likely to make reasonable market decisions—economists rejoice!

## Where Marketing Was and Where It Is Going

Throughout the twentieth century, marketing was largely a game of smoke and shadows. Marketers understood that consumers made decisions about products and services using relative quality proxies; in other words, using what was immediately available to them. Before the rise of the Internet, that amounted to very little.

In many cases today, consumers make decisions based on a global context, which amounts to a lot more. Broader comparisons can be performed, and they are not limited to your immediate experience. For one, you can access large repositories of information about a product or service from consumers just like you. This is the stuff that total unconditional evaluations are made of. It all brings us closer to accurate expectations about a product.

This isn't to say a product has some inherent, quantifiable, or describable value; rather, consumers can better evaluate their possible experience with a product without ever needing to come in contact with it. That, quite simply, is revolutionary.

This revolutionary spirit rides on the back of the technological revolution. At this point the term may very well sound like a platitude, but its effects cannot be understated, nor can their extent be presaged.

## Inside the Consumer's Armament

A number of tools have emerged that catalyzed the shift toward total unconditional value as an implicit norm of consumer behavior. Aggregation tools, advanced search engines, reviews from other users' social media, unprecedented access to experts and other emerging technologies. These and many other advances are conducive to more accurate and more fast-paced decision-making among this generation of consumers.

Consumers today have a varied and sophisticated armament of tools against the traditional ploys of marketing. There are apps that let you scan items in the store and compare the store price to online prices. There are apps that inform you about resale values of products, such as ShopSavvy and Bakodo. There are e-commerce sites and review sites dedicated to distributing goods and providing copious quantities of consumer feedback about products and services. Amazon, Yelp, and PCMag all fall in one or both of those categories.

This poses a problem for the obstinate marketer and significantly alters market culture at every level. Simply put, companies and marketers will have a hard time influencing consumers using traditional tactics and indirect cues based on the model of local context.

Their bag of tricks is old hat.

## Four Decades of Spring Cleaning for Marketers

Over the past four decades, a number of experiments in marketing have highlighted how susceptible people are to influence. The prevailing belief was that marketers could sway people to behave in irrational ways.

The modes of influence employed by marketers fell into three broad categories: framing effects, the way you present a product or service; choice context effects, contrasting one product or service with others of different prices; and task effects, the way in which consumers are asked to evaluate an offer.

These modes have lost their theoretical force in the age of information and technology. Consumers today can insightfully assess quality, compare their assessments with the experiences of others, and easily tap market information. This virtually amounts to noise that consumers make sense of, and all this noise turns those theories on their heads.

The reason is that all of this noise has pushed consumers to think more about their purchases. This has diminished the impact of marketing strategies based on those traditional theories. Consumers know there is a man behind the curtain.

There are still experiments emerging that add fodder to the belief that consumers are irrational and sheepish. Be wary of these claims! These studies are often performed in laboratory environments that cannot simulate the noise of the market. In a lab, experimenters have far more control over their subjects than a marketer does over consumers in the real world.

Some experiments have claimed the opposite. They hold that the increase in noise and distraction is turning consumers into deer in headlights, but that's a theory that may not hold water.

## New Decision-Making for a New Age

Consumers are still buying, they are still deciding, and they are doing it in a brave new world. The thought that they will simply grow weary and succumb to the wiles of marketers is overly optimistic for the marketer and pessimistic for the consumer.

Possibly in response to the increased noise coupled with access to tools and information previously unavailable to consumers, new decision-making trends among consumers can be observed.

As I see them, the three new decision-making trends can be described as couch tracking, faster verdict, and more from the head.

## Couch Tracking

*Consumers:* Couch tracking describes consumers who are not in the market for a particular product to address a particular need. They are simply keeping track of new products and sales, constantly consuming information about new products on the market and deciding when is the right time to purchase.

*Marketers:* What couch tracking means for marketers is that preferences about certain products are already formed well in advance of seeing the potential purchase item. Products, therefore, are not assessed solely of their own merits but against a bevy of unpredictable and unique information compiled by the couch tracker.

## Faster Verdict

*Consumers:* Faster verdict describes the perception that items directly searched for should be purchased quickly. This happens because the discovery step in the purchase chain now occurs more rapidly and more confidently than before. In the wake of this revolution, we can expect faster uncertainty resolution regarding product quality, preference fit, and acceptance. All this equals efficient purchase decisions.

*Marketers:* What faster verdict means for marketers is that they have a small window of opportunity to influence potential buyers, and much of their influencing must happen indirectly, way before the decision to buy even occurs. It must happen in the discovery phase in the noise.

## More from the Head

More from the head describes the shift from emotional content to matter-of-fact content. Reviews, marketing, and information about products and services tend to be less about subjective experience and more about the technical aspects of the product. Consumers are persuaded more by practical product considerations and less so by emotional cues. This is the result of consumer skepticism about marketing tactics, particularly those that arose from the modes of influence mentioned above.

This should dramatically affect marketing strategy. Marketers must change with consumer culture or risk falling out of touch. Here are some areas where improvements can be made.

## It's Not Me, It's You: Brand Loyalty

Brand loyalty is another thing of the past. With so many options, so many competitors, and so much information out there, purchases are largely considered transient transactions. Consumers see their relationships to brands as open, non-committal.

One phenomenon contributing to this trend may be that consumers see transactions with the same company as isolated from each other. Even if someone purchased a product from a company and had a positive experience, they do not assume that all of the company's products will be as good. They will usually go through the same decision-making to assess the relative merits of each product or service. This undercuts the attempts to foster customer loyalty on a fundamental level.

The bright side for companies is that the trend is ubiquitous. Everyone is feeling it. The way to counteract the effects of this is to provide value across the board and use facts to make it convincingly clear why your product or service is superior.

## Cut the Fluff: Communications

Positioning is a cherished marketing concept. It is rooted in the idea that product evaluations are predominantly dictated by communications strategies. The problem is that the concept is bankrupt for today's consumer culture.

Positioning statements created in conference rooms don't have the same persuasive force that they used to. If your product has an identifiable advantage over your competitors, that's the differentiating factor you must emphasize. It's the factor that consumers really care about.

The attempts at making products appear unique just won't fly with consumers anymore. Consumers are savvier. They don't care for fluff; they want concrete information.

## If You Build It, They May Not Always Come: Social Media

As social media grew and grew, marketers flocked to all channels, trying to stake their claim to user newsfeeds. It was envisaged as a Panacea of profits via connectivity. As more and more social media sites emerged, users began to scatter, so marketers started stretching themselves thin trying to keep up with the flight.

This approach to marketing is unrealistic and unwise. Not every consumer will be on every social media site. Success lies in targeting the place where your potential customers dwell and attacking it.

You must seek out your customers, not the other way around.

## A New Perspective: The Influence Mix Approach

Marketing and consumer culture have certainly undergone changes. So, too, should marketing strategies and systems of belief regarding customer behavior change.

The Influence Mix Approach addresses those points and a number of others.

The Influence Mix approach is comprised of three axes:

- The consumer's prior beliefs, preferences, and experiences (P)
- Fellow consumers and information platforms (O)
- And, last but not least, marketers (M)

This approach is aptly described as a zero-sum game. Reliance on one axis decreases the need to rely on another. In today's market, however, P and O are largely more influential than M. I don't mean to diminish the importance of M, but in terms of persuasive force, P and O take the cake.

The goal shouldn't be to choose one over the other. These axes are inter-affective not mutually exclusive. However, funds and time are limited, so priorities must be defined and enacted.

At a philosophical level, marketers should step away from the notion that they are behind the driver's seat. For example, consumers who are closer to the O side of the continuum may not depend on marketers' outputs to make decisions: their O features may primarily guide decision-making. Furthermore, some products and services are more O feature evocative than others.

In theory, an optimal application of this approach would hinge on marketer's understanding of their customer's current and future influence mix. The medley of P, O, and M should correlate with customer's purchase decisions and customer characteristics. These attributes will vary from market segment to market segment. Marketers should keep abreast of this.

The driving question of this approach is, "To what extent do my customers currently depend on O and on specific O features to make their purchase decisions, and to what extent might they depend on O in the future?"

Answers to that two-part question are always changing and always on a continuum.

## The Moral of the Story

If you have heard about the rising tide of content marketing, all this should help explain its existence.

The crucial takeaway is that marketers should recognize where they can exert the most influence; that is, where effective impact is localized. Marketers are moving away from modes of influence toward modes of communication and content dissemination centered on these trends and the Influence Mix approach.

Market research will also change. Tracking O features is hard work and time sensitive. Consumer preferences are not static, and for a marketing strategy to succeed, it must keep updated on O changes constantly.

Content marketers are learning how to do this. All marketers should learn how to do this.

# CHAPTER 116

## *Extracting Maximum Value When an Ad Goes Viral*

Going viral on social media for many of us is a mythical event, utterly unexpected and, as an unfortunate consequence, often a golden opportunity that is wasted. We spend a magical sleepless night (or two) watching all the adulation pouring in, but when the noise has subsided, life resumes as if nothing had happened because we don't do anything about it.

"Winning the Internet" means nothing if you have nothing to show for it.

The very top marketers (and that could be any of us if we consider our personal brands) know that "going viral" is never a certainty, but if they put out the right content to the right audience on a regular basis, it is always a possibility. They plan for that possibility, and they make sure that they squeeze every possible benefit from the short timeframe of their fame. Many also subscribe to the notion that "going viral" is a by-product of their work rather than an aim in itself. If you write with a specific intention of going viral, your work risks losing its authenticity.

So, plan for going viral, but don't live for it; life is too short, even for the 100mph digital marketing wizards. The content conveyor is a place of amazing creativity, but when the viral hit does come, you have to switch into an organized "make the most of it" mode. In my experience as a digital publishing executive, and in anecdotal discussion with digital marketing colleagues, this mode comprises four stages:

***Acknowledge.*** If your content goes viral for positive reasons, it is important that you are involved in the conversation as early as possible. Understand which platforms are most active, and let people know that you appreciate their attention. If the content goes viral for negative reasons, you only have one chance to make the right response. If you leave it too long, the haters will only grow in number, and you have a PR disaster on your hands. In both situations, you have to take ownership for what you have "chosen" to put out into the world; people want to feel like they are in a two-way conversation with you.

***Engage.*** Opportunities to reach out to your followers in an organic and genuine way are rare. In a world that is drowning in direct marketing and sponsored posts, crafting a meaningful response to as many people as possible is the least that a brand (or an individual) can do. This doesn't happen enough, and when someone feels that they are being listened to, they will retain an affinity for your brand. The more fans you have out there in the world, the better. Engaging with them is the first step to building a relationship.

***Build.*** If you understand why your piece of content went viral (by talking to people), it makes absolute sense to create a follow-up campaign to continue the conversations and debate. You might want to use different media and reach out to other social media platforms, and if this is done in a measured and considered fashion, it can easily prolong the visibility and message that you are trying to get across. It is important to avoid desperate "copycat" attempts, as the viral formula is unlikely to be repeated, but if you supplement rather than copy, there is every chance that the reaction will be positive.

***Measure.*** Return on investment. Yes, even marketers have to account for their place at the table—no MD sees marketing as a bottomless pit. A viral update offers the chance to give a large-scale injection of activity at the top of the sales funnel, and if this can be tracked down to concrete sales (etc.), the case is made for your marketing budget for the foreseeable future. Content marketing is notoriously hard to measure, but when a viral hit comes along, even the Financial Director will be smiling. Measure your success, communicate it to the wider business, and let them know that you are making a difference.

Going viral feels great, but it feels even better if you are in control and maximizing the opportunities to squeeze every last benefit from the windfall.

# SECTION 6 – INNOVATION

# CHAPTER 117

## Innovating in the Internet Age

We all want to innovate in some way. It doesn't matter what industry you work in. Innovation is about new solutions to problems and foreseeing opportunities for efficiency and greater value. Some people are equipped with heightened creativity and innovative potential. They approach problems with a hawk-eye, seeing beyond the trivial into the core of a matter, and, in that way—poised for revolution—upend business as usual.

This is the story we often hear about innovators. It's fluffed and romanticized to our detriment. Beyond that, it's archaic. This story resonates with the ancient interpretation of creativity.

For those of us who live in the present, creativity is not unattainable, it's learnable. Here's how.

In the wake of the European Renaissance, a new belief gained prevalence—the belief that great creative or scientific accomplishments were the direct result of a person's education, abilities, and hard work, not the work of some divine entity.

### Backstory

In a not too long ago past, people believed that creativity was a divine attribute rather than a human one. The Sumerians and early

Judeo-Christians believed that technological advancements were gifts from the divine powers as a show of favor and satisfaction. This was the pervasive attitude in many human civilizations for quite some time. Then, between the fourteenth and seventeenth centuries, that changed.

In the wake of the European Renaissance, a new belief gained prevalence. The belief that great creative or scientific accomplishments were the direct result of a person's own education, abilities, and hard work, not the work of some divine entity. This amplified human confidence and human potential. As a consequence, the Renaissance gave birth to a flurry of unprecedented technological, artistic, and cultural innovations.

What sparked this creative tide? How did so many people almost simultaneously awaken their creative abilities and innovate in such historic ways? These questions are worth exploration because their answers might inform how to inspire ourselves and others to change the way we live.

All of us have the mental capacity for idea generation and imaginative problem-solving, and all of us can improve our creative abilities.

## Creative Mindset

There were key traits present in every Renaissance thinker's creative process. Although their outputs and ends may have varied, they invariably had similar creative processes and approaches.

- *Contrarian.* They were willing to go against the grain. They challenged long-standing beliefs and assumptions to reinvent their worldview and that of those around them. There was a latent optimism there. They believed the world could be better.
- *Nonconformists.* They were disquieted by conformity and sought to revolutionize technology, philosophy, art, politics, and all that had stagnated around them.

- *Curiosity.* They were unafraid of novelty. These thinkers were open to new ways and thoughts. Granted, it wasn't paradise. There were still those who clung to tradition, prejudice, and bias. Nevertheless, the overarching mentality was to seek novelty through curiosity.

- *Systems Thinking.* There was a quantum leap from the analysis of inherent and distinct parts to broader systems, interactivity, and relationships. This yielded a change of view toward the natural world and toward human beings. Thinkers developed an attitude, an awareness, of our limitless capacity for creation, stretching and synthesizing resources like never before.

They were not superhuman. And these traits are not enigmatic. They are observable and reproducible traits that can inspire the innate spirit of curiosity, invention, and innovation in each of us. I believe that all of us have the mental capacity for idea generation and imaginative problem solving, and all of us can improve our creative abilities.

So, how do we increase everyone's inherent capacity to come up with innovative ideas?

It might seem that most creative geniuses walk around having "Aha!" moments, snatching brilliant ideas out of thin air. It's a pretty myth. In hindsight, seldom has that been the case.

## Reverse Engineer the Creative Mindset

Creativity is learnable. It takes some of us more time than others, but it is learnable nevertheless. There is enough information available about people regarded as creative geniuses to distill key attributes and reverse engineer a creative regimen.

My deep-sea diving into the wild world of creativity revealed the following hidden treasures:

***Space.*** Creativity works best in creative environments. If you are surrounded by lackluster, unimaginative, command-and-control-oriented people, your creativity will likely suffer.

***Objects.*** Look at the world in terms of relationships, connections, patterns, and overlaps. We usually endeavor to simplify things with facile labels and schemata (fixed systems of concepts and ideas). The mind reduces cognitive effort by fixing these labels and schemata, rendering the world seemingly predictable.

Unless an event or thought deeply challenges our preconceptions, we will retain existing labels and schemata. The creative mindset runs contrary to fixed anything. It is reflective.

***Mind.*** To rethink labels and schemata, we essentially have to change the way we look at the world. It's a catch-phrase—I know—but that doesn't make it un-insightful, just over-used.

- The *first step* is to identify orthodoxies, as in patterns of thought that appear immutable. Orthodoxies by definition are fixed. That isn't necessarily a bad thing. Yet, they can blind us to opportunity if unchecked.

- The *second step* is to embrace change. You may think you are adaptable and open to change. Be wary! Our very aversion to change brings about the delusion that small changes are bigger than they are. I'm not talking about changing your toothpaste; I'm talking about ground-shaking change.

Ask yourself, *What could I do drastically different without jeopardizing myself or others?* Once you have an answer, ask yourself *How?*

- The *third and final step* is to devise a creative process. It might seem that most creative geniuses walk around having "Aha!" moments, snatching brilliant ideas out of thin air. It's a pretty myth. In hindsight, seldom has that been the case. Most moments of insight and profundity come when we are steeped in a problem, entrenched in contemplation and frustration.

Remember that an insight is not a new idea—or even the recognition of a new idea—it is a fresh thought or an illuminating understanding that inspires a new idea.

## The Secret Weapon: Creative Process

Not all creative processes are created equal. They reflect the idiosyncrasies of the person who devised them. I want to share mine with you. It was inspired by countless articles and books on the subject.

- Frame a specific challenge, and focus on solving it.
- Research the subject, and learn from the work of others.
- Immerse yourself in the problem, and explore possible solutions.
- Reach a roadblock, and feel the creative frustration.
- Detach from the problem. Let it incubate in your unconscious.
- Come to an illuminating insight that fundamentally shifts your perspective.
- Build the insight (or insights) into a big idea, a new combination of thoughts.
- Test and validate the new idea. Try to make it work.

Does this still sound out of reach? Remember that an insight is not necessarily an original idea—or even the recognition of an original idea—it is a fresh thought or an illuminating understanding that inspires a new idea. An insight is a striking realization that fundamentally changes our thinking. Simply put, an insight is something you previously didn't know, or yet think about, that has the power to surprise and inspire you.

Once we accept that creativity is not a birthright of exceptional people but a skill that can be taught and acquired, we can begin to seriously tap into the latent innovation potential inside all of us and across our organizations.

## What About Group Creativity?

In the workplace, you may need to make giant leaps in creative thinking without the necessary intellectual stepping stones to get from insight to big idea.

The eight-step creative process above is applicable to individuals and groups alike, with a few variations that account for group dynamics and social psychology.

Assume you are tasked with creating a team that will innovate on company offerings. To accomplish this using the eight-step creative process, you must first create a core group from across the organization that can devote time to this critical challenge.

Then divide the group into four sub-teams. The goal is for each team to generate some new strategic insights using one of four pre-assigned lenses. One group will challenge deep-seated orthodoxies about who your customers are, what you offer them, how you deliver value, how you make money and how you differentiate from the competition.

Another group will identify and analyze trends with the potential for new benefits to customers or for disruption. The focus should be on developments that competitors have overlooked or ignored.

The third group will look for ways to leverage your company's resources into adjacent or perhaps radically different kinds of opportunities, or to make combinations between your own resources and those of external organizations in order to create new value for customers.

The fourth group will search for deep, unarticulated customer needs that could form the basis for compelling new offerings or quantum-leap improvements to your existing products and services.

Once each group has identified a problem, completed extensive research, and steeped themselves in their findings, they should have reached the point of creative frustration. That's when the sparks begin to fly!

After you've aggregated all your team's strategic insights, it's time for the ideas to start flowing. Now the teams should switch gears from gathering and steeping to building and generating. The teams then begin to "crash" or combine insights from the various lenses to produce a slew of unexpected ideas and business opportunities.

The bulk of the work is in clustering ideas that reinforce each other, adding them into domains. This further improves the creative output. Finally, sift through this pool of potential opportunities to select the ideas your company wants to seriously consider for experimentation and development.

## We Are All Innovators in Wait

The eight-steps, the history lesson, and the traits of past thinkers are all useless if you don't believe in your own potential to innovate. It won't come easily. It will take time and energy, but that isn't a reason to relent.

I truly believe that literally anyone can improve their creative thinking skills. Only when we accept that creativity is not a birthright of exceptional people, but rather a skill that can be taught and acquired, can we seriously tap into the latent innovative potential inside all of us and across our organizations.

# CHAPTER 118

## *Never Let Innovation Become Normal*

### "We're an innovative company."

You hear that phrase everywhere these days—in advertising, at trade shows, in corporate literature, and even listening into conversations in coffee shops. It is a badge of honor for the early twenty-first century, but, as with all popular assertions, the word itself is being devalued in its misuse by the underwhelming majority.

Innovation doesn't simply mean doing something differently; it means doing something completely new. Yes, completely new. One company may have a new method of running a meeting standing up, but hundreds of other companies have been doing that for years. This isn't innovation; this is iteration.

Doing something differently from the way you have done it before is part of the natural cycle of life. We change with the times, but you cannot call this innovation. It is simply what needs to happen for you or your company to keep your heads above the water. Life is changing at a breakneck speed, and if you too don't change, you will be left behind. There is nothing particularly impressive about this; it is just the way that things have always been.

So, for all the MDs out there who ask their staff what innovative things they have done this week, please, I implore you, don't make "innovation" as common as filling in your expense forms or compiling your Monday morning performance report. In my humble opinion, innovation should be a "Wow, I can't believe you did that!" type of feeling. It shouldn't be expected, and it shouldn't be measured—it is simply something to strive toward, something to believe in.

In a similar vein, the "innovative" start-up culture that has sprung up over the past few years has the same obsession with "innovation." There are only so many ways that you can build an app, which hooks you up with nearby drivers. The first big movers in the market were the true innovators (well done, Uber), but the subsequent competitors cannot truly call themselves innovative. Someone has been there and done it before them—they are simply building on someone's idea.

Innovation is about striving towards your idea—for yourself, for your team, or for your company. It is that unique and indelible mark that you will one day make on this life—a mark that will affect others in a way that they have never been affected before. We all have the chance to make this mark, but too many of us settle for second best when the going gets tough. We tell ourselves that we are being "innovative" in the little things in life, but actually when it comes to true innovation, too few of us keep the fire burning within us for long enough to make that difference.

Don't get me wrong, continuously striving to get better is a noble and very necessary pursuit. Life is sometimes so tough that many of us see merely standing still as a decent result, but every now and again we should all give ourselves a chance to dream, and chance to believe in something, in that far away but ultimately obtainable goal… to become an innovator.

# CHAPTER 119

## *The Nine Ingredients of Innovation*

Creating the right conditions for innovation is like baking a cake. There are essential ingredients, and they should all be added at the right time to ensure success. Every situation is different, so there is no set recipe, but in my experience, these nine ingredients should be included more often than not:

***Commitment.*** Without visionary business leaders standing behind the initiatives, innovation won't get far beyond the conceptual stages. If a program is allocated a hefty budget, it will automatically be taken more seriously. If innovation is managed on a "case-by-case" basis, then it is unlikely to get off the ground.

***Collaboration.*** Selecting the "talent" to work on the innovation project is crucial, but what is more important is how they collaborate with each other and the wider business. Innovation doesn't happen in a vacuum; soliciting opinions and advice from a wide range of colleagues and customers is crucial for success. Ideas need to be adopted before they can become reality.

***Risks.*** The correlation between taking risks, making mistakes, and achieving success is obvious. At the same time, another correlation exists: when you take risks, you expose yourself to unforeseen opportunities, which may open up whole new areas of possibility. Employees need to feel comfortable challenging one other and finding the best-fit solution, no matter which path they took to get there. Linear is not a word associated with innovation.

***Support.*** Commitment is one thing, but active support from particular stakeholders in the leadership team is another entirely. Unless an influential individual understands the subtleties of the program, the required steps will not be fully understood. Having an extra layer of protection from the "fallout" of the inevitable mistakes is crucial to achieving eventual success.

***Experimentation.*** In order to find the best ideas, you need to come up with a load of them (good and bad) and simply see what works. Most companies don't have a way to test small ideas and separate out the good ones, but experimentation is crucial to foster creativity. When mistakes are welcomed as part of the process, the wider business will be less judgmental and more accepting of your wacky ideas.

***Enthusiasm.*** There is nothing more important than encouraging a positive attitude within the team. Without enthusiasm and belief in the goal, influencing others will be impossible. It will help everyone get through the late nights and the nervous product launches, not to mention the regrets and missed opportunities. We all love to work with happy people around us.

***Diversity.*** In many situations, people tend to want to work with people who share similar ideas or beliefs. People with different experiences and from different backgrounds are crucial to discouraging group think, especially in a company with a strong corporate culture. If you find yourself agreeing with each other too much, you need to bring some fresh thinking in to shake things up.

***Implementation.*** Many ideas and projects are short-lived and end up living on the drawing board without the capability for delivery. The step from concept to roll-out should be as smooth as possible—with a view to evaluating success and failing fast if that seems to be likely. Innovators need to communicate what success looks like to all parties and let them know what role they play in that success.

***Customers.*** Innovation is worth nothing in a vacuum; involving the end customers is crucial to ensure that your ideas are worthy. Customers help determine perception of value, and they are the *raison d'etre* for any business. Ignore the consumer in your innovation efforts at your peril – don't assume that you know best. Their perspective will always add a different dimension.

# CHAPTER 120

## *How Can Companies Innovate in the Digital Era?*

"Friction-Free Innovation? Since when has anything been friction-free in a big corporation?" you might ask. "Simply getting them to switch coffee vendors is an uphill struggle."

Many large corporations are oil tankers, plowing through the waves with a relentless purpose, fueled by management consensus and a honed business strategy that has been developed and tweaked over decades. However, recent disruption from hungry start-ups has started to eat away at their market share, and they have to react or one day they will be ripped apart by an iceberg. Just look at the hotel industry—Airbnb is a prime example.

Many big companies are realizing that they have to compete on multiple fronts. Their core business needs to continue, but they also need to foster innovation from within to counter these external threats. GM's Volt only came about because of the threatening developments within Tesla Motors.

How are these corporate behemoths addressing this question? Some are successful, some less so, but all of them have the same broad challenges. Here are a few that come to mind:

One of the biggest issues that stifles innovation in bigger companies is their innate need for management by consensus. While this has helped them to steadily grow their market share, it has a tendency toward mediocrity in terms of testing the extremes of possibility. When you have a group of people who need to agree on something, the middle ground will always be the final choice. If companies were less democratic in certain circumstances, the best ideas would rise to the top and be less likely to be trampled.

For the innovative projects to flourish, the organizational structure of a company therefore needs to offer flexibility. In certain circumstances, there should be a VC type structure within the business, where the innovators can rely on the CEO for the "green light," rather than wading through layers of management (who aren't as invested in the process). This will speed up decisions and allow the innovators to compete with their lean start-up rivals. Many companies (even Disney) are setting up internal accelerator programs to enable these developments.

The best innovators foster a culture of experimentation, where it is possible for anyone to come up with an idea and test it out cheaply and quickly. Employees feel that their ideas are valued, and if they fail (which many will), at least they fail fast. When management allow this activity to sit alongside the daily "delivery" of their core business, they are giving their people additional opportunities to grow.

Recruitment policy is also a key part of a company's innovation strategy. It is no good if the company creates the right conditions but doesn't have the right sort of people to deliver. Companies have to take some risks on hiring the Type-A personalities who are likely to thrive in such environments. The normal "risk-averse" hiring strategies will not work, as they will simply lead to safe decisions in that fatal middle ground.

Companies need to put their money where their mouth are and invest in the big ideas, fully aware that a high percentage will eventually fail. VCs plan for a percentage of projects to fail—big corporates should be no different. The stigma of "failure" should be banished within these innovation circles. Companies need to balance the short-term volatility against the long-term vision.

Throughout history, companies and societies have changed in response to external threats. The current push for innovation is no different. Change your business model or risk "death by a thousand start-ups."

# SECTION 7
# - ENTREPRENEURSHIP

# CHAPTER 121

## *Start-Ups Need Momentum More Than Money*

Too many start-ups resemble a staccato lurch from funding round to funding round. When investment is readily available, it is easy to fall victim to the "who has the deepest coffers" game and forget your true calling. You have to build a viable business that will eventually thrive without the oceans of investment cash.

There are too many entrepreneurs who cite unexpected "burn" as the reason for their company's demise. They are, of course, talking about the fact that they got through the investment funds quicker than anticipated, i.e., they weren't making enough money off their own back. When any business is constantly analyzing burn rather than traction, you know that the day of reckoning is not so far away.

I am not denying the fact that some business models need to reach a critical mass before they can truly take off, and some need super-fast growth to ward off potential competition, but this is not the case with every business. There is much to be said for bootstrapping your business, growing with your customer base and building your momentum slowly but surely—safe in the knowledge that your fundamentals are tried and tested.

Nine out of every ten start-ups fail. Their product does not fill a need in the market, their leaders do not form a cohesive team, but the main reason is that they don't reach a critical mass of growth. Part of this is indeed their speed to market (investment certainly helps with this), but another part is the lack of focus from the founders on building something that actually works rather than strategizing about what would look best in the next investment deck.

Momentum should not be defined as the number of different ideas that have been attempted. Trying and failing is useful if there is a consistent direction, but if the goalposts change every month, each failure will lead to starting from the beginning over and over again. That is not progress… Far better to spend time carefully defining the overall plan and then iterating within that plan until you achieve success. The challenge is to find a way to make the original plan work (possibly with a few so-called "pivots" along the way). Momentum here is the ability to move toward a certain goal at a constant or increasing pace, albeit maybe with a few diversions along the way.

I sometimes question the "fail fast" mentality of many entrepreneurs around the world. Like I said, failing fast but then iterating along the same path is fine, but failing fast and then changing direction entirely shouldn't be encouraged. There are so many "failures" that were nearly an excellent business, and if they had had that little bit extra momentum (and belief) from their founders, they may have been a success. There is not the stigma attached to failure that there used to be; many entrepreneurs will move from failed business to failed business until they might finally hit the jackpot.

If they believed a bit more in momentum rather than chasing investor's money, maybe they might have gotten there a little earlier.

# CHAPTER 122

## *Lost Your Entrepreneurial Mojo?*

Perpetual motion is not the way of the entrepreneur. They ride the waves of their market, shooting down the face of the waves like a bullet after every great idea, enjoying the ride, then waiting until the next wave comes along to propel them to further glory. The ride is far from continuous; sometimes it involves significant amounts of waiting, false starts, and wipe-outs.

It is in those lulls between the waves that mojo can wane. They are entrepreneurs, used to being inches away from disaster, one wrong move away from a painful fall. Passivity (for whatever reason) does not come easily to them, but sometimes you have to bob up and down on that calm sea, waiting for the right wave. Retaining your motivation at these moments is crucial.

There are lots of reasons for losing motivation, but having to slow down can be the beginning of a chain reaction for a serial go-getter. When that "whatever" feeling starts to creep over them, they lose their sharpness, and when the opportunities do come along, they may not take advantage of them as they did before. A vicious circle ensues, and it is hard to break.

I find that the following things have helped when I sense that I am entering the doldrums:

***Feel the sun on your face.*** The moment your mind starts to stagnate, you need to take a stroll in the sun. Exposure to sunlight lowers blood pressure, increases oxygen levels in the blood, builds your immune system, and has been proven as weapon against the onset of depression. The ancient Greeks called sunlight therapy heliosis—in my view (in moderation), it is a good thing. A few hours out in the sun recharge your batteries and prepare you for the battle ahead.

***Get moving.*** Exercise and physical activity deliver oxygen and nutrients to your tissues and help your cardiovascular system work more efficiently. Exercise combats stress and releases endorphins to help get back that feel-good factor. It has even been proven that creativity receives a boost in the immediate aftermath of exercise—what better to break out of the monotony?

***Remember your Why.*** When things slow down, it is easy to forget why you are doing this all in the first place. Your victories seem ever more distant, and you start to wonder how you achieved it all in the first place. When you have little to be motivated about, you have to make an extra effort to reconnect with your joy. No one climbs Everest for the fun of it—everyone has their own reasons. If they forget their reasons, the urge to turn around becomes undeniable.

***Change your focus.*** Just because business is not motoring like usual doesn't mean that you need to lose your drive. Maybe it is the time to take up a new hobby or learn a new skill. This way, you can pour your energy into something worthwhile and keep your mind sharp until your business takes off on the next wave of growth. Business lessons don't only happen at the negotiation table—you can understand more about yourself, no matter what activity you're engaged in.

***Reconnect with people.*** Standing still can be a lonely place. Just because your particular business is going through a slow phase and you don't have any progress to report doesn't mean that you should avoid others. Yes, your friend may have closed out a huge funding round, but the doldrums will await him too at some point. Lean on your friends and recharge your batteries from their successes. Let them do the same when it inevitably happens to them. That is what friends are for.

# CHAPTER 123

## *Entrepreneurial Lessons from Black Swan Events*

Nassim Nicholas Taleb wrote about the effect of highly rare and unanticipated events in his book *The Black Swan*. These unexpected events can create a ripple effect of consequences that stretch far into the future.

I believe that the usually heavy snowfall each winter across the Eastern U.S. will have a significant knock-on effect on the entrepreneurial future of America.

One such weekend last winter was a time for teenagers to understand the impact of supply and demand. Rather than getting out their sleds, a few of the teenagers in my neighborhood were busy earning a healthy living clearing the driveways of their neighbors.

There was a lot of snow, and many of my more elderly neighbors may well have felt a little threatened by the accumulating snow piles.

Come to the rescue a couple of enterprising kids.

They must have been 17 or 18 years-old, dressed barely warmly, one with a snow blower and one with a shovel. I observed as they started to clear the driveway adjacent to mine, and I went out to play in the backyard with one of my children. I came back 20 minutes later to see that they had almost finished. The driveway was looking good.

All the other driveways were a white out, but I could already picture my neighbor adjacent sleeping soundly in the knowledge that he would (possibly) be able to get to work on Monday morning. He had a better chance than the rest of us, in any case.

These kids were providing a service that we all needed. They were the only ones doing it. They had cornered the market on our street. Naturally, I walked out to ask how much they were charging. Let's just say that they were employing a "surge pricing" strategy—it wasn't cheap, but I had to admire their attitude, so I paid up and set them to work on my driveway and stairwell.

By the end of an undoubtedly exhausting few hours, they had cleared seven driveways and earned a decent amount of cash.

Those two kids took advantage of the opportunity and enriched their lives because they were willing to go the extra mile and make a difference for others in their time of need.

As our world turns towards the "gig economy," increasingly more people are seeking to understand the needs of others and providing a service that fits those needs. When *Black Swan* events happen, you can easily charge a premium for those services.

I am willing to bet that those two kids will grow up to be entrepreneurs one day. What they do will make a difference to our world, and they will carve their own little niche into people's lives.

My drive sadly didn't stay clear for long; when the town started clearing the main streets, the industrial equipment blew the street snow right into my driveway. Fascinating to see the two kids kept an eye out for this opportunity as well and came right back for another bite at the cherry.

# CHAPTER 124

## *How Will Entrepreneurs Solve Their Problems?*

Give a curious entrepreneur a Rubik's Cube, and they will use every minute of their downtime in order to master it.

They won't get it out in investor meetings, and it certainly won't be visible during the morning email onslaught. They may not even bring it to work some days, but it will be waiting for them when they get home—a mix of color waiting to be unified.

No, they will decide to sacrifice a few minutes of aimlessly flicking through television channels in the evening. They might wrestle with it instead of watching some random YouTube videos or scanning their Twitter feed for interesting content. Time "wasted" daydreaming can now be put to better use; they will get to the bottom of the puzzle, and nothing will get in the way.

This is not only a "Big Idea" for entrepreneurs in 2016 (#BigIdeas2016), it should be considered by anyone who has a lot on their plate.

We need to use our downtime to grapple with our problems.

Some may say that after a long day in the office, the last thing that we want is to sit obsessing over our worries. Surely vegetating in front of the television is perfect for giving our brain a well-deserved break, right?

Well, yes and no. Those problems aren't going anywhere, and unless we address them, they will pile up until we throw in the towel and forget about them entirely. That is never going to end well, so rather than waste two hours in the name of relaxation, why not take 20 minutes to work through a pressing issue every evening? You will be all the more relaxed once the problem can be filed in the "solution" drawer, and you will sleep that little bit sounder that night.

I am not suggesting that entrepreneurs don't get any downtime; they simply get in the habit of working through their problems and organizing their lives when us mere mortals are already comatose on the sofa.

Entrepreneurs have a second habit when it comes to problem solving – they will always attempt to solve a problem in its entirety before moving on to something else. Many of us are guilty of jumping from one activity to another without fully finishing what we started. When problems are concerned, they only tend to grow if they are left unattended, so proactively (and fully) "ticking" them off the to-think-about list is crucial if you want to progress.

Critical thinking is crucial for any entrepreneur, but it is my view that it almost needs to happen in those moments of quiet when a person might otherwise be "wasting time." Much has been written about the power of creative thought in the shower, on your commute to work, or simply when out for a walk with the family.

Do you let your mind wander aimlessly at such times, or do you seek to dedicate at least part of that time to addressing something that is bothering you?

I can tell you what the best entrepreneurs will be doing with some of their free time.

# CHAPTER 125

## *Your Product Is Destined to Fail*

I have been to a lot of technology shows over the past 15 years.

The annual Consumer Electronics Show (CES) is held each January in Las Vegas. It showcases some of the brightest global minds, the founders of some of the most innovative companies on our planet—their solutions ranging from the sublime to the ridiculous. Their eyes and the eyes of their devout employees shine with the belief that their product will be THE next blockbuster.

However, whether their product is sublime or ridiculous, the chances of real success are infinitesimal in my opinion. Behind their shiny eyes probably lie countless past failures, and even though they have high hopes for the "next one," deep down they cannot fail to recognize that they face an uphill struggle to break through to the big time.

This is why I love going to shows like this, it is the people that make the show, not the products. There is nothing like meeting a whole lot of people who simply "keep going," against all the odds, against the impossible realities and improbable opportunities.

They know that their product is statistically destined to fail, but they never fail to enthuse about it to anyone who will listen. If you say those six words in the title, "Your product is destined to fail," they will react with an impressive mix of realism and determination.

"Well, you know… it could, but actually here is why I believe that it won't."

Working in an entrepreneurial company or on a groundbreaking project, you simply have to have an ability to keep your eyes open to spot all the obstacles in your way, while at the same time retaining the belief that you will get there in the end.

It is the ultimate test of human spirit that, despite their past failures, many of these people will eventually go on to work on that product or project, which will break through the glass ceiling of failure.

I'd like to finish with a story of a technology sector veteran who I once met at one of these shows.

He had worked as a sales manager for emerging technology companies all his life. He had silvery hair and George Clooney-esque good looks. He had a gentle manner about him and spoke in a quiet voice that made you want to listen harder. Amongst all the bustle and noise, he exuded a quiet confidence in everything he talked about. It was clearly his last role before retirement beckoned, and, with this in mind, one thing in particular totally blew my mind about him… He talked about his product with a passion that very few fresh graduates can muster. You might think that this isn't surprising, but I can tell you that the product that he was representing was probably one of the worst products I have ever seen.

I have often wondered about that man. Didn't he realize that he was trying to promote a dud? Was he trying to pull the wool over my eyes? I would say "yes" to the first question and "no" to the second question. He knew, deep down that the product would probably fail, but he had been in that situation so many times in his career that he believed that maybe, just maybe, I might be that magic customer to transform its fortunes and take it past that magical tipping point.

Unrealistic? Probably. Inspiring? Definitely.

I love going to trade shows.

# CHAPTER 126

## *The Five Golden Rules for Freelancers*

As the booming gig economy cuts a vast swathe through the corporate jungle and as clients judge more on value-add than on size, being a freelancer has never been more attractive.

In theory.

In practice, it is not all cozy lie-ins, exotic coffee, and casual attire. The potential rewards are there for people with the right product and the right attitude, but there are many hidden obstacles along the way that cannot possibly be anticipated. If you have never sat scanning your bank account for a crucial client payment to go through (so that you can pay your tax bill), you won't know what I mean.

I am not a freelancer myself, but a few of my close friends are, and these are the top five issues that they talk about over a drink or dinner:

***You have to get paid.*** It is all well and good agreeing on a contract with someone, but you have to be able to deliver what you promise to their satisfaction before they will pay you. There are many circumstances that will hinder this process, not all under your control, and sometimes people simply won't want to pay you. Another variant is that they aren't able to pay; pre-qualifying your prospects and turning down those who are overly price sensitive is crucial for a healthy cash flow. Getting paid is the oxygen of a freelancer—when it isn't flowing, it can get a little hard to breathe.

***You have to treat people right.*** Oh, this is a big one. Many freelancers will not sit in the same office as their clients, and they may not even be in the same country. The market for their services may not be huge, and word about the quality of their service will travel fast in the client community. If you put your clients first (in every situation), you give yourself the best chance of developing loyalty. If you are inflexible and antagonistic, you can wave goodbye to a stable future. Freelancers often need the client more than the client needs that particular freelancer.

***You can't plan too far ahead.*** It is nice to dream, but the reality is that freelancers have to spend 99% of their efforts on the day-to-day running of their business. It is important to understand the direction of your market so that you can adapt your current activity accordingly, but pinning your hopes on an uncertain future is highly risky. If there is one certainty about being a freelancer, it is uncertainty, and you have to be ready to roll with the punches. You may well retire early on a beach somewhere, but don't count on it.

***You have to have an off switch.*** This isn't only advice for freelancers, but given the nature of their roles and the ubiquity of communication devices, they have to be able to drop everything and forget about things for an hour or two every day. Many of them are working to secure the future of their young families, but at the same time letting family life pass them by because they are on a plane or buried in their laptop. Balance is hard to achieve.

***You have to prioritize ruthlessly.*** The "to-do" list for a freelancer can be a liberating tool, or it can be a weight around their ankles. There are so many things that they could be doing to promote their business or to achieve the desired goals for their clients, but they have to understand which activities actually work. No one finds it easy to admit defeat, but 80% of these activities won't be worth the time that is spent on them. Cross them off the list and don't go there again; if something didn't work the first time, it would be unlikely to work the second time.

If freelancers follow these five golden rules, they have every chance of being successful. My friends never want to go back to corporate life, but every now and again one of these issues comes up and bites them. It isn't as easy as it seems.

# CHAPTER 127

## *The Entrepreneur's Epitaph*

It is a modern phrase, but three small words sum up the ideal epitaph (the brief phrase that is written about you when you have passed away) for any entrepreneur on this planet.

Everything they do in their lives is geared toward making a mark on this world, and a true measure of their impact is whether that mark will live on when they are no longer with us. They dream of leaving a legacy, so the three words are

### *We Feel You.*

From the local deli owner leaving his popular business to his children to the billionaire mogul donating his fortune to charity and handing his business on to the next generation, we all want our lives that mean something. For the ambitious and driven entrepreneur, all their efforts mean nothing if they have nothing to leave behind.

Their legacy doesn't have to be a concrete product or a profitable business. It could simply be a feeling that "Wow, was I lucky to know that guy. He was always so inspirational to talk to." Entrepreneurs are the go-getters of life, and they touch far more people than they know. Everyone needs "outlier" examples of people in their lives to inspire them to take that next step, and the more people they know who are pushing the envelope, the more impetus they will have to make that extra bit of effort in their lives. You might be an entrepreneur in a struggling business, but you keep battling, and unknowingly, you might be setting an example to one of your friends who have a battle of their own. They will be "feeling" you, that is for sure.

So, all you entrepreneurs out there. Are you touching as many lives as you could? Do you share your knowledge or squirrel it away in a locked vault, never to see the light of day again. I can tell you one thing; it isn't going to do much good in there…

You naturally want to create an impact, you want tens of thousands (or maybe even millions) of people to be able to say, "We feel you," when you have passed on, but do you view your business through your own eyes or through the eyes of others? Getting insular and obsessive about how you want your business to develop is never going to lead to this outcome. Open your arms, welcome the world in, and your activities will be infinitely richer.

On a darker note, the phrase "We feel you" can have more sinister connotations. You have a duty to make sure that your legacy is a positive one, not a negative one. You don't want to make people feel worse because of your actions. Is your business environmentally friendly? Does it make a positive contribution to your society? Do you treat your employees fairly, or do you treat them like a commodity? Being an entrepreneur and a leader is a position of great responsibility—don't abuse it, or you will leave a less-than-positive legacy.

As a last point, it is impossible to understand what feelings you may leave others unless you look inside yourself and decide what you feel about what you are trying to achieve. Do you feel good about what you are doing? If you do, then the likelihood is that others will think the same.

Leave a legacy every day. Then many will say, "We feel you."

# CHAPTER 128

## The Top Ten Hires for Any Start-Up or New Project

It goes without saying that every start-up needs a certain amount of diverse functional expertise to help it get off the ground. The CEO is the decision-making hub, the finance guy crunches the numbers, the sales team do the schmoozing, the marketing team make everything look pretty, and the operations guys make sure that everything works.

It is far from easy to find people with the right functional experience, but in the white heat of a start-up atmosphere, I would like to argue that functional experience is far from the only hiring criteria.

You have to have a mix of the right personalities.

***The Catalyst.*** A start-up cannot function without ideas. It requires people who can think laterally and have the courage to challenge the status-quo. They need to compel influencers within the team.

***The Architect.*** Architects understand the overall plan and can describe how to construct it, but they are also incredibly detail-oriented. They understand the impact of various decisions on the direction of the whole. They are the rational "go-to" people when the CEO wonders whether something makes sense.

***The Slogger.*** These types hit their desks at 0700 in the morning and don't stop slogging until 0700 at night. They laugh at the concept of work-life balance, and although their habits are a little unhealthy, they set a high bar for the rest of the team.

***The Butterfly.*** No one wants to work in a stressful start-up where everyone is sitting with their headphones on, immersed in their work. The social butterfly acts as the social glue of the outfit, always suggesting lunch out and coordinating various activities where people can get to know each other better.

***The Dreamer.*** The deep thinkers of the start-up, the dreamers often drift off into their own little worlds, only for their sub-conscious to come up with the next amazing idea. Without lofty dreams, no matter how impossible, start-ups will wither and die quickly.

***The Scrooge.*** With "burn" cited as the number one reason for start-up failure (duh), there need to be people who are keen to calculate the ROI of various initiatives. Start-ups should be run with the intention of becoming a profitable business, but without a few Scrooges, this will never happen.

***The Finisher.*** With so many balls to juggle, it is inevitable that many will fall to the ground. Prioritizing is important, but even more important is having some completer-finishers on your team. It is all well and good having great ideas, but those great ideas have to come to fruition.

***The Encourager.*** Working in a start-up is hard work. There are days that your mind begs you to go and work in a comfortable corporate job, and you desperately need a few people around you to say, "It will all work out fine." Positivity is vital when failure is commonplace.

***The Wrecking-Ball.*** Sometimes there is no way around a wall, no way over it or even under it. You have to smash through it, and the wrecking ball personality delights in doing exactly that. No obstacle is insurmountable, and they do not flinch at the thought of hurting themselves in the process. No pain, no gain.

***The Believer.*** This personality type is the most crucial in my view. No matter what the difficulties, no matter how long it might take, they fervently believe that everything will work out as planned. Belief is contagious, and just a smile from the believer at a difficult moment can imbue the team with an extra sense of purpose.

# CHAPTER 129

## *Where Do Entrepreneurs Get Their Energy?*

I have been a huge fan of Sir Richard Branson ever since I was a student back in the early 90s at the University of Sheffield in the UK. This chapter is the result of my immense respect for his entrepreneurial passion, zest, enthusiasm, and commitment for the betterment of mankind and overall energy to go where no human has ever gone before.

I have always wondered where Sir Richard Branson got his energy to keep going at it all this while, and as I have pursued my own entrepreneurial adventures these past five years, I seem to have figured a few things out in the process.

When you have something to live for, the world seems alive with possibility, and it would be a crime not to explore every possible avenue.

The immense drive that any entrepreneur feels when they get up in the morning doesn't come from the thought of their bank balance at the end of the month. Their ability to pull 12-hour working shifts on a regular basis can't be put down to their dedication, their "to-do" list, or their desire to annihilate the competition… All these things, and many more, do indeed help to keep them moving forward, but their main source of energy (in my humble opinion) is this:

They don't know what is around the bend.

Being an entrepreneur is a seat-of-the-pants adventure of the best kind. You are trekking steep mountain paths, abseiling down deep crevasses, swimming across crocodile-infested rivers, or maybe simply paragliding to more fertile ground. Each step that you take is different than the last one, and you can be sure that the next hundred steps will be radically different from the last hundred.

One minute, your business might be structured in a certain way, and then market changes dictate that you have to pivot in a totally different direction. Only the hungry and adventurous entrepreneur will be able to make this change before their competitors, and they will thereby secure their advantage.

Their energy comes from a constant curiosity about what might be next. They know from experience that there is always something that comes along next—nothing is set in stone, and the more you explore what is around you, the more you will get a feeling for your landscape.

If your hearing is acute enough, you may hear the roar of the river rapids far before the others; the energetic entrepreneur is forever listening.

If your eyesight is sharp enough, you may see the clouds rolling in a few valleys away and get your wet weather gear on; the energetic entrepreneur is always looking forward.

The life of an entrepreneur is like a constantly evolving crossword; the moment you have solved a section, another section branches off it like a tree spreading its branches ever wider. Discovering which sections of the "crossword tree" you wish to develop is one of the joys of being an entrepreneur. It is your party, and you decide which direction you will take.

Whichever metaphor you prefer (there are many more where these come from), entrepreneurs find untapped reserves of energy because they know that they are going to find something worthwhile to spend it on. They believe in their cause, and, for them, they are motivated by every aspect of the journey.

Unlike the kids sitting in the back of the car saying, "Are we there yet? Are we there yet?", the entrepreneur simply says, "Where can we go next? Where can we go next?"

You can be sure that this energetic attitude will take them to some pretty amazing places.

# CHAPTER 130

## *Entrepreneurs Have to Learn to Kill*

The media is firmly to blame for romanticizing the life of an entrepreneur. You see polished specimens on Shark Tank, you leaf through their lives in the features sections of business magazines, and every second blog proceeds to hero worship their every move. The masses are spoon-fed with idyllic dreams of fast cars and faraway beaches.

Don't believe a word. The car windscreens are splattered with the blood of road kill that was in the way, and the beaches are littered with the bloated bodies of those who didn't quite make it. Would you save someone else if it meant you were risking drowning yourself? Would you swerve past that deer in the road and risk crashing, or would you grimace and plow into the poor creature? Many entrepreneurs simply have to put themselves first sometimes—that is how they get to the top of the greasy pole, by climbing on others.

The important word here is "sometimes."

Collaboration and compassion are still crucial in a tight-knit start-up community. You never know who your next partner in crime might be, and you are never sure where your money is coming from next. It pays to act the "good guy." You try to do the right things, say the right things, and portray the right image. But sometimes, just sometimes, you have to take another path… If you don't, you will be putting your company (and those that you work with) at risk.

You might have to take one of your competitors out of the equation. Market share is sometimes easier to gain if there are fewer mouths to feed. Sometimes. You reel them in like a helpless fish to the bank, denying them a gulp of precious water and any hope. Then, onto the bank and a dull thud over the head for good measure. You can't risk them slipping back into the water—the kill should be swift and efficient. After you have done it a few times, it will seem normal. Everyone does it, why shouldn't you?

Wild animals that travel for their survival cannot carry weak or injured passengers. They might try to help them, but ultimately, they will leave them. The most successful entrepreneurs cannot scale the heights if they are carrying too much extra weight. People who are not contributing will be fired, and they will often be fired swiftly. You don't often hear about staff turnover figures in start-ups… I wonder why.

There are many other gruesome instances where entrepreneurs need their killing streak (I am sure that you can think of some), but there are none more important than an ability to kill a bit of themselves when required. Writers are encouraged to "kill their darlings" and get rid of the superfluous prose. Equally, entrepreneurs should be ruthless with the thousands of ideas that pop up in their heads. Sometimes the core concept itself needs to be killed in order for another to rise like a phoenix from the ashes.

Entrepreneurs do need to learn how to kill. Could you do it?

# CHAPTER 131

## Seven Reasons Why Investors Won't Back Entrepreneurs

Seeking investors is nothing like showing up and getting picked for your local community youth football league. The chances of the average person being "picked" at all are infinitesimally small, and there are many reasons for potential rejections – those without a thick skin need not apply.

The most successful entrepreneurs are passionate about their idea, but they don't let it consume them. There are many practical reasons why investors won't touch them with a bargepole, even if the product itself is brilliant. Entrepreneurs have to be aware of these potential banana skins. Here is my take on the top seven reasons why people don't win investment for their business.

***They aren't a leader.*** There is so much written about leadership (too much, some may say), but there is no situation that requires leadership skills more than when managing an ambitious start-up. If the entrepreneur cannot inspire their people to follow them on the journey, how can an investor have any certainty about the security of their investment?

***Customers aren't interested.*** If there is no proof of actual or potential success, the growth story slides more into fantasy land. If there is no current market, very few products will be strong enough to create one by themselves. If entrepreneurs don't understand their customer base from day one, they are simply relying on luck in aiming to "meet" them somewhere along the way.

***Their team is second-rate.*** The entrepreneur themselves might be a super star, but unless their team are equally impressive, investors will get cold feet. Very few companies rely on the efforts of one person for their success, and unless the team has the talent to pull off the magic, progress will stall pretty quickly.

***They don't listen.*** Investors are buying into a business, and they need to be able to give the entrepreneur feedback and constructive criticism when required. If the business owner is not coachable, investors can feel like their money is disappearing into a bottomless pit with no hope of recovery. Listening to feedback and acting on it is the hallmark of the best start-ups.

***They don't know their stuff.*** If the investors know more about the product and its market than the founder, then the relationship is doomed to failure from the start. Investors will add all sorts of value, but the product expert should be the entrepreneur themselves. Being unaware of the broader market is the first sign of tunnel vision.

***They're all action, no thought.*** Entrepreneurs are often seen as 100mph make-it-up-as-you-go-along adrenaline junkie types who thrive on change. However, the best entrepreneurs can weigh up the consequences of their actions and test things out at 50mph before they get up to speed.

***Lack of a long-term vision.*** If the product or service doesn't offer the potential for scalable growth, most investors will pass. An entrepreneur's vision should be grounded in reality, and ideally involve growing revenue without growing overheads in the same proportions. Basic business sense 101. If investors have no sense of when they will see an ROI, they will run for the hills.

# CHAPTER 132

## Routine Is the Enemy of Entrepreneurs

According to various interviews, the new Twitter CEO Jack Dorsey used to "theme" his days—Management on Monday, Product on Tuesday, Marketing on Wednesday, etc. I'm not sure that his new responsibilities will allow him to stick to it these days, but he organized his work life like that for quite a while.

There are many other celebrated fans of routine. Medium founder Evan Williams takes a break from work in the middle of every day to go to the gym. Going back a few years, Winston Churchill rarely rose from his bed before 11am, reading the papers, dealing with correspondence, and even dictating to his secretaries. Barack Obama, on the other hand, seems to be a night owl, going back to the Oval Office most evenings after the family dinner to tie up loose ends and prepare for the next day (so that he can enjoy breakfast with his family every morning).

All this strict organization is fine if you are at the top of the food chain with your minions fitting their schedules around you, although I am not so sure that Churchill's secretaries enjoyed his bedroom dictations. However, the very nature of a "normal" entrepreneur's day means that while they need to understand which activities contribute to their success, having any sort of set routine is virtually impossible.

Such flexibility is championed by self-help guru and author of *The 4-Hour Workweek* Tim Ferriss, "I don't have to do anything in this schedule. I choose to do them because I like them. None of them are financially-driven or unpleasant obligations. If the chance to do something more fun comes up last-minute, I can cancel all of them." Ferriss also schedules very few things into his calendar so that he doesn't need to stress about multi-tasking to get things done. "The goal is to spend as much time possible doing what we want by maximizing output in minimal time."

The difficulties start when people feel obligated to do something because it is part of the routine, not because it needs to be done. To a certain extent, a routine does create a certain space for these essential tasks, but it can equally hamper their delivery. For an entrepreneur in an utterly fluid environment, they need to forget about routine and become experts in prioritizing for the moment.

There is one question that many entrepreneurs ask themselves at the start of each week and at the start of each day: What are the activities that will bring me closer to my goal?

If one of those activities falls on a Wednesday, but Wednesday is the "Marketing Day," then they will lose out on an opportunity. If a crucial investor meeting can only happen at lunchtime, what happens to the mid-day workout? You don't pass up on these sorts of opportunities if you are to get ahead.

Therefore, I would say that sticking to a set routine is pretty much impossible if you want to give your business every chance of success. The idea of routine is that it is regular—entrepreneurs live anything but regular lives.

Of course, everyone has a different definition of routine, and there are many grey areas in between. Routine is definitely easier in a "normal" office environment, but even then, I'm not sure that it is such a good thing.

I'd be really interested to hear your thoughts—I'm sure that there will be lots of different opinions out there.

# CHAPTER 133

## *Entrepreneurs Eat Failure for Breakfast*

There is an entrepreneur in each one of us. *Let failure into your mind but not into your heart.*

Breakfast is the most important meal of the day. Whatever your preferred fuel, most people can't function until that energy starts coursing around their body, transforming a stumbling wreck into a laser-guided missile, hunting for the best that life has to offer.

That's the way I feel, anyway—confessions of a breakfast junkie. Taking the metaphor a little further, I look at friends of mine in the entrepreneurial space, and it is obvious what fuels their day: Memories of failure and rejection.

Most people have started something new in their lives. It is daunting, scary, and causes you to wake at night with cold sweats. It might be a project, it might be a new job, it might be a house move, or maybe even getting married. However, entrepreneurs are a special breed; the nature of what they do means that these "new" feelings are an almost constant companion. They are always moving, always thinking, always refining.

The law of averages means that not everything you try will work out. You might put all your efforts into a project (to the detriment of everything else at work), and it will probably be fine. You might battle to make a go of your new job, have some early wins, and gradually settle into company life.

New personal relationships are equally hard work; how many dates do you have until you meet "the one"?

Now, imagine that you have multiple "new undertakings" on the go at once. Not all of them will work out. Some will crash and burn in flames, some will fail quietly and fizzle out, and a few will be lucky enough to stand the test of time. This is the life of an entrepreneur, and it is fair to say that they experience failure to some degree on a daily basis.

Now comes the breakfast idea...

You have two choices what you do with these feelings of failure. You can take them to heart, assume that they are "your fault," and let them eat you up from inside. Alternatively, you can let failure into your mind. When failure lives in your mind (and not your heart), it becomes a spur to do things differently and become better, and it takes you one step closer to perfection. If you create a special "failure vault" in your brain, you can dip in when you need that little bit of a push, remember what it felt like, make sure that you learn the lessons, and find a better solution.

Life has a tendency of repeating itself. The same situations come up in different guises, and unless we internalize our failures and learn from them, we can get into a vicious circle of mistakes, regrets, mistakes, and regrets.

Entrepreneurs understand that unless they eat (and enjoy) their failures for breakfast every day, they won't get very far. In order to be the best and come up with truly innovative ideas, they have to break through the pain barrier that deters all but the most determined and resolute.

The pain of failure is their friend. It is what sets them apart from others. They welcome troubled dreams because they know that they are part of the journey.

When you let failure into your mind but not into your heart, that is when you eat it for breakfast. Then it can provide the fuel for an amazing day.

*Let failure into your mind but not into your heart.*

# CHAPTER 134

## *Why Every Start-Up Needs a Spring Clean*

Entrepreneurs the world over are masters at perfecting their business models in an ever-changing competitive environment, but sometimes a developing business needs to focus on some of the more mundane areas of operations in order for it to remain the lean, mean, fighting machine of the early days.

Every now and again, start-ups need a spring clean.

There are many areas that might benefit from a polish, a dusting, or even a thorough scrubbing. In this chapter, I would like to borrow Osterwalder's nine-piece business canvas to segment what activity may be required in each critical area:

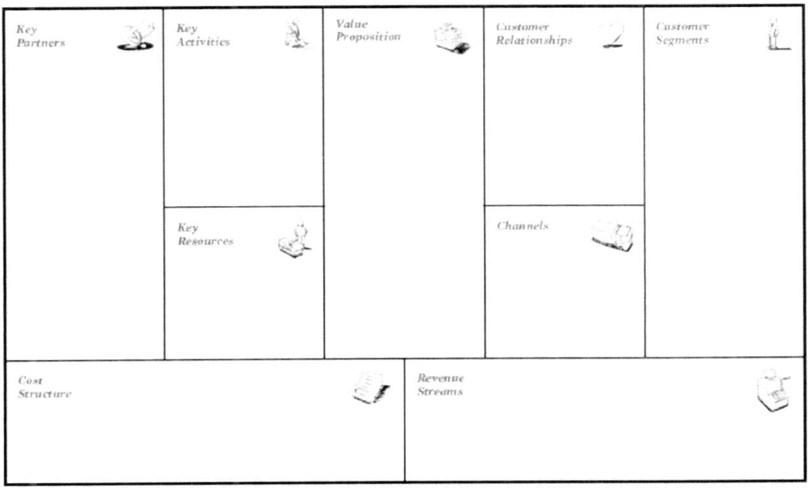

***Key Partners:*** Often a start-up's success is closely linked to the value-add of its partners. However, success on one side does not always equate to success on the other side. Entrepreneurs need to ensure that they are working with the best-fit companies at every stage of the way. Nostalgia for the early days shouldn't hold you back if your partner can't handle the increased demands.

***Key Activities:*** The priority tasks for year one of a business will be different to year two and year three. Any business with a rigid operating model will be shackled and unable to fulfil its potential. Getting an external view on how you might operate more effectively is crucial. Do it at regular intervals and don't give in to believing that you have the perfect model. It won't be perfect for long.

***Key Resources:*** Are you feeding your business the right diet to help it to grow? Have you got the right employees in place? Do you need to upgrade your facilities or give your sales force a company car? Is it about time you invested in some tech to improve company communications? Constant investment in the right areas will keep you ahead of the curve.

***Cost Structure:*** This is a big one, and it will vary hugely from industry to industry, but you can be sure of one thing: the fixed and variable costs involved in running a start-up will rarely be the same from year to year. Look to the past to understand what created value, and look forward to predict what might bring you the desired result. Be clinical in eradicating unnecessary spending.

***Value Proposition:*** The features and benefits of your product will develop along many potential avenues. The market may dictate certain changes, you may need to react to competitors, or you may need to pivot your business into a more profitable niche. Never assume that you hold the "perfect hand." There are always ways and means of improving on your offering.

***Customer Relationships:*** How you create and maintain customer relationships is the litmus test of any successful business. Finding new customers will become ever more important as the business develops scale, but keeping the loyal ones is the real key to success. How do you ensure that you grow with them?

***Channels:*** Delivering an ever more complex product or service needs efficient distribution and communication. Technology and social media are offering some cutting-edge solutions in this area; are you sure that your business is making the most of them? Are your channels keeping up with the growth?

***Customer Segments:*** Not enough businesses evaluate their customer base on a regular enough basis. They do heaps of market research initially, but customer habits change and companies can easily lose sight of their core customers in the haste to grow.

***Revenue Streams:*** Entrepreneurs are notorious for continually seeking new revenue streams to diversify the business, but sometimes the temptation to focus on the "new" can cause the neglect of the "old." Make sure that you are making the most of each area of your business, no matter how long you have been active in the market.

Evaluating some of these areas isn't seen as a priority because there are bigger perceived "wins" to prioritize. However, without a regular spring clean, there is always the threat of falling out of touch with why you started the business in the first place. Entrepreneurial housekeeping is always vital for the long-term health of any business.

I am sure that we all know a few companies in need of a spring clean.

# CHAPTER 135

## *Seven Battlefield Tactics of Successful Entrepreneurs*

Entrepreneurs today face unprecedented amounts of competition. In the age of the Internet, their moves are scrutinized in an instant, and they are always potentially one bad move away from implosion. The hostility of the business environment is so immediate that having the effective offense and defense battle plans in place is crucial for the survival of any company. Although the majority of entrepreneurs will act reactively most of the time, having a few strategies in the back pocket is never a bad thing.

Here are seven moves from the battlefield, which may come in useful:

1. *Tripwires.* It's the dead of night, but you know that no one will be able to sneak up on you. If they do, they will trigger a tripwire, and you will never be caught unaware... Entrepreneurs need to keep their eyes on their market to understand when various competitors are starting to encroach on their territory. Alarm bells should go off when a customer works with someone else or an employee moves to a mysterious start-up.

2. *Surprise attack.* Some of the most effective moves are entirely unexpected—entire armies can be routed in their sleep by the smallest force of assassins. An army that is not expecting attack is lulled into a false sense of security. For an entrepreneur, first mover advantage gives them precious weeks or months to monopolize their part of the market.

Meticulous planning behind closed doors allows companies to move at lightning-fast speed at the touch of a button.

3. *Sniper.* Silently they lie in wait, surveying the scene, assessing their targets and waiting for the right moment to strike. If they eliminate the head of the snake, the body will be useless; they simply have to take out the right person. In the entrepreneurial context, you could equate this to working out the movers and shakers behind their success and then headhunting them to join you. Not only do you harm your competition, you are also adding to your organization.

4. *Feigned retreat.* If the enemy thinks that you are backing off, they will likely consolidate their forces and relax. At the same time, you are sneaking around their flanks and about to strike them when they expected it least. For the entrepreneur, publicly backing away from a certain market can sometimes give you a chance to regroup and attack it from a different direction. Sometimes in order to take two steps forward, you need to take a step back first.

5. *Second wave.* The battle is fiercely raging, but suddenly, reinforcements appear to overwhelmingly turn the tide for one side. The defeated army capitulates with the numerical odds stacked against them as the victors dominate the battlefield. Entrepreneurs can dominate a competitive market by doubling down on their efforts. If the "brains" behind each competitor are equal, it is often the resources at their disposal that win the day. If one team has a sales force twice the size of the other (and equally well trained), they will inevitably win more business.

6. *Intelligence gathering.* Before you attack your enemy, you have to know your enemy. The more you know about them, the more effective your strategies will be, and the fewer lives will be lost. The entrepreneur who doesn't understand every intricacy of his market is making decisions with a blindfold on. They can be certain that their competition won't be making the same mistake.

7. *Stealth tactics.* Deception has long been a military tactic, and if your enemy can't see you, they can't defend themselves. The intelligent entrepreneur doesn't

want to let his competition know what he is doing and where he is doing it. The longer he can go incognito, the stronger he can make his business, and the more resistant he will be to attack when he does have to show his face.

I do not pretend to be a military expert, but I have, however, been an entrepreneur for a good number of years and used these tactics myself on multiple occasions.

*If you fail to prepare, you should prepare to fail.*

# *ABOUT THE AUTHOR –*
# ANURAG HARSH

Anurag Harsh, voted one of LinkedIn's Top Voices (#1 in Technology), is an entrepreneur, executive, management guru, blogger, author of several books, columnist for leading US publications, investor, and a classical vocalist who has performed two solo concerts at New York's Carnegie Hall. His business blog has hundreds of thousands of readers. His Carnegie Hall concert is one of the most watched world music videos online. His videos on digital technology are among the most watched on YouTube. Anurag holds an MBA & MS from the Massachusetts Institute of Technology and the Wharton School at the University of Pennsylvania.

@anuragharsh | blogbrain.org